AN INTRODUCTION TO THE STUDY OF CHINESE PAINTING

To LAURENCE BINYON

THE CH'ANG-LO PALACE, after Li Ssŭ-hsün
12¼ in. × 10 in. (See p. 140)

British Museum

AN INTRODUCTION TO THE STUDY OF
CHINESE PAINTING
BY ARTHUR WALEY

GROVE PRESS, INC.   NEW YORK

First published 1923, reprinted 1958

Library of Congress Catalog Card Number: 58-6228

Grove Press Books and Evergreen Books
are published by Barney Rosset at Grove Press, Inc.
795 Broadway   New York 3, N. Y.

Manufactured in the United States of America

PREFACE

I am deeply indebted to Professor Pelliot, who not only allowed me to use prints taken from his Tun-huang negatives, but also furnished me with information upon many points; and to Mr. Roger Fry, who lent photographs of the Takahashi Lohan.

Mr. Oscar Raphael, Mr. George Eumorphopoulos, Monsieur Charles Vignier and Monsieur Adolphe Stoclet kindly allowed me to reproduce paintings in their possession. Messrs. Yamanaka gave me permission to publish three paintings, one of which has since passed into a private collection. Plates XXIX and XXX are from the *Kokka*, and are republished by kind permission of Mr. Taki, the Editor.

Lej Tcheppa.
July, 1923.

CONTENTS

LIST OF ILLUSTRATIONS

LIST OF ILLUSTRATIONS

LIST OF ILLUSTRATIONS

LIST OF ILLUSTRATIONS

CHAPTER I
PRELIMINARY

CHAPTER I
PRELIMINARY

This book is rather a series of essays than a general survey of early Chinese painting. To attempt such a survey at the present time would, I think, be dangerous owing to the lack of those detailed and special studies by which general works are usually preceded. As an example of what I mean let me cite Sir Charles Eliot's *Hinduism and Buddhism*, the most accomplished general account of a wide subject that has appeared in recent years. That author's task consisted to a great extent in gathering together and co-ordinating information which was either scattered among the pages of learned journals—French, German, and English—or buried in old and unprocurable books. Had he been obliged to undertake for himself all the researches which he summarizes in his history, the writing of it would have required not one but several lifetimes.

A few special studies of particular Chinese artists or paintings have from time to time appeared. They have, however, with one or two exceptions, failed to reach the standard of scholarship set by European art-research. The danger of demanding symmetry and completeness from a historian who has not the necessary material at his command is well illustrated by many Histories of the obscurer literatures. A writer, let us say, undertakes to compile a history of the literature of some remote country. He himself is perhaps interested in fiction, but only moderately in poetry, and not at all in philosophy; there exist no preliminary researches to guide him. He will write sensibly of fiction, perfunctorily of poetry, and ludicrously of thought.

Conscious of this danger, I have confined myself so far as possible to topics of which I have special knowledge. I have tried, moreover, to mention as few rather than as many artists as possible, lest my book should become a mere dictionary. I have no doubt omitted some very important names; but they will be found in my *Index of Chinese Artists*,[1] which is, in effect, a biographical dictionary of Chinese painters. A considerable part of this book is occupied with the history of Chinese art-tradition, æsthetic, and taste; an attempt is also made to give in the broadest outlines a history of early Chinese civilization in general. If anyone says that the knowledge of these things is irrelevant to the study of art, I answer that in human beings, as we know them, sensitivity to art is usually accompanied by some degree of intellectual curiosity; that enjoyment of a work of art leads not only to the question, Who made this?

[1] British Museum, 1922.

3

but also to the question, What sort of people did he live among？ What were their feelings？ Now if, with regard to any age or country, these last questions can be answered at all, it will be largely through the study of literature, and principally, of poetry. Hence in writing this book I have sometimes been helped by knowledge gained from the study of Chinese poetry. Moreover, in supplying a certain literary background, I am justified, I think, by the intimate connection between poetry and painting which from early times existed in China.

CONNOISSEURSHIP IN CHINA

By connoisseurship I do not mean appreciation of the æsthetic qualities in a work of art, but only the ability to decide who brought it into being. Such ability, so it seems to me, depends much more on knowledge than on sensitivity ; it is the fruit of a science, not of inspiration. The æsthete may be as unreliable an authority upon the work of art which he admires as a lover upon the qualities of his mistress. In fact, a process frequently takes place which is entirely analagous to Stendhal's " crystallization." It may even happen that a man has quite erroneous ideas about the content of a picture which he has studied at frequent intervals for years —a work that he has been in the habit of praising with an almost idolatrous adoration.

The essential condition of connoisseurship, then, is not emotion but knowledge ; and such knowledge can only be acquired through conditions of study similar to those under which the European science of *Kunstgeschichte* has grown up. The student must have access either to some representative national collection or to a large number of small private collections. The second condition could never be adequately fulfilled in China, where private collections were scattered over such enormous distances that no individual could possibly make a complete study of them. " Le critique d'art en Chine, malgré son zèle et malgré son goût, a manqué de points de repère solidement établis."[1]

Only at one period in Chinese history did a representative national collection exist, that of Ch'ien Lung, which was accessible to the members of the Court, and no doubt to aristocrats and high officials in general, from 1730 till 1901.[2] But it was arranged in a way calculated to make systematic study as difficult as possible. The paintings of any individual

[1] Pelliot, *Mém. concern. l'Asie Orientale*, I, 121 (1913).
[2] When, during the Allied occupation of Peking, a large part of the Imperial Collections was either looted or destroyed.

4

artist were distributed among a number of different buildings and apartments; moreover, secular paintings were kept apart from religious ones. Nevertheless, it was probably during the 18th century, and owing to the existence of this vast collection, that connoisseurship reached its apogee in China. The only other great representative collection which ever existed was that of the Emperor Hui Tsung. But it seems to have been made somewhat uncritically; moreover, its existence was extremely brief, for in 1127 the Capital was sacked by the Tartars[1] and the treasures of the Palace were destroyed. A certain number of paintings (among which, if we believe in its genuineness, we must reckon the *Ku K'ai-Chih* roll now at the British Museum) was carried south by the retreating courtiers; but it was only a minute fragment of the vast collection.

The Chinese connoisseur was beset by difficulties connected not only with external conditions of study, but also with the nature of Chinese painting itself. The Chinese have a mania for classification; partly indigenous, it was certainly stimulated by contact with Indian thought. But mixed with an intellectual prompting to analyse and codify was a preference for enumeration as a mere figure of rhetoric, similar to its use in Hebrew literature (" There are six things which the Lord doth hate "). Some early writer, then, partly because it pleased him to roll off the enumeration, would enunciate six ways of painting fir-cones; with the result that subsequent painters of fir-cones paused to consider which of these categories they should conform to.

Hence arose a tendency to codify styles and technical processes. As applied to poetry this tendency reached its zenith in the 13th century. It does not imply a purely external and mechanical view of art, as is strikingly illustrated by the writings of Yen Yü,[2] in which it goes hand in hand with the most esoteric Zen mysticism. In painting the tendency towards classification and technical analysis developed somewhat later, culminating, towards the end of the 16th century, in the writings of Tung Ch'i-Ch'ang,[3] the past-master of classical procedures. Painting took on the formality of, say, harpsichord playing, as opposed to the free, graduated touch of the piano. It was as though a modern British landscapist, instead of struggling merely to realize his own vision of a tree, should necessarily

[1] I know of no authority for the statement of some European writers that the Tartars preserved Hui Tsung's collections and transmitted them intact to the Mongols. For testimony to the contrary, see *Burlington Magazine*, XXX, 4.

[2] For an extract from this important writer's *Discourse on Poetry*, see *The Dial*, September, 1922, p. 274.   [3] See below, p. 247.

have before him the alternatives of painting it in the style of Gainsborough, Girtin, Turner, Crome, or Constable. The Chinese artist turned on a "Chao Ta-nien" tone just as the harpsichordist turns on his lute-stop. Particularly the technique of rendering mountain contours (and though there are vast plains in China, hardly a landscape has ever been painted there that lacked hills) was analysed with the utmost minuteness, and we shall see that it was the use of contour lines (*ts'un-fa*)[1] which above all else guide the great connoisseurs in their attributions.

This habit of technical analysis, combined with the constant copying of ancient masterpieces which formed the basis of art-training, made of every artist a potential forger ; while in modern Europe (where manual dexterity still abounds) mere technical ignorance would make it impossible for the vast majority of painters to imitate deceptively any work but that of their contemporaries. The *Li Yüan Ts'ung Hua*[2] has the following grim passage on forgers : " The art of forging calligraphy and paintings is an ancient one. In the T'ang dynasty Ch'ēng Hsiu-chi forged the writing of Wang Hsi-chih, and in the Sung dynasty Mi Fei forged the writing of Ch'u Sui-liang. But these forgeries were both made as a joke, not for commercial purposes.

" At the beginning of the Manchu dynasty there lived in the Chuan Chu Lane at Soochow a family called Ch'in. Father, sons, young and old, were all expert in picture-forging. The alleged masterpieces by Sung and Yüan painters, by Hui Tsung, Chou Wēn-chü, Li Lung-mien, Kuo Chung-shu, Tung Yüan, Li Ch'ēng, Kuo Hsi, Hsü Ch'ung-ssŭ (grandson of Hsü Hsi), Chao Ta-nien, Fan K'uan, Chao Po-chü, Chao Mēng-chien, Ma Ho-Chih, Su Han-ch'ēn, Liu Sung-nien, Ma Yüan, Hsia Kuei, Chao Mēng-fu, Su Ta-nien, Wang Mien, Kao K'o-kung, Huang Kung-wang, Wang Mēng, Ni Tsan, Wu Chēn—rolls and hanging pictures of all sizes —are more than half of them the work of this family. . . . I remember when I was young seeing a man of this name selling calligraphy and paintings at the Tiger Hill.[3] Although he was a miserably poor, starved creature, I do not doubt that he was a descendant of the famous forgers whose name he bore.

" After the time of the Ch'in family the fashion grew apace and forgers became more numerous every day. Those whom I myself have known

---

[1] See Petrucci's *Encyclopédie de la Peinture Chinoise*.

[2] By Ch'ien Yung. Preface dated 1825. (Page 156 of Shanghai reprint.)

[3] A famous view-point about two miles N.W. of Soochow ; but the name is often used as a designation of Soochow itself.

were the twins Shēn Lao-hung and Shēn Lao-ch'i, Wu T'ing-li, and Chēng Lao-hui. Whenever a genuine old picture came their way they hastened to make a reproduction of it. In the case of calligraphy they traced the outer edges of the brush-marks and filled in the space afterwards; in the case of paintings they made an exact, line-for-line copy. Their industry was handsomely rewarded."

European collections of Chinese painting must be very rich in examples of the Ch'in family's art—one which is indeed deserving of every encouragement, since it not only provides its exponents with an easy affluence, but also gives much harmless pleasure to its patrons. I should like to have published some of these elaborately documented antiques, but I am not sure that their owners (some of whom were kind enough to supply me with photographs of them) would relish this form of publicity.

JAPANESE CONNOISSEURSHIP

Chinese painting is very unevenly represented in Japan. The Japanese have at all periods tended to bring back from China what was at the moment out of fashion there, and hence easy to acquire. T'ang cult-figures came to Japan at a time when Zen was replacing the idolatrous sects. The Zen painting of Southern Sung, in which Japan is particularly rich, became a drug on the Chinese market from the 14th century onwards. But paintings which the Chinese themselves have at all periods admired—the landscapes, for example, of the great Southern School masters such as Chü-jan and Li Ch'ēng, of the Four Masters of Yüan, or of the Four Wangs in the 17th century—these the Japanese were seldom able to acquire.

Thus ample materials exist in Japan for the study of Southern Sung painting, and of all but a few phases of painting from the 16th century onwards. They have not till the last few years been fully utilized. Much of the material has been admirably reproduced, but little of it critically examined. The scientific study of Chinese painting in Japan has, in fact, only just begun.

Particular difficulties attend the study of Zen paintings, owing to the fact that the owners are reluctant to display them except during the celebration of the Tea Ceremony. The European *Kunstforscher* has been too much inclined to regard works of art solely as archæological documents. The Japanese have perhaps erred in the opposite direction, so that their connoisseurship (at any rate, in old days) had in it something of the pontifical character. The great Kanō masters were credited with the

7

power of deciding *ex cathedra,* by virtue of their office, upon the author-ship of every kind of Chinese picture. In many cases their quite arbitrary attributions are still misleadingly attached to the works upon which they pronounced judgment.

AIMS OF THIS BOOK

It has been suggested above that no very complete connoisseurship of Chinese painting has hitherto existed either in China or Japan. Much less has it existed in Europe, and, as I have said, this book is in the main a history of art-tradition rather than an account of Chinese painting as represented by the works that survive to-day. So to a great extent are the works of Giles and Hirth; hence it comes that I have sometimes translated the same texts as these two writers. Very often my translation differs widely from theirs, but I have not in each case noted the fact, lest I should give to my book that controversial air which has sometimes irritated me in reading the books of others; for often in informative works the name of some previous writer is savagely dangled from footnote to footnote, like the scalp that a triumphant Indian wears always at his waist.

It is not likely that at present any work upon Chinese painting will be written in which there do not occur considerable lacunæ, for the subject demands qualifications which are seldom combined in one person. The ideal writer would know both Chinese and Japanese, which under existing conditions[1] requires a special talent for languages; he must possess both the means and the leisure for extensive travel and prolonged residence in the East; he will require, if after successive rebuffs he is at last to get sight of closely guarded treasures, a certain degree of *aplomb* and social persistency. It is essential that he should be a person in whose life art plays an important part; otherwise, however great his scholarship, it will be impossible for him to sift to any intelligent purpose the vast mass of documentary material at his disposal. Finally, he must be able to write.

I possess very few of these qualifications; but so little is at present known of Chinese art or of Chinese civilization in general that there is some case, at any rate in Europe, for fragmentary and imperfect works. My one claim to consideration is that I have not attempted to hide the gaps in my edifice by a delusive façade of omniscience.

[1] There is no institution in London which teaches the kind of Chinese required for this purpose.

PRELIMINARY

NOTE ON TRANSLITERATION AND ILLUSTRATIONS

For Chinese words I have used the Wade system. In Sanskrit words I at first intended to use the one sign " sh " for both ś and ṣ I found, however, that this gave too strange an appearance to familiar words and therefore restored the ś, except in the name of Shākyamuni, which is fairly familiar in that spelling. I have throughout used two words in their Japanese form, in each case because this is the form which is best known to European readers : the first is the name of Amida ; the second is the term Zen.

The choice of illustrations was to some extent determined by factors beyond my control. Thus with regard to the colour-plates it became apparent that satisfactory results could only be obtained if successive proofs could be continually corrected by the originals. This made it necessary that the pictures reproduced in colour should be near at hand and constantly accessible—conditions fulfilled only by the British Museum Collection. The other pictures which I have reproduced are certainly not all masterpieces ; but they need not, I think, fear comparison with those that illustrate previous books on the subject. A work which deals principally with the great early painters—with Ku K'ai-chih, Chang Sēng-yu, Yen Li-pēn, Wu Tao-tzŭ, Li Lung-mien—can no more be adequately illustrated than could a book about Zeuxis, Protogenes, and Apelles. The Japanese collections (as I have said) are rich principally in ink-paintings of the 13th century, many of which have been published in Japan. I have not, except in a few instances, thought it desirable to re-produce them, for they have already been freely (and often piratically) utilized by European writers. I regret the absence of any illustration from the Freer Collection, Washington. During the time when this book was being written the Freer Museum was not accessible. I also have to apologize for the absence of any technical information about the nature of the pigments used by Chinese painters ; as I know nothing of science this subject lies wholly beyond my reach. I hope that the question will before long be studied by some competent specialist.

9

CHAPTER II
FROM CHOU TO HAN

CHAPTER II
FROM CHOU TO HAN

The earliest Chinese pictures which have survived are manifestly the product of an art long practised, a civilization already mature. Concerning the development of this art history tells us very little that is important. Many anecdotes attest that image-making of some kind existed from the earliest times; one such story even refers to the 14th century B.C. But where the word *hua* ("drawing") is used, it must not be assumed that actual painting is meant. For *hua* originally meant no more than to scratch or "trace" (as one traces a pattern on the ground with one's umbrella), and in early times often refers to incisions on wood or stone.

Most of the anecdotes which refer to painting in early times have already been translated. They chiefly concern portraits; with regard to the materials used or the way in which they were handled, no information whatever is given. It is not possible, then, to give any account of the stages by which Chinese painting developed into the state in which we find it when we examine the earliest specimens which survive. But it will perhaps be worth while to give some account of Chinese civilization in the periods which preceded this mature art.

Many of the books which purport to give an account of these early times are of doubtful authenticity and meagre interest. But one, the *Odes*, is not only indisputably genuine, but also portrays in a vivid and varied manner the life of the Chinese at a remote period. The *Book of Odes* is an anthology of songs most of which were made between the 13th and the 6th centuries B.C. Two subjects predominate—the miseries of love and of war. The little China[1] of those days was beset on all sides by hostile tribes. Song after song records the agony of endless combats :

> *We pluck the bracken,*
> *The new bracken,*
> *The bracken springing from the earth . . .*
> *" Home, home," we cry,*
> *For the old year's ending . . .*
> *We have no home, no house,*
> *Because of the Hsienyün . . .*
> Odes II, 1, VII.

> *The Hsienyün blaze out upon us ;*
> *We must make haste to meet them.*
> *The King has called us to war,*
> *To deliver his lands.*
> Odes II, 3, III.

[1] For its extent, see Hirth's *Ancient History of China*, 2nd ed., New York, 1911.

13

CHINESE PAINTING

Marshal of the troops,
We are the King's teeth, we are his claws.
Why have you led us into misery,
Why have you robbed us of our rest?

Odes II, 4, I.

Here is one of the love-poems :

All day the wind blew wild.
You looked at me and laughed ;
But your jest was lewdness and your laughter, mockery.
Sick was my heart within.

All day the wind blew with a whirl of dust.
Kindly you seemed to come,
Came not, nor went away.
Long, long I think of you.

The dark wind will not suffer
Clean skies to close the day.
Cloud trails on cloud.   Oh, cruel thoughts !
I lie awake and moan.

The sky is black with clouds ;
The far-off thunder rolls ;
I have woken and cannot sleep, for the thought of you
Fills all my heart with woe.

Odes I, 3, V.

As a boat is danced
Where the waves will,
So I on my bed
In torment tossed
Lie long awake ;
Nor wine, nor sport
Can ease my pain.

Oh that my heart were a glass
Wherein I might read !
To my brothers I went,
Sought help and found it not,
But anger only.

My heart is not a stone
To be rolled aside ;
My heart is not a mat,
To be folded away.
What have I done?   If I a jot have erred,
Show me my fault !

14

My heart is dull with dread ;
I am girt around
With the scorn of little men.
Much torment have I seen,
Much insolence endured,
Have sunk in idle thought
And, waking, beat my breast.

O Sun, O Moon,
Why have you dwindled and changed ? . . .
Sorrow to my heart
Clings like an unwashed dress ;
I am borne down
By useless thoughts, and cannot
Take wing to fly away.   Odes I, 3, I.

There is in the original a grace and lightness which are even more difficult to recapture in English than its absolute simplicity of diction.   In the first of the two long poems the writer paints human passion against a background of storm.   In many of the odes (as in other folk-poetry) each human feeling recorded in the poem is prefaced by the description of some parallel manifestation in nature :

Thick grow the weeds on yonder bank,
And tangled are the sorrows that clot my breast.

This tendency to bring human things into relation with Nature, common enough in primitive literature, survived as one of the most prominent characteristics of developed art and poetry in China.   I have said that the songs are written in an age of incessant war.   Many passages prove that it was also an age when social inequalities were already a bitter grievance :

They drink good wine,
They eat fine food,
Build houses side by side,
Kinsmen by marriage,
They make cause together.
But I am all alone,
In sorrow and dismay.

Those churls have houses,
Those coxcombs, corn !
But the people have no sustenance,
With the rod of disaster
Heaven has laid them low.
The rich still may live,
But woe to him that is poor and alone !
        Odes II, 4, VIII.

15

Some had fields and lands,
But you have taken them away.
Some had serfs and servants,
But you have laid hands upon them.
Some were innocent and you have bound them ;
Some were guilty and you have pleaded for them.

Odes III, 3, X.

" If this is life," says one of the later sages, " would that I had never been born ! "

" If this is life," say in effect other songs, " let us snatch from it what pleasures we can."

The cricket chirrups in the hill ;
The year is drawing to its close.
I will make merry, I will sing,
Ere the days and months be fled.

Odes I, 10, I.

There grows an elm-tree on the hill
And by the mere, an alder-tree—
You have a coat but do not wear it,
You have a gown, but do not trail it,
You have a horse, but do not ride it,
A coach, but do not drive it,
So will it be till you are dead
And others can enjoy them !

There grows a gum-tree on the hill,
And by the mere, a chestnut-tree.
You have wine and food, why do you forget
Sometimes to play your lute,
Sometimes to laugh and sing,
Sometimes to steal new playtime from the night.
Shall it be so till you are dead
And others have your house ?

Odes I, 10, II.

The latest of the Odes belongs to about 600 B.C. From that period onwards the Chou dynasty, which had held together the states of China in a loose confederation, began to lose its controlling power. To the perpetual discomfort of nomad incursions was added the horror of constant civil war. It was at this gloomy epoch that there arose two teachers whose influence was so far-reaching that no book upon any phase of Chinese civilization could afford not to give an account of them.[1]

[1] It will be apparent to Chinese readers that my account of the *Odes* was written under the influence of Hu Shih's *History of Chinese Philosophy*.

16

CHOU TO HAN

LAO TZŬ (*c.* 570–*c.* 490 B.C.)

A study of the *Book of Odes* shows that the religious conceptions of the ancient Chinese were not very different from those of the Aryans. Chief of gods is the Sky (*T'ien* or *Ti*). The Sky-god watches over all the actions of men. By nature he is amiable and indulgent ; but sometimes a storm of capricious ill-humour will overspread his face. He can then only be appeased by copious offerings of oxen and sheep. Next in importance comes his son Hou Chi, the Harvest-god, borne to him by a mortal princess and venerated as the ancestor of the Chou dynasty.

If we turn from the *Odes* to Lao Tzŭ, we find that the conception of a supreme personal deity, a capricious and moody potentate of the sky, has completely vanished. The universe, says Lao Tzŭ, is governed by an impersonal principle, a primal force that is not angered by neglect, nor placated by sacrifice.[1] The old conception of a supreme anthropomorphic deity was no doubt still current. But from the time of Lao Tzŭ it gradually dwindled, and it has played an inconspicuous part ever since.

The early Chinese conception of God was derived from experience of earthly kings. From them he borrowed his exacting and capricious temperament. On the other hand, the ideal monarch of Lao Tzŭ's philosophy is an earthly copy of the passionless impersonal Force which rules the world.

Thus from his metaphysic Lao Tzŭ derives his political philosophy. The king must not rule ; that is to say, he must not make sporadic sentimental efforts to improve the condition of his subjects, any more than the sun stops in his course to shine longer on those that shiver than on those that sweat. He must allow the wheels of state to turn unimpeded either by pity or anger.

Lao Tzŭ was no believer in progress ; for he regarded every civilized complication of life as a step away from the simplicity of Nature, and with Nature he identified the primæval *tao* or " principle " upon which his whole philosophy was based. His political ideal was " a small kingdom with few inhabitants. Let there be machines capable of doing ten men's, a hundred men's, work ; but let no one use them. . . . Let there be ships and carriages, but let no one side in them. Let there be breastplates and swords, but let no one arm himself with them. Let the people again use knotted ropes[2] instead of writing."

[1] Like Blake's God, " He is not a Being of pity and compassion, He cannot feel distress."
[2] The *quipus* of the Mexican Indians.

Lao Tzŭ's book is so well known to Western readers that I need not here give a detailed analysis of his doctrines. Of the forty-odd translations which exist, many suffice to give a general notion of his philosophy. Certain passages will always remain unintelligible, for the book was clumsily patched together at a comparatively late period out of a floating mass of " sayings."

CONFUCIUS (551–479 B.C.)

Like Lao Tzŭ, Confucius looked towards the past. He believed in a Golden Age dominated not by the " natural man " of Lao Tzŭ, but by a series of supernaturally wise and disinterested monarchs. Like Lao Tzŭ, Confucius did not believe in a personal deity. It has often been assumed that, because the Chinese have discarded the conception of God, they lack the emotions which we are accustomed to associate with religion. It seems to me that they have merely transferred these emotions to another object. In parent-worship the Chinese have found an outlet not only for the main stream of normal religious feeling, but also for all the minor morbidities and perversities which form the backwaters of religion. Developed Confucianism, which is of much later date than Confucius himself, measures a man's worth by two tests : with how utter and prostrate a devotion does he serve his parents while they are alive ; with what self-inflicted miseries, tortures, and penances does he mourn for them when they die ? Read the sections on Mourning in the *Book of Rites*. Doubtless it is for very different conscious motives that the fakir, the dervish, the Christian mystic, reduce themselves to that same state of emaciation, weakness, and filth, which is also the crown and glory of the Confucian mourner. But in each case the same inner psychological need is being satisfied.

Important, however, as is the instinct of self-abnegation which finds its outlet in parent-worship, it is second to an even more vital craving—the desire for self-extension, for the enlargement of individual personality by contact with some wider entity. This instinct (satisfied in the mystic religions by the conception of union with Buddha, Tao, or God) finds its Confucian expression in the cult of ancestors. The worshipper learns to look upon himself, not as a mere fate-blown wisp, but as the last link of a venerable chain.

From this cult of the past sprang inevitably the conception of a static civilization. The work of the statesman is to preserve what the Ancestors have transmitted. Whatever change is made can only take the form of restoration. If an organization is to remain intact, each element in it must have a clearly defined function. These functions can be scheduled and tabulated, so that henceforward each member of the community may know exactly what are his public duties. But public and private life are closely interwoven, and even when all conflict has been removed from the machinery of state the home may yet produce frictions which will ultimately cause harm to the common weal. It is therefore necessary to regulate every domestic contingency down to the minutest detail of table-manners—" if there are herbs in the soup, chop-sticks must be used; if there are none, it must be drunk out of the bowl."

The immense importance attached to minutiæ of personal conduct may be seen in many passages of the Confucian *Analects*, particularly in the tenth book, which describes the domestic habits of Confucius—how he walked, how he lay in bed, how he ate, and how he fasted. Even the shape of his night-gown is recorded. His passionate conservatism, his adoration of discipline, and established order, even his cult of neatness, were without doubt reactions against the state of frenzied anarchy into which the weakening of the Chou supremacy had plunged the whole country. But they were also reactions against the antinomian and dis-integrating philosophies which were then current.

Impressive as was the metaphysical side of Lao Tzŭ's mystic teaching, its political applications were childish. Mysticism belongs to the sphere of poetry, of emotion; and it is as poetry, not as political science, that its Utopias must be judged. In this respect Lao Tzŭ fails; for, at any rate in the form in which they have reached us, his political theories are pro-pounded in a language wholly devoid of imaginative beauty. The hiero-phantic vagueness which is perfectly appropriate to the transcendental portions of his work becomes intolerable in his political disquisitions. What precisely is the famous *wu-wei* (" Inactivity ") by which the ideal monarch rules? Certainly Lao Tzŭ did not mean to signify, as certain European interpreters have supposed, merely a species of Whig *laissez-faire*. It was something much more positive, and yet something wholly negative! Lao Tzŭ was not a solitary thinker propounding a theory of his own invention. He was the representative of a school of thought which had been long established in China. It is easy to imagine the exasperation which such loose doctrines aroused in the neat Confucian mind.

TĒNG HSI AND THE "SOPHISTS."

We read that Tēng Hsi (who was a contemporary of Confucius) could conjure with words " till wrong seemed right and right wrong." A man of whom this is said may be a mere rhetorician; on the other hand, experience teaches us that a serious logician will appear just in this light to the crowd. Tēng Hsi was regarded as a " sophist," and this is the label which one philosopher invariably attaches to another whose thought is subtler than his own. When Confucius speaks of those " whose sharp tongues would subvert the State," we may guess that he has Tēng Hsi in mind.

The book which bears his name is almost certainly a fabrication; his figure, a mere shadow. He was succeeded by a whole band of speculative philosophers whose works and reputations Confucianism has obliterated almost as ruthlessly as St. Patrick destroyed the learning of the Druids. Most of these philosophers we know only through vituperative allusions to them in the works of Confucian writers. A certain feudal prince was in the habit of holding long colloquies with the sophist Kung-sun Lung. His courtiers, fearing the visitor might be corrupting their master's morals, deputed one of their number to listen through the key-hole and report what was going on. To his horror the eavesdropper found that the prince and his instructor were solemnly discussing " whether a white horse is a horse "!

From all that we know of Kung-sun Lung it is apparent that he was a perfectly serious logician. To most of his contemporaries, as to the eavesdropping courtier, he seemed to be merely a lunatic. When in the 2nd century B.C. Confucianism had finally and completely stifled speculative thought, the works of the so-called sophists were either lost altogether or (owing to faulty copying by scribes who did not understand the subject-matter) preserved in so corrupt a form as to be unintelligible. Thus the portions of Mo Tzǔ's[1] book which deal with logic became, a few centuries after his death, entirely incomprehensible to his countrymen, and remained so until in recent years the Chinese became acquainted with Indian and European philosophy. It was then possible to reconstruct a good deal of Mo Tzǔ's terribly mutilated text.

Early Chinese philosophy suffered the same fate at the hands of Confucianism that Greek Lyric poetry suffered at the hands of Christian bigotry; it is hard to estimate the scope and importance of what we have lost.

---

[1] Born, *circa* 495; died, *circa* 420. His works have recently been translated in full by Professor A. Forke.

CHUANG TZŬ (b. *circa* 350; d. *circa* 275 B.C.)

The survival of that arch-heretic Chuang Tzŭ, where so much other heretical writing was destroyed, is something of a paradox. But the Chinese have generally allowed literary appreciation to override their orthodoxy. Chuang Tzŭ is rather a mystical poet than a philosopher; and it has been to his writings that generation after generation of Chinese poets have turned as a refuge from the aridity of Confucian ritualism.

The basis of his doctrine is that we must not accept as real the world which our senses present to us. For in that world everything is relative. Are you old? So you may think, but Methuselah would consider you a child. Is your shirt white? Lay it upon the snow, and it will appear as a dark patch.

But behind this world of contraries Chuang Tzŭ, like Blake,[1] divines a state of being in which contraries are identical. It may be apprehended by *ming*, " illumination " (Giles's " light of nature "), which corresponds to Blake's " imagination," but not by the physical senses. In a legend surprisingly like those of Blake, Chuang Tzŭ tells how the God of the North and the God of the South, having been kindly treated by Chaos (God of the Centre), were trying to devise some way of rendering him a service. Having noticed that his body lacked the seven apertures of the senses (eyes, ears, nostrils, and mouth), they proceeded to bore holes in him. " So every day they bored one hole; but on the seventh day Chaos died."

THE KINGDOM OF CH'U.

The early Chinese inhabited the basin of the Yellow River. The Yang-tze basin was still in the hands of " Jungle Barbarians," whose country was known from the 7th century B.C. onwards as Ch'u, " The Land of Thorns." These people were not wholly different from the Chinese either in speech or race; the relation may be compared with that of Rome to the Italic tribes. Their descendants still inhabit the wilder districts of Hunan, Ssechuan, and Yünnan. The Land of Ch'u was colonized by the Chinese at least as early as 1000 B.C. It was ruled by kings who claimed kinship with the Chinese Imperial family. In 334 B.C. the King of Ch'u conquered Yüeh, a non-Chinese state which lay near the mouth of the Yang-tze, and expanded his frontiers till they included parts of the

---

[1] See especially *Milton*, Bk. II, " There is a place where Contraries are equally True . . ." and *Jerusalem*, XLVIII, 13, " Beneath the bottoms of the Graves, which is Earth's central joint, there is a place where Contrarieties are equally true."

modern provinces of Kiangsi, Fuhkien, Kuangtung, Honan, and Shen-si. For a few decades Ch'u was the most important state in the Far East. The conqueror of Yüeh was Wei Wang, who ruled from 339–329 B.C. His son, Huai Wang (329–299), attempted to continue his father's policy of expansion, but was defeated by the King of Ch'in at the battle of Hankow in 313 B.C. Henceforward the fortunes of Ch'u steadily declined.

THE ARTS IN CH'U

The latest poems in the *Book of Odes* date from about 600 B.C. During the three hundred years which followed, the art of poetry seems to have made no progress. Literary poetry (as opposed to song-writing) first appears about 300 B.C., not in China proper, but in the semi-foreign state of Ch'u. Here arose a literature of almost Indian exuberance, wildly fanciful and romantic, which was destined for several centuries to deflect Chinese writers from the limpid Classicism which seems to accord with their national genius. It is probable that not only the poetry, but also the painting of the Han dynasty was derived from the Land of Ch'u. Ch'ü Yüan, the earliest of the Ch'u poets, has left a curious work called the *Heavenly Questionings*. It consists of a long series of questions concerning cosmogony and mythology, not apparently arranged in any coherent order : Who parted Light from Darkness ? How came a virgin to bear nine children ? Where is the forest of stone trees in which all the beasts can talk ?

Here is a story which sounds more Indian than Chinese : The River God, in order to amuse himself without constraint, assumed the form of a white dragon. The archer Hou Yi shot at him and wounded him in the eye. The River God complained to the God of the Sky, saying, " Hou Yi must be punished ; he has blinded my left eye." But the God of the Sky answered, " Hou Yi is not to blame. If a God stoops so low as to assume the semblance of a beast, he must brave the hunter's bow."

The Han dynasty editor gives the following account of the circumstances under which the *Heavenly Questionings* were written. When Ch'ü Yüan was wandering through Ch'u, he saw the Ancestral Temples of the former Kings of Ch'u and the Ancestral Shrines of the ministers ; upon their walls were painted all the marvels of Heaven and Earth, Gods and Spirits of the hills and streams, ancient sages and their wondrous doings. . . . So looking up at these pictures, he wrote upon the wall, and breathing upon it asked these questions."

The explanation is as obscure as the *Questionings*; but the tradition is important because it implies the existence of mythological wall-paintings in the country of Ch'u. With such wall-paintings the *Heavenly Questionings* seem to have some connection. It is impossible to read them without recalling the Han dynasty sepulchral reliefs. It is therefore, as I have said, not improbable that the art as well as the poetry of Han derived from the exotic culture of Ch'u. The luxuriant, "tropical" character of this culture, which some[1] have attributed to Indian influence, is probably due rather to a resemblance of *terrain* between the two jungle civilizations.

THE CH'IN EMPIRE

In the 3rd century B.C. a new power arose in the north-west and drove the Ch'us from their capital. This power was the state of Ch'in, a wild and bellicose people whose blood was much mingled with that of the Tartar tribes on whose borders they dwelt. By 221 B.C. the whole of China, not the small feudal China over which the Chou kings had ruled, but a vast imperial China which included the semi-Chinese states of the Yang-tze basin and mouth, had fallen into their hands. The King of Ch'in became First Emperor ("Shih Huang-ti") of a realm almost as great in extent as that over which Alexander had a hundred years before held such brief sway. Determined not to lose the fruits of his great conquest the First Emperor devised a scheme which should hold both vassals and enemies in perpetual impotence. To render his empire impervious to foreign attack he began to encircle[2] it with a huge wall, the Great Wall of China, which many centuries later was still incomplete. Every instrument of warfare throughout China was to be surrendered to him and all this vast mass of metal smelted into the form of two huge statues of iron.

Moreover, he would not be pestered with the precedents of a legendary past. He knew that his vast Empire could not be handled as the paragons of ancient times had managed their small feudal kingdoms. He therefore proscribed the Confucians whose wisdom consisted in perpetual adulation

[1] See Conrady, *Indischer Einflüss in China im 4. Jahr. v. Chr.* (Zeitschrift d. Deut. Morgenl. Gesellsch., Bd. 60, pp. 335–351). The only convincing example which he cites is the legend of the Hare in the Moon, which is to be found in the Jātakas and is also alluded to by Ch'ü Yüan; the rest of the article consists of vague parallels and resemblances. Evidently Conrady has not quite got to the bottom of the matter, for the legend of the Hare in the Moon is shared with the Indians and Chinese by the Mexicans and even the Hottentots!

[2] Parts of this wall-system were already in existence.

of the past, and burnt all written records (213 B.C.). The object of the Burning of the Books was probably the extinction of local patriotism. We know that in feudal times each state kept its own annals. None of these annals, except Confucius's history of the state of Lu, survives to-day. There is no reason to suppose that any pure literature perished in the Burning. Poetry, apart from folk-song, seems to have existed only in the state of Ch'u. Much heterodox (that is to say, non-Confucian) philosophy has certainly disappeared, but this was chiefly due to the indifference or hostility of Han dynasty scholars.

The Ch'in dynasty lasted only eighty years. The First Emperor, having carried out with apparent success his grandiose scheme of permanent and inviolable empire, discovered that it was marred by one flaw: he himself was mortal. But surely the Emperor who had defeated and disarmed the millions of China, who had girt its vast confines with unassailable ramparts, could frustrate so small a thing as death? He sent out wizards to search in remote islands for the " herb of immortality." After many failures they at last returned in triumph. He ate what they had brought, fell ill and died. Soon afterwards the Empire of the Ch'ins collapsed.

CHAPTER III
THE HAN DYNASTY AND BUDDHISM

THE HAN DYNASTY AND BUDDHISM

THE HAN DYNASTY

The Ch'ins had overthrown the feudal system and set up a rigidly centralized government. The Han dynasty partly reversed this policy. China was parcelled out into a number of fiefs which were put under the rule of the Emperor's kinsmen. The courts of many of these princes became important centres of art and learning. Under their patronage the culture destroyed by the Ch'ins was gradually reconstituted. The intellectuals of China lived in a state of perpetual excitement, as book after book was rediscovered and translated into the current script. As no one knew what had been lost, the wildest expectations prevailed as to what would be found. It was believed that " magic " books were somewhat concealed, capable of conferring upon the reader every species of divine and demoniac power.

The books which actually reappeared may be divided into two classes : (1) Northern works, the products of Confucian didacticism ; (2) Southern works, the products of the equally didactic, but more passionate and dithyrambic school of Ch'ü Yüan. The poetry of the Han dynasty, which was largely the work of southerners, was entirely founded on the latter class. Meanwhile the Confucian works were made the basis of a new state philosophy.

I have hitherto spoken of Confucianism as though it were a complete doctrine framed and perfected by Confucius himself. This requires modification. The only book which indubitably represents the actual teaching of Confucius is the *Analects*. The Book of Changes, the three Books of Rites, the Book of History, were all substantially " edited " by their rediscoverers, who, having slipped their own views into these venerated texts, denounced all other philosophies as heterodox.

Most influential of those who travestied the doctrines of Confucius was Tung Chung-cho. He is the inventor of absolute conservatism. Confucius tends to idealize the past, but his sayings are not the eternal panegyric of Yao and Shun which constitutes the backbone of later Confucianism. To Tung Chung-cho the past is a law, and any deviation from it a crime.

When, in 140 B.C., the Emperor Wu Ti ascended the throne at the age of sixteen, Tung Chung-cho had no difficulty in persuading him to proscribe all study but that of the Confucian Classics. Taoist mysticism never came effectually under this ban. But the schools of speculative philosophy, which might have struggled back into existence, were crushed for ever.

NEO-TAOISM

The early Taoists, Lao Tzŭ and Chuang Tzŭ, were mystic philosophers. During the 3rd century B.C. there arose a set of magicians who professed to have discovered the Elixir of Life, and to be possessed of all kinds of marvellous powers. As their patron saint they took Lao Tzŭ (a choice almost as irrelevant as that of the mediæval wizards who regarded themselves as the descendants of Aristotle). Consequently they are known as Taoists. Having first supported rigid Confucianism and then dallied for a time with literature, the Emperor Wu Ti fell completely into the hands of these marvel-mongers, who supplied him with an endless series of impressive " psychic phenomena." But the Taoist Church proper begins with the Heavenly Master, a mystagogue who about 142 A.D. set up a clinic on the Mountain of the Singing Crane in Ssechuan. Each patient brought with him a present of five pecks of rice, and was given in return a talisman inscribed with mystic formulæ. He was instructed to think of his symptoms while tapping his head, and to drink water in which the talisman had been held.[1]

So began a long line of glorified witch-doctors—popes of a mysterious " Higher Thought." The adepts of the society were graded according to their spiritual proficiency; the famous poet Li Po was the proud recipient of one of these Taoist diplomas.

Gradually the superstitions of the new Taoism were codified into a religion strongly resembling popular Buddhism, with a complete canon of hastily fabricated scriptures.[2]

Taoism having now become a revealed religion, its philosophic doctrines were no longer required and went a-begging. They were to a large extent annexed by the Han Confucianists. The bridge between the doctrines of Lao Tzŭ and Confucius was the *Book of Changes*.

The theory of the *Changes*, an ancient cabalistic work edited and enlarged by Confucius, is that the apparently complex phenomena of the visible world conform to certain simple and easily intelligible patterns. By correlating any group of phenomena to the " type " to which it belongs, one can predict the future development of this group.

[1] Most of the patients improved. The rest were told that they lacked faith (*pu hsin tao*).

[2] A collection of them is now being published by the Commercial Press, Shanghai. Some of the earlier scriptures may prove to be less wholly devoid of interest than has been supposed.

The " types " or patterns are formed by a combination of two elements, the Complete and Incomplete. These, under the guise of male and female, positive and negative, good and bad, are inherent in all worldly phenomena. Before their appearance there existed only a vast un-differentiated Chaos. For some reason (and the weak point of their philosophy was that they did not satisfactorily explain why) this Chaos split into the two elements which I have mentioned; and they between them spawned the vast brood of phenomenal existence. Lao Tzŭ (in his 42nd chapter, for example) expounds much the same theory. Thus the *Book of Changes* became a bridge between Taoism and orthodoxy, and we find Yang Hsiung, the chief exponent of this synthesis, giving to the undifferentiated primal unity the name of *Hsüan*, Mystery, a term borrowed from Lao Tzŭ.

THE SCIENTIFIC SPIRIT

Geography was the first branch of learning to emerge from mythology into science. The discoveries of the explorer Chang Ch'ien[1] had proved for the first time that, however infallible the transcendental teaching of the Ancients may have been, their knowledge of terrestrial facts was very incomplete. The mere discovery of the fact that the Yellow River does not flow down from Fairyland discredited the whole corpus of Confucian learning in much the same way as the discoveries of Tyndall shook the faith of our ancestors not only in Genesis, but in the whole Creed.

The scepticism of Han dynasty intellectuals is reflected over and over again in the great *History*[2] of Ssŭ-ma Ch'ien. It is expressed in its most concentrated form in the *Lun Hēng*[3] of Wang Ch'ung, who approached in a spirit of relentless criticism every belief held sacred by his countrymen. Lao-tzŭ? Confucius? What can be known of them? Their works were transmitted by ignorant scribes who have eliminated every vestige of sense from their writings even if we are to assume that they ever wrote sense. Ghosts? Who has seen one? Dragons? Mere crayfish.

His contemporary Chang Hēng is the first Chinese painter of whom we have any considerable knowledge. But we know of him chiefly as an astronomer, mathematician, and poet. In 132 A.D. he constructed the first seismograph. Eight copper dragons on springs sat round a bowl. Each held a copper ball in his mouth. In the middle of the bowl squatted

---

[1] *Circa* 138–126 B.C.   [2] Completed *c.* 90 B.C.
[3] Translated by Alfred Forke; composed in the 2nd century A.D.

a toad with wide-open mouth. When there was an earthquake, the dragon nearest the direction from which the shock came dropped his ball into the toad's mouth. On one occasion a dragon released his ball, but no shock was felt and there was no news of an earthquake. The Confucians of the Capital who regarded Chang Hēng as an impious charlatan were delighted that his contrivance should have proved to be fallible, but in a few days a messenger arrived from a remote province announcing that there had been an earthquake.

HAN POETRY

Han poetry is derived in the main from the literature of Ch'u, but has not the same seriousness. The luxuriant vocabulary of the South is used for purely decorative purposes, as in the astonishing word-embroideries of Ssŭ-ma Hsiang-ju. I have given an account of this poetry in the introduction to *The Temple and Other Poems*.[1] The poet who here concerns us most is Wang Yen-shou.

He was the son of Wang I, editor of the *Ch'u Elegies* (his text is that which is most commonly used to-day). Yen-shou was born in the south, but was taken when still a boy to the province of Shantung. Here he visited the famous palace built in the middle of the 2nd century B.C. by one of the Emperor Wu's brothers. The great palaces at the Capital (Ch'ang-an) had all been destroyed at the time of the great revolution which divides the first Han dynasty from the second. But this provincial palace, preserved owing to its remoteness from the great political centres of China, was the work of a prince whose life-passion was architecture, and it vied in magnificence with its prototypes at Ch'ang-an.

Wang Yen-shou's *Description of the Ling-kuang Palace* was probably written before he was twenty. A few years later he was drowned while crossing the river Hsiang.

In his poem he described the wall-paintings in the great hall of the palace :

Upon the great walls
Flickering in a dim semblance glint and hover
The Spirits of the Dead.
And here all Heaven and Earth is painted, all living things
After their tribes, and all wild marryings
Of sort with sort ; strange spirits of the sea,
Gods of the hills. To all their thousand guises

[1] Allen and Unwin, 1923.

Had the painter formed
His reds and blues, and all the wonders of life
Had he shaped truthfully and coloured after their kinds.
First showed he the Opening of Chaos and the beginnings of the Ancient World ;
The Five Dragons with joined wings ;
Nine-neck, the Lord of Men ;
Fu Hsi with his scaly body,
Nu Wo serpent-limbed,
Vast formless presences,
At first unmarked, but to the steady gazer's eye
Rising in luminous bulk ;
Huang Ti, T'ang and Yü,
Each crowned as he was crowned and robed as he was clad,
The Three Kings were there, many riotous damsels and turbulent lords,
Loyal knights, dutiful sons, mighty scholars, faithful wives,
Victors and vanquished, wise men and fools,
None was missing from his place. . . .

The Ling-kuang palace has long ago disappeared, but not many miles from its site are two series of grave-reliefs which were evidently reproductions in stone-incision of the palace-paintings which Wang Yen-shou describes. The earlier series bears the date 129 A.D., and is thus contemporary with the poet's visit to Shantung ; the second series is dated 147–149 A.D. They will be discussed by Mr. Ashton in his forthcoming book on Chinese Sculpture.

By piecing together what we can learn from Yen-shou's poem and from the grave-reliefs which still exist we can get some notion of Chinese mural decoration in the 2nd century B.C. We can at least rebut M. Grousset's assertion that but for Buddhist influences Chinese painting would never have existed.

Wall-painting may have been practised much earlier than the 2nd century, but we have no evidence that it was so. The only information which we possess concerning painting under the Ch'in dynasty concerns the art of an unidentified foreign country : " Lieh I "[1] was a native of the kingdom of Ch'ien-hsiao,[1] the king of which country sent him to the Chinese court in the second year of Shih-huang (220 B.C.). He put red into his mouth and spat it out on the wall in the shape of dragons and other beasts. He could draw lines on the ground with his finger as straight as though he were using a plumb-line ; circles and squares as accurately as if he had measured them with a compass and rule. In the space of a square inch he drew the Five Mountains and the Four Oceans,

---

[1] Ancient pronunciations approximately " Liet I " and " Gan-siev."

31

marking every country. He painted phœnixes so life-like that one expected to see them take wing and fly away.[1]

The wording of the Chinese text makes it quite clear that Lieh I was a foreigner, and we shall probably not be wrong in assuming that his native country lay towards the West. We should have been more interested in him if he had been an artist and not a conjuror. His story is only of importance because it shows that outside influences may have affected Chinese art long before the arrival of Buddhism.

BUDDHISM

We do not know when Buddhism reached China ; we do not even know when it reached Central Asia. Were there Buddhists in the countries visited by Chang Ch'ien in the 2nd century B.C.? We have no reason to suppose so. The Tibetan *History of Khotan*[2] places the conversion of the Khotanese to Buddhism in the year 83 B.C. Chinese legend places the introduction of Buddhism into China at a much earlier date. A devotional work[3] of the 6th century tells how a priest called Li Fang came with seventeen wise men to convert the First Emperor of the Ch'in dynasty. They were all cast into prison, but delivered during the night by a huge and luminous figure who battered down the prison gates and set them at liberty.

The first authentic date is 2 B.C., in which year a Chinese courtier received an account of Buddhism from an envoy of the Yüeh-chih or Indo-Scythians who had recently founded their great Central Asian and North Indian empire. It is certain, too, that about the middle of the 1st century A.D. a Chinese prince, the King of Ch'u (half-brother of the emperor Ming Ti), was an ardent Buddhist. The story of how in response to a Heaven-sent vision Ming Ti fetched missionary priests from India is obviously the work of pious pens. But there is no reason to doubt that about the year 70 A.D. Buddhism first received some kind of official recognition. In the next century it became an accepted and familiar institution.[4] In a poem written about 120 A.D. Chang Hēng speaks of dancing-girls, " whose beauty not the Confucian ascetic Chan Chi nor the *śramanas* of India could resist."

[1] *Ming Hua Chi* IV, 1 verso, quoted from the rather unreliable *Shih-i Chi* of the Taoist Wang Chia (died *c.* 386 A.D.).

[2] See Japanese translation (1921), p. 107.   [3] The *Li Tai San Pao Chi.*

[4] But till the 4th century its adherents were mostly foreigners.

THE HAN DYNASTY AND BUDDHISM

AMIDA BUDDHISM

From 148–177 A.D. there lived at Lo-yang, the capital of the Latter Han dynasty, a Parthian prince named An Shih-kao, perhaps a son of Mithridates IV (Wieger identifies him with Parthamasiris, son of Pacorus II).

It is difficult to disentangle him from the mass of legend which has gathered round his name; but it seems at least possible that it was he who introduced into China the worship of Amida, God of Boundless Light. The mild ethical and philosophic teaching imported by the 1st century missionaries was calculated to arouse the interest of a few sensitive students, but it could never have become the basis of a popular religion. About the year 170 A.D. the Parthian visitor translated a very different book, the Sūtra of Paradise.[1] This work belongs to the class of " accommodated " scriptures, in which the abstract doctrines of Buddhism are clothed in concrete language for the benefit of the unlearned. The bliss of Nirvāna is allegorically depicted under the guise of a sumptuous Oriental palace, whose gardens are green with an eternal Spring. Exquisite music, delicate fragrances, delicious food and drink—in fact, every sensual pleasure but love—perpetually delight the inhabitants of this abode, who are all young, intelligent, and of the male sex. Over this happy realm presides Amida, a timeless, spiritual Buddha, commonly regarded as the incorporeal aspect of Shākyamuni:

> Once upon the Vulture Peak He turned the Wheel of Law,
> Now Lord of the Western Land He sits in Paradise.

The description of Amida's Palace is to a large extent borrowed from the description of the earthly king Sudassana's palace in the *Sutta* of the Great Decease. It became part of the stock apparatus of Indian literature, reappearing in the Mahābhārata.

The Indian framers of this allegory hoped to excite the imaginations of common men by offering to them in a future life such splendours as only their kings and rulers enjoyed on earth. The prospect was no doubt attractive, but it lacked, for those who had seen something of their raja's court, the essential elements of mystery, exotism, incomprehensibility.

Upon the mind of the Chinese masses these luxuriant descriptions made a very different impression. All was strange and fascinating—the lotus-ponds, the unfamiliar jewels and trees with their luscious Sanskrit names,

---

[1] *Sukhāvatī Vyuhā Sūtra.* There is some evidence that the worship of Amida may have originated in Central Asia under Iranian influence. See Eliot, *Hinduism and Buddhism*, III, 218.

33

the scents, the spices, " golden waters lapping white sands ; silver waters lapping golden sands." In the land of its imaginers the Paradise of Amida has been forgotten for a thousand years ; but for many millions who belong to another climate and race it is still the spiritual goal.

THE FIRST BUDDHIST TEMPLE IN CHINA

Like all foreign visitors to China, the early Buddhist missionaries were given accommodation in public buildings. The word *ssŭ*, afterwards used to denote a Buddhist temple, implies this fact, for it originally meant " office " or " bureau." A very unreliable legend attributes to the Emperor Ming Ti the building (*c.* 70 A.D.) of the White Horse Temple at Lo-Yang. The building of a temple is also part of the An Shih-kao legend, but it seems that he is here being confused with the magician An Hou, who lived in the 3rd century A.D. About the year 190 A.D. we come to actual history. A certain Chai Jung was employed to collect rice-tithes in the Yang-tze valley. Availing himself of the state of disorder into which the country had fallen, he appropriated the tithes and with the proceeds built a temple at Hsü-chou in Kiangsu. " The courtyard was large enough to hold some three thousand worshippers. The idols were covered with gold and clad in brocades and colours. Each time Buddha was washed a great supply of food and drink was arranged at the road-side. Those who came to eat and look on were sometimes more than ten thousand."[1]

Soon, however, the rising power of Ts'ao Ts'ao (founder of the next dynasty) made Hsü-chou unsafe. Jung, with ten thousand young men and girls and three thousand horses, decamped to Kuang-ling, where he took to commerce. The remaining years of his life were packed with adventures which concern neither Buddhism nor art.

[1] *Annals of the Latter Han Dynasty,* 73, 9.

CHAPTER IV
THE THREE KINGDOMS AND CHIN

CHAPTER IV
THE THREE KINGDOMS AND CHIN

TS'AO PU-HSING AND THE SOGDIAN PRIEST SENG-HUI[1]

In A.D. 220 the Han dynasty broke up into three rival kingdoms—Shu, Wu, and Wei. Sun Ch'üan, the first emperor of Wu, made his capital at Nanking. In 247 there arrived at the city an Indian ascetic who, building himself a thatched hut, set up an image in the corner of it and began to preach strange doctrines. The emperor ordered an enquiry to be made, and was told that this was a priest of the same foreign religion which Ming Ti of the Han dynasty had imported from the West a hundred and eighty years ago. The stranger said that his name was Sēng-hui and that he was by race a Sogdian. He had come from India (where his family had for some while been settled) by way of Canton. Buddhist priests, long familiar to the inhabitants of the west and north-west of China, had never been seen in the neighbourhood of Nanking. The Court was soon converted and temples built.

There is a tradition[2] that one of Sēng-hui's converts was the Court painter Ts'ao Pu-hsing, to whom he is supposed to have given lessons in Buddhist iconography. But it is as a painter of dragons that Ts'ao Pu-hsing is known to history.

DRAGON-PAINTING

There was once a man called Tzŭ-kao who said that he had a passion for dragons. He was always talking about them and had them painted all over the walls of his house. " After all," he said, " there is nothing pleasanter to look at than a dragon." One day a huge, shiny, slimy paw flopped on to his window-sill ; soon a green and golden, scaly face reared itself up at the window and grinned a dank greeting. Tzŭ-kao, the lover of dragons, was beside himself with terror. He fled shrieking to the hall, where he tripped over the oozing, slithery tail which the monster had thrust in friendly salutation through the doorway of the house. The story is told as a warning against insincere enthusiasms.

Tzŭ-kao, an historical character, was Lord of the Heaths (*Yeh-kung*) in the land of Ch'u about the year 500 B.C. The earlier versions of the story tell us that his dragon-decorations were carved, not painted. It is Wang Ch'ung, writing in the 1st century A.D., who calls them paintings ;

---

[1] See Chavannes, *T'oung Pao*. Sér. II, Vol. X, 199–212.
[2] Dating from the 10th century, see *Shu Hua P'u*, XI, 26.

37

from which we may infer that sculpture was a commoner form of decoration than painting in early times. The sequel to the story, in most of its versions, was that the land of Ch'u lay under water all that summer; for the dragon is *yü-shih* (" Rain-master "), and floods follow in his train.

The Chinese dragon is a synthesis of two elements, the Divine Horse and the Divine Fish. (A third element, that of the Divine Snake, was imported from India with Buddhism.) The dragon which in Chinese myth draws the chariot of the Emperors and divinities is a kind of Pegasus; the dragon of pools, whom the peasants placated with offerings of sucking-pig and wine,[1] is a kind of glorified octopus, many-tentacled, sometimes many-headed, pink-whiskered, and goggle-eyed. The clouds, as well as the rivers and pools, are his domain, and in pictures his slithering coils are shown half-hidden in banks of fog and mist. The first historical dragon-painter is Ts'ao Pu-hsing; but long before his time rain-bringing dragons must have been painted on farmers' barn doors. He also painted huge figures on strips of silk joined together; these may have been Buddhist paintings, but we are not told so. His work did not long survive, for about 500 A.D. the critic Hsieh Ho was able to see no specimen of it except one dragon's head.

Ts'ao Pu-hsing's pupil, Wei Hsieh, is a much more definite figure. Most of his pictures illustrated Chinese legends (" Gods and Fairies," " Heroines,"[2] " The Upper Park at Ch'ang-an, in black and white," etc.). His Seven Buddhas of Langkā is also mentioned and a set of illustrations to the *Book of Odes*, which for a time belonged to a son of the famous writer Han Yü and were seen by the art-historian Chang Yen-yüan in 841 A.D. " All previous painters," wrote Hsieh Ho, " had worked in a rough summary style. Wei Hsieh's paintings were the first to contain fine detail."

If this is true, he initiated a tendency very dangerous to Chinese art, which has frequently suffered from over-elaboration of detail.

PAINTING ON VASES AND BRONZE BOWLS

The earliest Chinese painting which exists is perhaps to be found upon certain earthenware vases, dating from the 1st century onwards. Some of these are decorated only with formal ornament, others with conventionalized dragons[3] or flowers. Two much more elaborately decorated

---

[1] See *A Hundred and Seventy Chinese Poems*, p. 121.
[2] Or one might translate it " Famous Ladies of History."
[3] One such is in the Collection of Mr. Eumorphopoulos.

specimens were brought to England recently. They seem to date from about the 3rd century A.D. One of them (now in the British Museum) shows a mounted huntsman with bow and arrow pursuing a tiger and other creatures, mocked at the while by a strange imp or marsh-demon. The same imp reappears in the second vase, a photograph of which I reproduce on Plate II. This time the horseman is armed with a long lance. His lean and long-legged steed reminds one of some of Honoré Daumier's Rosinantes. There are many stories of hunters meeting with imps and bogeys; such, for example, as that of the Duke Huan of Ch'i,[1] who when hunting in the marshes saw a demon " broad as a cart-wheel and long as a shaft."

The drawing on these vases has not much general design (less in fact than appears to be the case in the photograph), but great vividness of representation. Such casual artisan productions do not, of course, give us any notion of contemporary Court art—of the painting of Ts'ao Puhsing, for example.

There is in the collection of Baron Sumitomo at Ōsaka a cylindrical bronze bowl (*Lien*) which is attributed in *Kokka*, 332, to a period later than Han and not later than the Six Dynasties. One gathers that the writer of the article would place it in about the 4th or 5th century A.D. The inside of the cover[2] is coated with vermilion upon which a phœnix is painted in light blue, with line-work in black ink. Not much of the red groundwork survives, and the design is partially effaced. The bottom and sides of the interior of the bowl were decorated in the same way; on the bottom a dragon is just discernible; the sides seem to have been covered with decorative patterns. Traces of similar decoration remain on the inside of a bronze bowl belonging to Mr. Eumorphopoulos. It is quite uncertain whether the painted vases described above are in reality earlier than the painted bronzes. Both may, however, be said to belong to a period between the 2nd and 5th centuries A.D.

THE CHIN DYNASTY, 265–420 A.D.

Wei Hsieh lived on into the next dynasty, dying probably in the early years of the 4th century. In 280, after fifteen years of conflict, China was again united. The Western Chin dynasty made its capital at Lo-yang. In 317 it was replaced by the Eastern Chin, which succeeded in reigning for a hundred years at Nanking. The lower Yang-tze had been colonized

---

[1] Chuang Tzŭ, Chap. XIX.   [2] Reproduced in colours, *Kokka*, 333.

by the Chinese at a comparatively late date. The city of Nanking had under various names belonged successively to the non-Chinese kingdoms of Wu and Yüeh. The people of this region have always regarded themselves as absolutely distinct from the inhabitants of Central and Northern China, who seem to them solemn, slow-witted, and clumsy. Among this gay race Confucianism had made little progress, and conversation pleased them more than scholarship.

It was at Nanking in the 4th century that these pursuers of the exquisite invented the pastime of *ch'ing-t'an,* " abstract talk," in which purely fanciful subjects were discussed with whimsical earnestness, the only rule of the game being that nothing should be said that had the remotest connection with reality.

It was an age of alchemy and magic—not the greedy hocus-pocus of the Han wizards, but a languid and decorative occultism, half-childish, half-humorous. Unfortunately these gentle æsthetes existed only on sufferance; all around them flourished violence and folly. An endless succession of military adventurers plagued China in that age just as to-day, while to the north and west the Chinese Empire was steadily crumbling. No less than seventeen different barbarian " Empires " were established during the Chin dynasty within the frontiers of China, in Chihli, Shansi, Shensi, and Kansu; six by Hsienpi Tartars, five by Tibetans, three by Hu, two by Huns, and one by the Turkic adventurer Shih Lo. It was at the court of a Tibetan chieftain who had established himself at Ch'ang-an, the former capital of China, that the great Buddhist translator Kumārajīva[1] made his versions of the Lotus and Vimalakīrti Sūtras. Finally, in 386, a chieftain of the Toba clan of the Hsienpi Tartars welded all these petty kingdoms into one great Tartar Empire.

The instinct of cultivated and sensitive men, cast into the midst of all this violence and turmoil, was to fly to the wilds, to hide themselves far from the road upon which armies marched and the cities where upstart kings were crowned and slaughtered every week. But hunger soon drove them back to the world, and into the service of some ambitious Jackboot or ephemeral kingdom.

Typical of these would-be hermits was the great poet T'ao Ch'ien,[2] beset on the one hand by his loathing of bureaucratic life, and on the other by the urgent necessities of his family. Four times he took office;

---

[1] 344–413 A.D. His father was an Indian, his mother a princess of Kucha in Eastern Turkestan. He was educated partly in Kashmir.
[2] 365–427 A.D.

once he was at Nanking for six years. But all the while his heart was torn with longing:

> *Oh to be home again*
> *Ere field and garden to a wilderness are grown !*
> *Why do I loiter ?   I that wantonly have sold*
> *The Spirit to be Matter's slave !*

Late in life he made the acquaintance of Hui-yüan,[1] Abbot of the Eastern Wood Temple on Mount Lu, of whom some account must here be given.

Hui-yüan studied the Confucian and Taoist classics till he was twenty-one. Dissatisfied, he became a priest. After studying Buddhist philosophy in many temples, he became first Abbot of the Eastern Wood Temple, which was built for him by the musician Huan I.[2] Here he founded the White Lotus Society, a mixed guild of laymen and monks. Of the 123 members of this society many were Confucian scholars from the neighbouring town of Kiukiang; its object was the mystic worship of Amida. For thirty years the Abbot had never left the grounds of his monastery. It was said that he had vowed never to set foot in the " World " again. One day two visitors to the monastery were returning to the town. The Abbot escorted them through the gardens and the three fell into earnest conversation. Suddenly the two laymen realized that something terrible had happened : the Master had forgotten his vow and walked with them across the boundary bridge. Turning to him in consternation, they saw to their relief that he was laughing ; and the three of them stood together on the little bridge laughing immoderately at the absurd mishap.[3] One of these two laymen was the poet T'ao Ch'ien, who sought at the temple brief glimpses of the peace for which all his life he had longed in vain.

Had he lived in the next century T'ao Ch'ien would have been a priest. For it was in the monasteries that henceforward all thoughtful and uncombative souls sought refuge from a world made hideous by the tramplings of Tartar and Avar.

---

[1] 333–416 A.D.   [2] See p. 240.
[3] There are chronological inconsistencies in the usual version of the story. But there is no reason to discredit it entirely.

CHAPTER V
KU K'AI-CHIH

CHAPTER V

KU K'AI-CHIH

Ku K'ai-chih was born in the year 344 or 345 A.D. In 364 the Tile-coffin Temple was founded at Nanking. The priests called together a meeting of townsmen and asked for subscriptions towards the cost of completing the work. Many grandees and Ministers were present, but no one put himself down for more than 100,000 cash. When the list was handed to Ku K'ai-chih, this very young painter, who was known to be as poor as a mouse, startled the company by putting himself down for a million cash.

When the priests came to collect the money, Ku K'ai-chih said to them : " First give me the use of a wall." They showed him into a small build-ing to the north of the temple. Here he shut himself up for more than a month and painted a single figure of the Buddhist saint Vimalakīrti.[1] When he had finished the picture and was ready for the final ceremony of " putting in the eyes," he sent for the priests and said : " On the first day you must charge 100,000 cash for admission ; on the second day, 50,000 ; on the third day let visitors subscribe what they please." When the doors of the chapel were opened a radiance burst from the walls ; the thronging sightseers stood speechless with wonder ; in a few minutes the gate-keepers had taken a sum which enabled Ku K'ai-chih to fulfil his fabulous promise.

This story is told in the *Record of Temples at the Capital*.[2] What else we know of his life is chiefly contained in the *New Stories Told in the World*,[3] a collection of anecdotes published twenty years after his death. " He was of wide erudition and proud of his attainments." Some one once asked how his own *Description of a Harp* compared with Chi K'ang's *Description of a Lute*.[4] He replied : " Those who lack real appreciation of literature neglect my poem merely because it is later in date ; but a few men of genuine feeling have realized that it is a work of lofty inspiration."

The famous statesman Huan Wēn sent for him, made him one of his

---

[1] Vimalakīrti, lying a fragile hermit in his bare white cell, was the patron saint of Exquisiteness.   [2] *Ching-shih Ssŭ Chi*. 6th century ?

[3] *Shih-shuo Hsin-yü*. These stories are summarized, sometimes in an unintelligible manner, by the *Annals of the Chin Dynasty*. Chavannes's translation of the Life of Ku K'ai-chih, extracted from the Annals, contains several mistakes.

[4] Still extant. Chi K'ang was a celebrated musician, alchemist, and dilettante of the 3rd century, one of the Seven Idlers of the Bamboo Grove.

military secretaries, and showed him every mark of affection. When Wēn died, Ku K'ai-chih composed an elegy in which he said :

> When mountains crumble and vast oceans cease,
> Where shall the birds shelter, or the fishes find their home ?

Some one said to him, " You who leant so much upon Wēn's support and valued him so highly, how piteous a spectacle must your grief have presented ! " " My sighs," he answered, " heaved like an earthquake. They rent the very hills. My tears ran swift as a great river ; they swelled the waters of the sea."

His fondness for jesting and play made him the favourite of all who knew him.

He next became the military secretary of Yin Chung-k'an[1] and lived on terms of great intimacy with him. Yin was a man of singular open-mindedness. The first time he was shown a Buddhist book he examined it carefully, and then, looking up, he said, " These are just the topics which philosophy ought to discuss."

When they were at Ching-chou,[2] Ku obtained permission to go home on leave. In those days sails were not generally used on this part of the Yang-tze. Ku begged the sailors to hoist one, and got his way. At the island of P'o-chung (" Break-tomb ") a gale sprung up and the boat capsized. Ku wrote to Yin saying : " They call the place Break-tomb, and truly I escaped from death by breaking the hulk that entombed me. The traveller held fast to his gear, and the sail was none the worse for its wetting."

When he returned to Ching-chou some one asked him what he thought of the scenery in Kuei-chi. He replied : " A thousand peaks vie in tapering grace ; ten thousand valleys contend with rival streams. Trees and grasses, like misty clouds that rise and gather, film them with a cloak of green."

Once when Huan Hsüan (Huan Wēn's son) was with Ku at Yin Chung-k'an's house they played at the game of inventing phrases to express the idea of " finality." Ku began with the phrase, " A flat plain burnt by a great fire, when the last spark has smouldered out." Next they invented phrases to express the idea of danger. Ku's was " A new-born child asleep upon the cross-bar of a well." A certain secretary improved upon this with the immortal, " A blind rider on a sightless horse galloping

---

[1] His father had given similar employment to Ku's father.
[2] In Hupeh ; Yin was Prefect there.

upon the margin of a deep lake." Yin, whose own sight was failing, cried out in horror, " That touches too closely," and the game was stopped.

When he ate sugar-cane, he always began at the wrong end, saying that he liked to " enter gradually into Paradise."

Above all, he excelled in the handling of colours ; his pictures were remarkably fine. Hsieh An[1] thought very highly of them, and considered Ku the best painter the world had ever seen.

When he had finished a portrait he often waited several years before putting in the eyes. Some one asked him the reason of his hesitation, and he replied : " It is true that beauty of frame and limb can be expressed independently of these delicate parts ; but delineation of character depends entirely upon them."

He was once attracted by a girl who lived near, but she would not have anything to do with him. So he painted her portrait on the wall and stuck a thorn in it where the heart would be. The girl at once began to feel a stabbing pain in her heart. Ku again made love to her, and this time she yielded. He then removed the thorn from her portrait and the pain ceased.

He admired Chi K'ang's poems in lines of four syllables and was fond of illustrating them. He used to say : " The line *My hand sweeps the five strings* is quite easy to illustrate ; but the line *My eye follows the wild geese on their homeward flight* is difficult."

He was a great portraitist. When he painted Hsieh Kun he placed him among jutting crags. Some one asked him why he had done so, and he replied : " Hsieh himself once said[2] that among hills and valleys he showed to greater advantage. So I have thought it best to put the fellow among his hills and dales."

He wanted to make a portrait of his patron Yin Chung-k'an, but Yin refused, saying, " I am too ugly ; it would not be worth while." " Illustrious Prefect," answered Ku, " it is only your eyes that are at fault.[3] When I have marked the pupils I will brush a thin film of white over them, so that they may look like the sun when it is covered by light clouds."

[1] A great general, 320–385 A.D.

[2] Kun once said to the Emperor, " As regards correct tenure at Court and the marshalling of a host of officials, I am inferior to Sou Liang. But give me the hills and dales, and you will find me the better man." Giles (p. 19) has misunderstood and romanticized the episode, saying that Ku's picture shows " a conception of man's place in nature to which there is hardly a parallel in European art."

[3] Chavannes, " C'est précisement à cause de vos yeux que je veux faire votre portrait."

He once left in Huan Hsüan's charge a box sealed up in front with a wafer; it contained all the pictures which he valued most highly. Hsüan opened the box at the back, took out the paintings, and sent it to Ku, saying for fun that it had not been opened. When Ku saw that the wafer had not been touched, but that the pictures were gone, he said resignedly: " Beautiful paintings are things bewitched; it is not strange that they should change their form and fly away, like holy men who are transformed into fairies." He showed no resentment or surprise.

He was given to fantastic boasting, and the young men used to amuse themselves by paying him mock compliments in order to draw him on to new absurdities. He was fond of reciting poetry, and declared that in this art he had rediscovered the lost style of the ancient rhapsodists. When some one asked him to sing one of the Lo-yang student-songs, he replied indignantly, " Am I to demean myself by making noises like the droning of a charwoman ? "

At the beginning of the period I-hsi (405–418) he was appointed Attendant-in-Ordinary to the Light Cavalry.[1] One night when he and Hsieh Chan were on watch at adjoining posts in the palace and a bright moon was shining, Ku kept on singing while Hsieh encouraged him with applause. The more he exerted himself by his singing the less he remembered the fatigue of his night-watch; but Hsieh soon began to get sleepy and persuaded a lictor to take his place. Ku did not notice that there had been a change in his audience and went on singing till dawn.

He believed in magic, and thought that by its means he could obtain anything he desired. Huan Hsüan once gave him a willow-leaf and, to make fun of him, said: " This is the leaf under which the cicada hides. Cover yourself with it and you will become invisible." Ku was delighted, and firmly believed that when he wore the leaf no one could see what he was doing.

In early days when he was serving under Huan Wēn it used to be said of him: " K'ai-chih is compounded half of real madness, half of conscious buffoonery. One cannot understand him without making allowance for both." It was commonly said that in three ways he excelled all men —as a wit, as a painter, and as a fool.

He died in office at the age of sixty-two. His prose works and *Record of Darkness Dispelled*[2] were published and circulated.

Three treatises attributed to Ku K'ai-chih are preserved,[3] but in a corrupt

---

[1] Once a military title; in Ku's time it merely implied Court rank.
[2] Neither of these works survives.   [3] In the *Ming Hua Chi*, Ch. 5.

and fragmentary form. The first consists of notes on his own paintings of various historical subjects, and begins with the general observation that human figures are the most difficult things to paint; next, landscapes; next, gods and horses. Buildings are the easiest of all.

" In painting my small figures of the Heroines[1] I gave the faces an appearance of suffering and emaciation . . . in painting the Seven Idlers of the Bamboo Grove only Chi K'ang need be made handsome; the rest will do well enough even though they be somewhat coarsely rendered. Compared with any previous picture of the Bamboo Grove mine will be found superior."

The second essay gives rather obvious directions for " tracing " old pictures :—

" Silk that has stretched awry is useless, for after a while it will stretch straight again. . . . When silk is traced on silk, the two silks must be allowed to find their own natural shape and then fixed down tight. If the brush and eye travel boldly forwards, the copy will not be a mere reproduction, but will contain something of the copyist's own. . . . In painting portraits, once you have arranged the accessories upon which the sitter's gaze is directed, you must not move them. Men do not wave a friendly hand or look interested, when there is nothing in front of them. . . ."

Finally, there is Ku's essay *How to Paint the Cloud Terrace Mountain*, an elaborate description of a Taoist picture :—

" I would make purple rocks looking something like solid clouds—five or six of them astride the hill. And ascending between them there should be shapes that writhe and coil like dragons. Catching hold of sharp rock-points, they are hauling themselves up to the high mountain-top. . . . As eastern neighbour to these rocks I would set another peak, and opposite to it, crags of fang-like and tapering form. The red cliff to westward drops down to a steep ravine, and where it overhangs the torrent-bed, symbol of dizzy danger, it must tower precipitous and vast. Here sits the Heavenly Master.[2] The rocks on which he leans and those which shadow him stand well within the ravine. Beside him peach-trees grow amid the rocks. Lean-limbed would I paint him, aloof and wild. . . . He is pointing at one of the trees. His head is turned a little to the side. He seems to be speaking to his disciples, among whom are two that

---

[1] His forerunner Wei Hsieh had painted a set of large Heroines. The " small Heroines " set seems to go back to Ts'ai Yung (2nd century A.D.). See p. 38.

[2] Chang Tao-ling, founder of the Taoist Church, *c.* 142 A.D. See above, p. 28.

lean forward and gaze into the abyss. They are in great trepidation, sweat pours from their temples, they are very pale.

" Wang Chang sits in an attitude of awe ; the Master is questioning him ; Chao Shēng, eager and attentive, watches the peach-tree to which the Master is pointing. At a distance from them are the attendants of Wang and Chao, one almost hidden behind a slanting rock, the other seen full length in his cave."

We do not know whether this conception was ever carried out. It was perhaps intended as wall-decoration for some temple.

EXTANT PAINTINGS

The " Admonitions." (Painted on a roll of silk and measuring $136\frac{1}{2}$ by $9\frac{3}{4}$ inches.) By strange good fortune the British Museum possesses a painting which, even if it is not the work of Ku K'ai-chih, at any rate preserves one of his designs. It was brought to the Museum in 1903 as " an old Chinese painting," and purchased upon the recommendation of Sir Sidney Colvin for a very small sum. It illustrates the *Admonitions of the Instructress to the Court Ladies,* a tract written by Chang Hua, a well-known poet who lived from 232 till 300 A.D.

It is incomplete, the first two sections having been lost, probably during the 12th century. It began[1] originally with a long passage of text serving as an introduction. The first picture represented the Lady Fan refusing to taste the flesh of birds newly slaughtered by her husband, King Chuang, who was addicted to excessive hunting. The second showed the daughter of the Marquis of Wei refusing to listen to the licentious music provided for her entertainment by her husband, the Duke Hsüan. One musician sat beating a gong, while others on each side of him played on the stone chimes.

The third picture (the opening scene of the roll as it exists to-day) represents the heroism of Lady Fēng, concubine of the Emperor Yüan of the Han dynasty, who rescued her husband from a bear that had broken loose from the circus-ring. (Pl. III.) Next comes the scene in which Lady Pan refuses to ride with the Emperor Ch'ēng (32–5 B.C.) in his litter, " lest she should distract his thoughts from affairs of state." The objection was evidently one of principle rather than expediency, for the Emperor's thoughts are already occupied by a young girl who is seated by his side. (Pl. IV.)

[1] A copy of the painting was made while it was still complete by the famous Sung painter Li Lung-mien. This copy is described in the Ch'ien Lung Catalogue.

Hitherto the painter has had the relatively easy task of illustrating concrete stories. The text, after the above series of edifying narratives, continues : *In Nature there is nothing high which is not soon brought low. . . . When the sun has reached its noon, it begins to sink ; when the moon is full, it begins to wane. To rise to glory is as hard as to build a mountain out of grains of dust ; to fall into calamity is as easy as the rebound of a tense spring.*

How will the painter tackle this difficult task? The fifth scene is thus described in the Ch'ien Lung Catalogue : " A precipitous mountain. On its right a crow, symbol of the sun ; on its left the hare, symbol of the moon. The mountain teems with precious birds, strange beasts, plants, grasses and wondrous trees. A man is kneeling with his bow drawn, in the act of shooting."

The " strange beasts " are a horse (appearing from behind a rock) and a tiger of relatively enormous size ; on a terrace of rock in the right foreground two hares are sporting. On the other side of the mountain are two phœnixes, one in flight. Most of the things mentioned in the text (sun, moon, mountain, tense spring) appear in the picture, and no doubt Ku K'ai-chih felt that he had acquitted himself quite creditably in his task. But he was evidently embarrassed by the number of miscellaneous elements which the picture had to include, and the design is weak.

The sixth text says that " Men and women know how to adorn their persons ; but few know how to embellish their souls." The picture shows a group of ladies adorning their persons.

The seventh text runs : " If the words that you utter are good, all men for a thousand leagues around will make response to you. But if you depart from this principle, even your bed-fellow will distrust you." The picture shows a lady in a curtained bed ; she is conversing with a bearded man who is sitting in an easy posture on a bench outside the bed—a very inadequate illustration to the text, but a most engaging design. (Pl. V.)

The next picture shows a gentleman with a large family ; it illustrates the concluding words of the text, " Your race shall multiply."

The ninth picture shows a lady listening to her husband's reproaches. It illustrates the text, " No one can endlessly please ; affection cannot be for one alone ; if it be so, it will one day end in disgust."

No. 10. A lady kneels in an attitude of " calm respect," illustrating the " Fulfil your duties calmly and respectfully " of the text.

No. 11. A lady stands writing upon a tablet which she holds before her. Two court ladies stand in front of her, exchanging glances and

emphasizing her words by significant gestures. The inscription runs:
" Thus has the Instructress, charged with the duty of admonition,
thought good to speak to the ladies of the harem."

THE TEXTS

At the side of each picture except the first (the text which tells the story
of Lady Fēng and the bear was probably torn away at the same time as
the first two sections of the painting) is written the relevant portion of
Chang Hua's tract.

Japanese experts have asserted that these texts were written in the T'ang
dynasty. But, at the time when these assertions were made, beyond a
few alleged T'ang copies of 4th-century cursive calligraphy, very little
early Chinese writing existed in Japan. On the other hand, Mr. Taki,
the editor of the *Kokka*, has declared the writing to be a Sung imitation
of T'ang style. It does not appear that either in China or Japan sufficient
material has existed to render possible a systematic study of Chinese
handwriting between the 4th and 10th centuries. *Typical* 4th-century
writing and *typical* T'ang writing can be recognized, and that is all. The
texts on this roll are not typical of the 4th century, nor do they coincide
with the most familiar type of T'ang writing as known to us through the
Buddhist sūtras; on the whole they seem most probably to belong to the
8th or 9th century. But I do not think we can say positively that they
were not written by Ku K'ai-chih himself. The great critic Tung Ch'i-
ch'ang[1] expressed at different times two opinions about this question. In
the *Hsi Hung T'ang Fa T'ieh* (" Classic Scripts of the Sportive Wild-goose
Hall ") he attributes the texts to Ku K'ai-chih. In a volume of miscel-
lanies[2] he ascribes them provisionally to Wang Hsien-chih, son of the
great calligraphist Wang Hsi-chih, and notes that the hand very much
resembles that of the *Thirteen-line Script* (a passage from the Lo Shēn
Ballad written out by this Wang Hsien-chih).

The writer, whoever he was, did not perform his task very carefully.
At several places he impinged upon the painting, and in one place reversed
the order of two characters, a slip seldom made in anything but a careless
rough draft.

CONDITION OF THE PAINTING

The two missing scenes were torn jaggedly away. The painting as it
exists to-day begins with a strip of restoration. The first figure, from

[1] 1555–1636 A.D.   [2] *Hua Ch'an Shih Sui Pi*, I, 37 recto.

the bust downwards, is very hazily sketched in on fine regularly woven silk of the same type as that which was used throughout the roll to repair the jagged edges of the picture. Part of the second figure also belongs to this strip of restoration.

Another very indifferent piece of restoration is the train of Lady Fēng's dress (she is the lady who stands near the soldiers). Equally formless is the train of the mysterious lady who stands with her back to the bear. I cannot help thinking that the lower half of her figure has been wrongly restored. As it is, she iterates in a clumsy and pointless way the figure of the virtuous concubine who walks behind the litter. Granted that the picture was once in a very fragmentary condition, it is not impossible that this figure really belongs to one of the lost scenes and was inserted here by mistake.

The skirt of the virtuous concubine herself has been a good deal restored, but it is not an inert mass like those of the two figures already discussed. But the picture has not suffered only in places where the old silk has been replaced. The line-work has in many parts been clumsily refreshed, and all the solid masses of red and black are comparatively modern. By this reckless doctoring the tone-values of the painting have been wholly destroyed. Particularly crude examples occur in the " Numerous Posterity " scene. It is obvious that in many places, particularly towards the bottom of the picture, the original outlines had so faded that the restorer had to rely on his imagination. One of the best-preserved sections is the Bedroom scene. The perspective does not, of course, follow our Western system, but forms and planes are expressed with a complete and graceful mastery. Contrast with this the false archaism of the Toilet scene, in which the figures indeed retain their charm, but the mirror-stand and toilet-boxes have been deformed by a crude and insensitive hand.

DATE OF THE "ADMONITIONS"

(1) *The silk.* Attempts have been frequently made to date Chinese paintings by the silk upon which they are painted ; it has been said, for example, that the oldest repairs to the " Admonitions " are painted on Sung silk, and that the picture itself must therefore be older than Sung. Even were our knowledge of the different types of Chinese silk much more complete than it is, this method would be of very limited application. It might be possible to say that a particular type of silk first began to be manufactured at a particular date, and that a picture painted upon

such silk could not be earlier than that date. But the fact that a picture is painted upon ancient silk does not prove that this is an ancient picture. For a modern painter may choose to paint on ancient silk. Actually, our knowledge of early painting-silk is very scanty. In the British Museum, for example, the " Admonitions " is the only picture which claims to be earlier than T'ang. Of T'ang paintings we have only those of the Stein Collection, works produced in a remote corner of the empire. From these we cannot safely deduce the nature of the materials used by the metropolitan painters of Ch'ang-an, Lo-yang or Ch'ēng-tu. Still less have we accurate knowledge of the various types of Sung silk. Apart from the Ku K'ai-chih the Museum possesses no picture which may with certainty be regarded as earlier than the 15th century. A very large number of specimens would be required to establish what types of silk were prevalent during the pre-Mongol period. It is possible that in Europe and America a sufficient number of such paintings exists ; but no useful work can be done in this direction until a higher standard of connoisseurship prevails among collectors and custodians.

It is sometimes stated in Chinese works on painting that the silks of Sung, Yüan, and Ming are identical. If this is true, we must abandon such arguments as that because a painting is repaired with " Sung " silk it must necessarily be as early as Sung. And, in any case, might it not occur to a restorer to use ancient silk in restoring an ancient painting ?

(2) *Seals and Inscriptions*. It has also been customary to judge the date of Chinese paintings by the " seals " which they bear. Against this method there has lately been a considerable reaction. It has been pointed out that seals can easily be forged. This may be so ; but it is certain that they are usually forged very unskilfully. The seals of mediæval collectors were exquisitely cut and dexterously inked. Modern imitations of these seals are, in most cases, at any rate, crudely cut and unevenly imprinted.

An artist's seal is in China[1] very generally accompanied by his signature, so that the seal loses its importance.

Collectors' seals are only useful when the owner in question happened to be a man of importance ; otherwise it is impossible to discover any facts about him. An owner's seal will often consist of two characters, forming his tzŭ or literary name. Such names, though not as stereotyped

[1] Many Japanese paintings have been identified by seals. I speak only of such Chinese paintings as survive. No doubt the practice of putting a seal instead of a signature was at certain times not uncommon in China.

as Christian forenames, were not confined to one bearer. Hence the seal "Tzŭ-ching,"[1] which is now known to be that of Hsiang Yüan-pien (1525–1590), was mistaken by Bushell for that of Sung Ch'i (998–1061), who also had "Tzŭ-ching" for his literary name.

However, collectors did not only put their own seals on paintings which came into their possession; sometimes, to indicate the distinguished provenance of a picture, they would imprint the seal of a former owner. Seals were considered an intrinsic part of a painting, and when an artist copied an old picture he also reproduced the seals which were stamped on it.

The seals on the "Admonitions," which must number upwards of a hundred, have almost all been deciphered and most of them have been identified. As regards the history of the painting they confirm what we learn from Chinese art-records and catalogues, but (assuming their genuineness) they do not tell us much more. The only seal earlier than those of Hui Tsung (reigned 1101–1125) is the seal Hung-wēn ("Vast Culture"); it is that of a department in the Han-lin literary college. The *Ming Hua Chi* (c. 847 A.D.) gives it as one of the seals found on ancient paintings, and says that it was used by the department which in his day was called the Tung Kuan ("Eastern Shrine").

It would be extremely difficult to ascertain when the seal "Hung-wēn" ceased to be used by a department of the literary college; it might have been used on works of art long after it ceased to be the official name of the department concerned. Moreover, the combination of characters "Hung-wēn" is a very natural one, and many private individuals known to history bore it as their "literary name."[2]

I have dwelt upon this point in order to show how little positive information can be obtained from evidence of this kind. I now come to the question of inscriptions.

The practice of calligraphy as an art enabled Chinamen to write in various different styles and techniques. The classification of strokes and methods made imitation easier than it would be in the case of our antinomian scrawl, and every schoolboy could imitate the handwriting of the Old Masters.

It is therefore often difficult to tell whether an inscription comes from

---

[1] It occurs about twenty times on the "Admonitions."

[2] E.g. Kuo Shih-chien of the Sui dynasty, in whose house "seven generations dwelt together in amity." Professor Fukui points out to me that the seal on our picture appears to have been cut in metal and thus resembles some of the earliest Japanese seals.

the hand of the person who signs it. In the case of most pictures which are brought to Europe and America the difficulty does not occur. For it is transparent that the numerous inscriptions which purport to be penned by eminent persons from the Sung dynasty downward were all written fairly recently by one hand. Scholars have made the mistake of supposing that the importance of a work of art consists in what is written upon it. They have pored over some third-rate 17th-century copy as zealously as if it were a clay tablet from Carchemish.

Inscriptions nevertheless have a certain value, chiefly negative. Pictures which have 18th-century dates (as do several paintings in the Wegener Collection which were supposed to be Sung) are not likely to be earlier than that century, though they may possibly be later.

It is difficult also to decide how much importance is to be attached to " signatures." Often they are mere labels scribbled in one corner of the picture by ignorant or interested persons. At Soochow, where many of the paintings now in European collections were forged, Chao Mēng-fu and Ch'ien Hsüan were local heroes. Hence it comes that their names are upon so many of the paintings sold by Chinese dealers. The horse-paintings go to Chao Mēng-fu, and the landscapes, birds and flowers, etc., to Ch'ien Hsüan.

To return to the " Admonitions," the signature is in this case obviously a late addition. It is probable that the painting was not ascribed to Ku K'ai-chih until the 12th century. The *Ming Hua Chi*,[1] which gives a long list of Ku's works, makes no mention of the " Admonitions," and even in the 16th century the painting is sometimes spoken of as an anonymous 4th-century work.

At the end of the roll are two long inscriptions. The first,[2] in bold square writing, consists of the last three sections of the " Admonitions " text written out as a calligraphic exercise. The Ch'ien Lung Catalogue tells us that the writing is that of the 12th-century Emperor Hui Tsung. The second long inscription[3] is by Ch'ien Lung. It begins with a quotation from Ku K'ai-chih's biography, and subsequently tells us that the roll formerly belonged to a " Mr. Secretary Ku." This is Ku Chēng-i, a famous collector who lived about 1600.

[1] 847 A.D.

[2] This is the inscription which Giles described as " eighteen lines of poetry praising the excellence of the Admonitions of the Imperial Preceptress."

[3] The seals and inscriptions will be fully discussed in the *Catalogue of Chinese Paintings at the British Museum*, which is now being prepared.

(3) *Style*. I have tried to show that the evidence which can be obtained from silk, inscriptions, and seals is of a very uncertain kind. It remains to examine the painting itself. Here we are upon much surer ground. The painting is in a style so evidently intermediate between the 2nd-century grave-reliefs in Shantung and the 6th-century wall-paintings at Tun-huang,[1] that, apart from all other evidence, one would have guessed that it embodied a pre-Wei design. Moreover, if we examine details of costume, landscape treatment, etc., we find that it stands much closer to the Tun-huang frescoes (which are probably " backward " in style) than to the Han reliefs ; so close, indeed, that, had no tradition connected our painting with the name of Ku K'ai-chih, we should still have regarded it as at any rate founded upon a 4th-century design.

ACTUAL DATE OF THE PAINTING

As regards the actual date of the painting, I think we are safe in assuming that the picture in the British Museum is the one which the Emperor Ch'ien Lung possessed, and which the great connoisseur Tung Ch'i-ch'ang[2] admired. Whether it is the same which belonged to the Emperor Hui Tsung in the 12th century is much more doubtful.

Supposing that the picture is a copy, when could such a copy have been made ? Not even the most sceptical students of the painting have suggested a date earlier than Sung. We know of at least one Sung copy— that made by Li Lung-mien in the 11th century. This, however, was not a reproductive copy, but a " translation " into black-and-white. We have already seen that Ku K'ai-chih himself did not regard " copying " as a reproductive process, and it is true that when Chinese painters copied ancient paintings for amusement they generally improved freely on the old theme.

But from the earliest times a more sinister form of copying also existed.[3] We read, for example, that towards the end of the 7th century Chang I-chih, favourite of the Empress Wu-hou, stole all the pictures in the Imperial collection and replaced them by forgeries. The technical skill of the old Chinese painters was immense. We may well believe that when they turned their hand to actual forgery they made a pretty good job of it. We must not therefore assume that, because some pictures which we know to be Sung copies frankly display their true nature, all Sung copies will be easy to recognize. The " Admonitions " may, then,

---

[1] See Pelliot, *Les Grottes de Touen-houang*. Geuthner, 1920, etc.

[2] 1555–1636.   [3] See above, p. 6.

be a Sung copy, but I confess I should be extremely surprised if this turned out to be the case. Such a thing as an " absolute copy " does not exist in art. *La main se trahit.* One feels that a Sung hand would somewhere have betrayed itself.

I believe that the general opinion of experts tends to be that the painting is a T'ang copy. Against this theory, which of course cannot be proved, no valid argument can be brought. Indeed, a 14th-century writer tells us that in the Shao-hsing era[1] Wu Tao-tzŭ's copies of Ku K'ai-chih were often mistaken for originals. " But by whom ? " one asks. And this involves the whole question of Chinese connoisseurship, which I have briefly discussed in my first chapter.

Another hypothesis is this : the painting is not a copy ; but it has in successive generations been so often repaired and repainted that not all the silk and hardly any of the line-work and colouring which meet the eye are original. At the same time the original design has, except in a few places, been successfully preserved. Towards the bottom of the picture the line-work had, especially in the opening scenes, become at some period so indistinct that the restorer was obliged to trust a good deal to his own inspiration. I think this theory fits the facts, but I should gladly welcome any other if it could be supported by solid arguments.

HISTORY OF THE PAINTING

If we accept the genuineness of the " Admonitions," we may provisionally trace its history as follows :

(1) Painted by a Chin artist *c.* 390–400 A.D.

(2) Owned by the Hung-wēn Kuan, a department of the Hanlin College, 8th century (?).

(3) Belonged to Liu Yu-fang (of whom nothing further is known), end of the 11th century ; now attributed to Ku K'ai-chih.

(4) Belonged to the Emperor Hui Tsung, first quarter of the 12th century.

(5) Belonged to Yen Fēn-i, a famous collector, middle of the 16th century.

(6) Belonged *c.* 1570 to Mr. Secretary Ku Chēng-i, who also possessed three famous pictures by Li Lung-mien.

(7) Belonged to Hsiang Mo-lin (Yüan-pien), most famous of all Chinese connoisseurs, from about 1580–1590.

[1] *Circa* 1130 A.D.

(8) Belonged to the statesman and poet Liang Ch'ing-piao,[1] who, having served both Mings and Manchus, died in 1691.

(9) It bears a seal indicating that it belonged for a time to the Korean amateur An I-chou, author of the *Mo yüan Hui Kuan*,[2] a list of paintings and scripts which the writer had seen. This list includes the "Admonitions."

(10) Another seal indicates that the painting was *seen* (not possessed) by the famous amateur Yang Shih-ch'i, probably between 1693 and 1700.

(11) Many of the most important paintings in the Emperor Ch'ien Lung's collection had previously belonged to Liang Ch'ing-piao. Among them was the "Admonitions." It is not at present known under what circumstances this and other paintings from Liang's collection were acquired by the Emperor. The "Admonitions" remained in the Palace till it was looted during the Boxer Rising of 1900.

(12) It was sold to the Trustees of the British Museum by Captain C. Johnson in April, 1903.

OTHER EXTANT WORKS ATTRIBUTED TO K'AI-CHIH

The *Lo Shēn* Roll. A painting with this title belonged to the first Emperor of the Southern Sung dynasty (1127–1162), and subsequently passed into the possession of the Director of Worship, Han Ts'un-liang, who lived in the 16th century.[3]

It is possibly this same painting which is described in Vol. XXXVI of the Ch'ien Lung Catalogue. But the painting which Ch'ien Lung possessed is in any case not the same as that which was formerly in the collection of Tuan Fang, Viceroy of Chihli, and is now in the Freer Museum at Washington.

The Ch'ien Lung painting was 178·7 Chinese inches long. This (judging from other measurements in the Catalogue) means about 133 English inches. The Freer painting measures only 122⅛ inches. But Chinese

---

[1] To whom a certain mystery attaches, for his name is excluded from the ordinary biographies in spite of the fact that he closed a highly successful public career by the pomp of a State funeral. Professor Pelliot generously communicated to me his notes on Liang Ch'ing-piao; they will be more fully utilized in the *Catalogue of Chinese Paintings at the British Museum*.

[2] See J. C. Ferguson, *Journal of the North China Branch of the Royal Asiatic Society*, Vol. 45 (1914), p. 11.

[3] The *Shu Hua P'u* (100'8) gives a list of 99 paintings which belonged to this important collector.

measures are very tricky, and the numerals in the Ch'ien Lung Catalogue are not very accurately printed. A more decisive proof that the two paintings are not identical is that at the end of the Ch'ien Lung roll, and immediately after the picture, came a text of the Lo Shēn poem, written out by the great calligrapher Chao Mēng-fu[1]; whereas at the first inscription at the end of the Freer picture is a note by Tung Ch'i-Ch'ang.[2] The description of the Ch'ien Lung picture and its inscriptions is very minute, and if there had been an inscription by Tung Ch'i-ch'ang it would unquestionably have been mentioned.

THE LO-SHĒN POEM

The poem was written by Ts'ao Chih, third son of the founder of the Wei dynasty,[3] in A.D. 222. It is an imitation of Sung Yü's *Goddess*,[4] written about 180 B.C.

In the preface the poet tells how once, when he was travelling back from the Court to his country estate, he camped at sunset by the shores of the River Lo. Suddenly he saw the figure of a woman moving along the edge of the cliff. Who could she be, so fair a lady in so desolate a place? *"They say,"* said his charioteer, *" that there is a goddess of this river whose name is the Lady Fu. Perhaps it is she whom my lord sees. But tell me first what face and form are hers, and I will tell you if she is the goddess or no."* Then I said: *"She moves lightly as a bird on the wing; delicately as the rain-elves at their play; she is more radiant than the sun-flowers of autumn, more verdurous than the pine-woods of the spring. Dimly I see her, like a light cloud that lies across the moon; fitfully as swirls a snow-wreath in the straying wind.*

"Now far away, she glimmers like sunshine peeping through the morning mist. Now near, she glistens like a young lotus, a bud new-risen above the waters of the lake. . . .

"Her shoulders are as chiselled statuary; her waist is like a bundle of silk. Her body is anointed not with perfumes, nor is her face dabbed with powder. The coils of her hair are like cloud-heaps stacked in the air. Her long eyebrows join their slim curves. . . .

"I was enamoured of her beauty; my heart was shaking and would not rest. There was no matchmaker to lead us to our joy; so to the little waves

---

[1] 1254–1322. [2] 1555–1636.

[3] The early native dynasty of this name; not the dynasty set up in Northern China by Tartars in the 5th century. The two are constantly confused by writers on Chinese art.

[4] See *The Temple and Other Poems*, Allen & Unwin, 1923. Introduction, p. 32.

of the stream I gave a message for her ear. And that I might forthwith give a pledge of kindness, I took a pendant from my girdle and cast it to her.

"She sighed acceptance of my vows, of my gift and my fair words. With jasper she requited me and with the milk-white Stone of Truth; she pointed into the river depths in token that there she would meet me. Then I was afraid, for I thought 'Should I be joined in amity with her, then might this Goddess despoil and delude me.' For I remembered how Chiao-fu[1] once was deceived. I was cunningly forearmed and wary as a fox. I hardened my heart, I looked sternly upon her, I held her back from me.

"Then the Lady of the River was ashamed; piteously she havered. The flames of her godhead glimmered fitfully; on tiptoe she stood, tense as a bird that in a minute will have flown away. At last, as she turned to go, she uttered a cry of sorrow so fierce and desolate that at the sound of her voice all the Spirits of the river came flocking down the stream, some splashing in the clear waves, some winging through the haunted islands. One stooped to pluck from the waters a many-coloured stone; another, to cull a halcyon-feather from the shore. Then, to move the stranger's heart, they sang the doleful song of the Ladle-star that knows no mate, and the ballad of the Herdboy's lonely place. . . .

"The Lady of the River raised the silken flutterings of her light mantle, covered her long sleeves, and for a moment paused. Then, swift as a hawk in flight, again a Goddess, she sped upon her way; and as she skimmed the waters, wave-spray like a fine dust flecked her damask shoes. . . .

"The Storm-god lulled the winds to rest; the Lord of Waters stilled the waves. P'ing-i beat his drum; the fairy Nü-wo sang with shrill, clear voice. She summoned the Fish King from the depths and bade him guard the Lady's flight; she called upon the Jade Phœnix to flutter by the Lady's side.

"Then dragons, six abreast in flawless line, were harnessed to her chariot of cloud. The whale and the dolphin gambolled at her wheel-side. Water-fowl lent winged escort to her train.

"She has crossed the Northern Rivulet, passed over the Southern Mound . . . and now she turns her white neck, gazes back with clear brow. Moves her red lips, speaks quietly; speaks of Love and the Great Chain that binds men heart to heart; 'Alas that between men and gods no converse can endure! Alas that they are vanished, those lusty days of mortal[2] youth!' . . .

---

[1] He fell in love with two river-spirits and gave them the precious gem he carried at his girdle. Whereupon they vanished.

[2] Like most gods, she had once been a mortal. Some say that she was the spirit of a woman who was drowned in the river.

"Suddenly I could not see her ; her bright divinity was changed to darkness and all that radiant vision folded up in night."[1]

It is generally agreed by all who have seen the Lo Shēn painting that it is in a different category from the " Admonitions " and may well be a Sung copy. However that may be, it, too, certainly goes back to a pre-T'ang design. The first part of it illustrates a passage quite near the end of the poem : " P'ing-i beat his drum ; the fairy Nü-wo sang with shrill, clear voice." The next scene shows " dragons six a-breast in flawless line " drawing the Lady's chariot through the sky. The existing picture, then, illustrates not the whole poem, but the *finale*, which we may call " The Departure of the Goddess." It is very unlikely that the original painting did not illustrate the whole story ; it is doubtful whether even the Ch'ien Lung version, which may have embraced some additional scenes, was quite complete. The suggestion that the picture illustrates not the Lo Shēn poem, but the *Nine Songs* of Ch'ü Yüan, seems to me quite unnecessary.

THE HEROINES

Liu Hsiang in the 1st century B.C. wrote a book called *Lives of the Heroines* (or " Famous Ladies of History "). It was illustrated in the 2nd century A.D. by Ts'ai Yung in a set of paintings known as the Small Heroines. We have already seen that Ku K'ai-chih's forerunner, Wei Hsieh, painted a set of Large Heroines ; Ku speaks of his own set as founded upon that of Wei Hsieh.

In the 11th century the *Lives of the Heroines* was printed with wood-block illustrations. This edition has naturally become very rare, but a reprint made in 1825 is not uncommon. The illustrations are usually said to be based upon paintings by Ku K'ai-chih and have been cited by European critics as examples of his style.

If, however, we examine the book itself we find that Wang Hui's preface, dated 1063, attributes the pictures to " some *amateur*." It is the editor of the modern reprint who, writing in 1820, attributes the illustrations to Ku on the ground that they resemble " a copy by Chao Mēng-fu of Ku K'ai-chih's *Lives of the Heroines*."

The writer of the third preface (1825) quotes from the *Manual of Bibliography* (*Tu-shu Min-ch'iu Chi*) of an 18th-century writer, Ch'ien Ts'ēng : " The *Lives of the Heroines* printed in the Sung dynasty has the colophon

---

[1] The text of the *Wēn Hsüan* appends to the poem a long political tract ; this is excised in the standard edition of *fu* poems published by the Emperor K'ang Hsi.

Pictures by Secretary-to-the-Grand-Marshal Ku K'ai-chih of the Chin Dynasty." But Ch'ien Ts'ēng does not make it clear whether he had himself seen a copy with this colophon, and the writer of this third preface admits that the architecture, trees, and rocks (e.g. the library in the picture of Mencius's mother, I. 11 verso) show traces of T'ang or even Sung workmanship. The story of Lady Fēng and the bear (the subject of the first section of the " Admonitions ") is told in the eighth volume of the Heroines. It is illustrated by a design, which, if it is by Ku K'ai-chih, must certainly have been made before he became acquainted with bears. But the eighth volume is labelled " supplementary," and may not have existed in Ku's time. Ch'ien Lung possessed part of a roll illustrating the lives of the Heroines and attributed to Ku K'ai-chih. It consisted of eight scenes, each with a text. The roll appears once to have consisted of fifteen scenes. The earliest inscription is dated 1225 A.D. It does not seem that this was regarded as so important a work as the two other Ku K'ai-chih paintings in Ch'ien Lung's collection.

THE INCISED STONE AT CH'Ü-FOU

In the Confucian temple at Ch'ü-fou, once capital of the ancient state of Lu, are three incised slabs. The first and second represent the Master standing alone, and reproduce a painting by the 8th-century artist Wu Tao-tzŭ ; the third represents Confucius followed by his disciple Yen Tzŭ, and is after a design by Ku K'ai-chih. All three were cut by order of Kao Tē-i, Governor of K'ai-chou, in 1191 A.D.[1] The two figures on the third slab were probably taken from Ku K'ai-chih's painting entitled " Sages of Antiquity," which was the fifth of the nine paintings by him which belonged to the Emperor Hui Tsung in the 12th century. Taken in conjunction with Ku's other surviving designs, this incised stone is of some interest. But it is so roughly executed that it would not by itself have enabled us to form any estimate of Ku K'ai-chih's style.

Several other paintings have been attributed to him—a Vimalakīrti[2] at the Tōfukuji, Kyōto, and a landscape roll representing the " hills of Kuei-chi " at the Metropolitan Museum, New York. But it is not probable that either of these works has any connection with Ku. The landscape would naturally have been attributed to him because of his famous eulogy upon the Kuei-chi hills ; the Vimalakīrti, because of his exploit at the Tile-coffin Temple.

[1] See the *Tung Yu Chi* by the 13th-century writer Yang Huan, quoted in the *Chin Shih So* ('Enquiry into metal and stone objects,' 1821.) [2] See *Shimbi Taikwan*, XIV, 5.

CHINESE PAINTING

LOST PAINTINGS BY KU K'AI-CHIH

We know of about sixty paintings, of which about a dozen are portraits. Only three or four represent Buddhist subjects—for example, " An Assembly of Priests," " Distribution of the Relics," " Vimalakīrti," " Heavenly Ladies" (Apsaras). There are many paintings of lions, dragons, tigers, wild-geese, etc., many representations of the Taoist Immortals. There are illustrations of early legend, such as " The Great Yü Draining the Empire," " Huang Ch'u-p'ing turning Stones into Sheep." Among illustrations to poetry may be mentioned the " Wandering in the Western Garden on a Clear Night," illustrating a poem by Ts'ao Chih, author of the Lo Shēn *fu*.

IMPORTANCE OF KU

Chinese Estimates. It is strange that, though Ku K'ai-chih is the earliest Chinese painter about whose style we can form any conjecture, we know more about his life and work than about the careers of many much later men. This is due to the fact that, besides being the greatest painter of the day, he was also one of the outstanding characters of his time. We might almost put " character " in inverted commas ; for Ku was a " character " in the peculiarly English sense of the word, which is as much as to say " an inspired eccentric." The Chinese have at all times (and never more than in the 4th century) pursued the cult of the whimsical and absurd ; and Ku K'ai-chih is not only the father of Chinese painting, but also the patron saint of Chinese absurdity.

There is some reason to suppose that Ku's reputation as a painter was enhanced by the glamour that surrounded his mysterious personality. Hsieh Ho, the famous critic of the 5th century, places him in his third category, saying : " Though he never used his brush idly, but employed it always for the expression of abstruse and spiritual mysteries, yet his execution fell short of his conception, and we must own that his reputation is beyond his merits."

Li Ssŭ-chēn, a critic of the 7th century, protested against this verdict : " Ku with his superhuman talents stands in heroic isolation. How can Hsieh Ho have made the mistake of putting such triflers as Hsün Hsü and Wei Hsieh at the head of his list ? The fact that even Ts'ao Pu-hsing is placed above Ku shows that Hsieh Ho was a very inept critic. Ku's mind dwelt close to that of the Creator ; by contact with the supernatural he had acquired mysterious potency. . . . How can talents of this order

64

be forced into the mould of classification? In any case, one is not justified in putting him in a low class."

However, Chang Yen-yüan, the author of the *Ming Hua Chi*,[1] sensibly observes: "A painter should be judged by his paintings. What have other talents got to do with it? His Excellency Li's remarks lack point."

Chang Huai-kuan, of the 8th century, though in less downright terms, expresses Hsieh Ho's suggestion that it was in imaginative force rather than plastic creation that Ku excelled: " The operation of his thoughts was subtle and abstruse; the mysterious depths of his nature was unfathomable. His skill left behind him a monument of ink and brush; but his spirit soared high above the misty skies. The beauty of a man's soul cannot be expressed in his paintings."

It is true that Chang Huai-kuan goes on to compare Ku with other painters and exclaims at last: " Who but he has expressed the soul's very essence stripped of all outward encumbrance?" But throughout these appreciations we detect a note of apology for Ku K'ai-chih's actual performances.

The critics who express this disappointment tended to regard painting solely as illustration. If we compare Ku's conception of the Cloud Terrace Mountain Picture[2] with the mountain scene in the " Admonitions," we can easily imagine that his spoken or written descriptions of his paintings were sometimes more impressive and romantic than the paintings themselves.

As Artist and Illustrator. The Chinese specialized in illustration and took quite for granted an illustrative skill which surprises and delights us. The " Admonitions," in spite of the mutilated form in which we possess it, contains passages of astonishing illustration. For example, the Bed scene. This king, lolling in careless converse, is regal without pomposity; he makes no show of dignity, yet one feels that beside him Louis XIV might have seemed a trifle low and awkward. Turning to the purely plastic side of the painting, it should at once be said that it is not, and is not intended to be, a continuous whole like the later Chinese scroll-paintings. Viewed by itself, the Bear scene is a fine design; so is the Litter scene, with the wave-like rhythm of the bearer's feet; and so is the Bedside scene of which I have spoken above. Many of the other scenes suffer from repainting, and also possibly from mutilation.

This, the earliest of Chinese paintings, exemplifies much that is typical of Chinese art. Design and illustration are evenly balanced. In every

---

[1] Published 847 A.D. [2] See p. 49.

secular Chinese painting there is an element of narrative, lyricism, or romance ; and in every painting there is at least some striving for formal beauty. Never at any moment has the plastic side of art been entirely subordinated to sentiment, as it has been in Europe by popular artists since 1850. Never has so great a formal beauty been achieved in Chinese painting[1] as is seen in the works of such artists as Della Francesca, Chardin, or Cézanne.

[1] So far as it is at present known to us.

CHAPTER VI
CALLIGRAPHY AND THE BEGINNINGS
OF ART PHILOSOPHY

CHAPTER VI

CALLIGRAPHY AND THE BEGINNINGS OF ART PHILOSOPHY

The earliest Chinese inscriptions which exist belong to the Shang dynasty (1766–1122 B.C.). They are cut upon pieces of bone, which were found in 1899 at the site of an early temple in the province of Ho-nan. The characters employed are for the most part simple geometrical forms. Some of them no doubt began life as pictograms, but they have, in the Shang inscriptions, already travelled a long way upon the path of conventionalization. Others depend upon various kinds of symbolism and were never directly pictorial. Thus the character for " return " is a ring ; " up," " down," " middle," are expressed by an obvious geometrical symbolism. The numerals seem to be derived from patterns made by string looped in various ways. We know from Lao Tzŭ that ideographic writing was preceded by a system of communication by variously knotted ropes—*quipus,* as the South American Indians call them—and more characters than is now evident may be derived from this system. Superficially the earliest Chinese writing bears a strong resemblance to the earliest Sumerian. But very few signs indeed—and only the most crudely pictorial—have the same meaning in both scripts. As for sound-values, we have not the least idea how early Chinese was pronounced ; we cannot fix the sounds even approximately until about the time of Christ. The sound-values of the Sumerian signs are perhaps rather less uncertain, but still very doubtful. We have therefore no reason at present to look outside China for the origin of Chinese writing.

In the West writing is a convenience ; in the East it is almost a religion. Some of the most passionate stories in Chinese history concern the art of calligraphy. Chung Yu, who died in 230 A.D., learned that a courtier named Wei Tan possessed a book which revealed the secret of Ts'ai Yung's[1] skill. He begged for the loan of it, but Wei Tan would not let him have it. In rage and despair Chung Yu beat upon his breast till blood flowed from his mouth. He was saved from death by a drug sent from the Imperial medicine-chest.

Not long afterwards Wei Tan died and the secret book was buried with him ; but Chung Yu, committing a crime which posterity has approved, broke open the tomb, stole the book, and became the greatest calligrapher of antiquity.

[1] A famous calligrapher of the 2nd century A.D. See pp. 49 and 62.

69

Or again, take the story of the *Lan T'ing* Scroll. On a spring day in the year 353 a party of friends were picnicking together. Among them was the great calligrapher Wang Hsi-chih, whom they asked to write a preface to the poems which the friends had improvised that day. It was then that he wrote the famous Lan T'ing scroll, named from the place where the picnickers had met.

"That day the sky was cloudless ; the wind blew softly where we sat. Above us stretched in its hugeness the vault and compass of the World ; around us crowded in green newness the myriad tribes of Spring. Here chimed around us every music that can soothe the ear ; was spread before us every colour that can delight the eye. Yet we were sad.

"For it is so with all men : a little while (some by the fireside talking of homely matters with their friends, others by wild ecstasies of mystic thought swept far beyond the boundaries of carnal life) they may be easy and forget their doom. But soon their fancy strays ; they grow dull and listless, for they are fallen to thinking that all these things which so mightily pleased them will in the space of a nod be old things of yesterday. . . ."

This scroll came into the possession of the 7th-century Zen-master Pien-tsai, from whom the Emperor T'ai Tsung,[1] a great collector of Wang Hsi-chih's scrolls, tried in vain to procure it. Finally he sent a certain Hsiao Hui to Pien-tsai's monastery, disguised as a Shantung student. Hsiao treacherously cultivated the priest's friendship, and one day, when Pien-tsai was out for his afternoon walk, stole the scroll from its hiding-place amid the rafters. Going back to his lodgings, he changed his academic gown for the gorgeous robes of an Imperial envoy, commandeered stage-horse and postilions from the Governor of the Town, and in a few hours was speeding back to Ch'ang-an with the Lan T'ing scroll in his sleeve. When Pien-tsai discovered the treacherous trick that had been played upon him, he fainted with horror. " When he recovered from his swoon, he found that he could not swallow. It is said that a sudden fright or sorrow will sometimes thus close the passage of a man's gullet, so that he can get no more nourishment than a sip of broth. So at last it was with Pien-tsai, who died before the year was out."

Till about the 6th century B.C. writing was usually carved on hard substances such as metal and stone. This was the monumental phase of Chinese calligraphy. I reproduce on Plate VI an epitaph which is said to have been designed by Confucius. It consists of ten characters, which read : *"Alas ! Here is that noble gentleman Wu Yen-ling's tomb."*

[1] 627–650 A.D.

CALLIGRAPHY AND ART PHILOSOPHY

In sheer beauty of form not even the noblest Cufic script ever excelled these ten majestic letters. But with the invention of the writing-brush a new art of calligraphy arose. It advanced slowly, because both ink and brushes were still very imperfect; even at the close of the Han dynasty the commonest form of writing was to scrawl with a blackened stump on thin wedges of wood.

But in the 2nd and 3rd centuries the new means of writing spread rapidly through China, and, drawn with the hog's-hair brush on fine-woven silk, the archaic letters lost their stiffness. At last (probably in the 3rd century) a cursive style developed, and in the 4th century arose the greatest cursive calligrapher of all time, that Wang Hsi-chih[1] of whom I have spoken above. Of the 243 scripts by him which were in the collection of the Sung Emperor Hui Tsung, only seven were in " square " writing. About forty were in the semi-cursive or " running " hand. The script which I reproduce on Plate VII belongs to the Japanese Imperial Household. It is thought to be a T'ang copy of Wang Hsi-chih's writing. It is known as the Riot Script, because it begins with the words : " Hsi-chih bows his head and announces that the prevailing riots have now reached their climax." Henceforward painting and calligraphy went hand in hand. The painter's outline, which had hitherto been a mere boundary to the form which it contained, became expressive, " calligraphic."

LU T'AN-WEI

The first artist who applied the cursive line to painting was Lu T'an-wei, who flourished in the second half of the 5th century. He is said, indeed, to have " done for painting what Wang Hsi-chih did for calligraphy." The Emperor Ch'ien Lung possessed a scroll entitled " Buddha's Mother," which was considered to be an original painting by Lu T'an-wei, and another of " The Five Mountains " which is catalogued as a copy.

His painting of a lion on a wooden panel was destroyed at the burning of the Kan-lu Temple in 1098. Another of his paintings, " Prince Hsüan's Queen,"[2] was still extant at the end of the 11th century. His " Descent of Mañjuśrī, with attendant Divinities," existed in the 14th century.

---

[1] 321–379 A.D.

[2] Lady Chiang, the virtuous wife of Prince Hsüan of Chou (8th century B.C.). She placed herself under arrest, saying that it was her fault the Emperor got up so late in the morning and consequently neglected public business. When he heard that she was in Long Lane (the women's prison) he felt very much ashamed of himself, and for some years spent less time in bed.

71

Mr. Ferguson reproduces on page 217 of his *Outlines of Chinese Art* a painting of a lion led by two Indians. It may be a copy of the lion-panel which was destroyed by fire.

HSIEH HO

Hsieh Ho, who also lived in the second half of the 5th century, was a figure-painter of some importance, but he is chiefly known as the enunciator of the " Six Canons " of painting.

As these are to some extent the basis of subsequent art criticism it is important to understand them. The word hitherto translated " canon " or " method " is regularly used as an equivalent to the Buddhist term *Dharma,* " component part." I think it is here meant in its Buddhist sense. It would therefore perhaps be more accurate to speak of the " Six Component Parts " rather than the Six Canons or Methods of painting. They are (in pidgin-English) as follows :

(1) Spirit-harmony—Life's motion.
(2) Bone-means—use brush.
(3) According to the object depict its shape.
(4) According to species apply colour.
(5) Planning and disposing degrees and places.
(6) By handing on and copying to transmit designs.

Petrucci[1] saw in the above sentences an expression of profound Taoist doctrine. We need not, I think, credit Hsieh with anything more than a modicum of Confucian (not Taoist) philosophy. He was himself (as we know from the 6th-century writer Yao Tsui) a realistic portrait painter. His doctrines were not very different from those of popular 19th-century artists in our own country.

Let us take the easiest " Canons " first : (3) and (4) tell us that the painter must accurately reproduce the colours and forms of the objects he depicts. (5) refers to composition in the broadest sense. (6) is peculiarly Chinese. A work of art must contain an echo of the past. It must be " classical." Copying as a separate art is not what is here referred to, but rather the observance of traditional design. Thus if an artist paints the " Tortures of Hell," he should not try to imagine the scenes for himself ; his picture should grow out of the standard master-

---

[1] *La Philosophie de la Nature dans l'Art d'Extrême Orient,* p. 89.

pieces which illustrate this subject, such as the famous wall-paintings of Wu Tao-tzŭ.

We are left with Canons (1) and (2). What " Spirit " is it that Hsieh means? Certainly not the Way of the Taoists; for if so, why should he not call it *tao*?

Mr. Sei-ichi Taki has shown[1] that it is rather the Confucian " spirit of heaven and earth," the " subtle spirit " of the *Book of Changes*, that is here referred to. Indeed, Hsieh Ho actually quotes from the Confucian commentary on the *Book of Changes* when (later in his book) he is criticizing the work of Lu T'an-wei.

The spirit sets in motion the phenomena of the world as the hand of a harp-player sets in motion the strings of the instrument. Instead of " harmony," another character is often used which means " revolutions," " influences." I would therefore translate " The Operations of the Spirit." The use of the words " rhythm," " rhythmic," etc., is very misleading, for nothing like symmetry of design or balancing of forms is meant.

These " operations of the spirit," then, produce " Life's motion "; and it is this process which the painter must illustrate. The " spirit " is here something objective, something outside the artist. But with the spread of Zen Buddhism, which regarded the Ideal as something to be sought by each man within his own nature, the first Canon was differently interpreted. Sung writers such as Kuo Hsi and his son Kuo Ssŭ speak of the " spirit " as operating from within, as a quality of the artist himself.

Canon (2) means " the use of the brush in outline-drawing; *ku-fa* might almost be translated = bone-work "; *fa* does not here mean " law." Petrucci's " La loi des os au moyen du pinceau " is surely meaningless.

The six sentences are, in fact, an enumeration of tests by which a painting is to be judged. If it were not for the first canon we should conclude that Hsieh Ho had the ideals of a colour-photographer. He saves himself by telling us that the painter must (before all else) " show the operations of the spirit producing life's motion."

Each age and time has made its attempt to define æsthetic beauty, has produced its convenient phrase (Disegno, Grand Gust, Significant Form, etc.), and grown tired of it. Who shall say that Hsieh's formula is any

[1] In *Kokka*, 338.

more nebulous than the rest? An attempt[1] has been made to connect the Six Canons with the *Shadanga* or " Six Limbs " of Indian art. There is very little resemblance between the two sets of Canons. But if I am right in taking *fa* (" method," " canon ") in its Buddhist sense, it is possible that the idea of a sixfold classification, though not the actual wording of it, may have come from India or the West.

[1] *Ostasiatische Zeitschrift*, III, 375–377.

CHAPTER VII
THE SIX DYNASTIES: THE WEI
TARTARS AND THEIR ART

THE SIX DYNASTIES: THE WEI TARTARS AND THEIR ART

(Liu Sung, 420–479 ; Southern Ch'i, 479–502 ; Liang, 502–557 ;
Ch'ên, 557–587 ; Northern Ch'i, 550–577 ; Northern Chou, 557–581)[1]

After the fall of the Chin dynasty (under which Ku K'ai-chih lived) the North of China fell entirely into the hands of the Wei Tartars, who in 534 separated into two branches, the Eastern and Western Wei. In 550 a Chinese of Tartar extraction named Kao Yang turned the Eastern Wei out of K'ai-fêng Fu, their capital, and founded the Northern Ch'i dynasty, whose rule, though semi-barbaric, was regarded as slightly less humiliating to Chinese pride than that of the Wei Tartars. Meanwhile the Western Wei, with its capital at Ch'ang-an in the north-west, metamorphosed itself, under the guidance of another semi-Tartar, into the Northern Chou dynasty. The four southern and wholly native dynasties, like the Chin which had preceded them, had their capital at Nan-king.

THE WEI TARTARS

Who were these barbarians, under whose rule was produced some of the greatest art that the world has ever seen?

The *History of the Wei Dynasty* was compiled about 560 A.D. by a minister of the Northern Ch'i, who had themselves overthrown the power of the Wei in Central China. The account there given of the Wei makes them the kinsmen of the Chinese : " The Yellow Emperor, when he apportioned his lands, gave the North Country to his youngest son, whose successors took the clan name *T'o-pa*, ' Earth-sovereign.' " The conquerors of the Wei had no reason to flatter them, and the fact that the historian regarded them as of like origin with the Chinese must not be brushed aside as mere mythology.

As regards language (which is no test of race) the Weis seem to have spoken a dialect akin rather to Old Turkish than to Mongol.[2] The Chinese, on the other hand, speak a dialect of the great Sino-Tibetan family of speech which stretches from China to Burma, and includes the languages of the aborigines who still maintain independence in the southern and south-western provinces of China.

---

[1] Some enumerations make the Six Dynasties begin with Wu and Chin, omitting Southern Ch'i and Northern Chou. There are other variants.

[2] See Pelliot, *T'oung-pao*, XX, 328, Note 3.

It is not impossible that the Chinese, like the Weis, were Turko-Mongols who, having invaded China from the north, mingled with the inhabitants and borrowed their speech. Chinese legend, it is true, says nothing of such an immigration. But such silence is of little significance; Indian legend gives no account of the entry of the Aryans into India, an event which was certainly much more recent than the rise of the Chinese.

We read that in 442 an envoy came from the " ancient home of the Weis " to the Wei Court in Northern China urging the Emperor to renew the ancestral worship which his people had carried on in the cave-temple at Wu-lo-hou. The *Wei History* tells us that this ancient seat of the Wei Tartars was 800 miles away from the northern frontier of China, in a low and swampy country to the south-east of the Northern Lake. Wieger[1] is probably right in assuming that this lake was Lake Baikal, and that " Wu-lo-hou " stands for Orkhon.

The Wei, therefore, came from Siberia. Trekking southwards through Mongolia, they made their first appearance upon the Chinese frontier about the year 260 A.D. At the time of their arrival, as we learn from the last book of the *Wei History*, they had no knowledge of Buddhism, but worshipped the spirits of the dead. They had no writing, but communicated by means of symbolic wooden tallies.

During the hundred years after their arrival on the frontiers of China they gradually established an ascendancy over the minor kingdoms of the North and absorbed their semi-Chinese culture. At last, in 398, the Wei king set up his capital at P'ing-ch'ēng, well within the Chinese frontier, began to ape the pomps and ceremonies of a Chinese court, and commanded his warriors to wear Chinese dress.

Perhaps the most important step in the cultural progress of the Wei was their conquest, about 425 A.D., of the kingdom which called itself " Latter Ch'in."

This principality had been established by a Tibetan chieftain in 384. Its capital was at Ch'ang-an, in Shensi. In 405 there arrived from India, by way of the Tarim basin, the great Buddhist teacher Kumārajīva, many of whose translations from the Sanskrit are still standard texts. He settled at Ch'ang-an and witnessed there a tremendous outburst of Buddhist enthusiasm. Nine-tenths of the inhabitants were converted; the Master's theological lectures were attended by over a thousand pupils.

In 417 Ch'ang-an became for a time part of the main (southern) Chinese Empire. But in the first quarter of the 5th century it fell into the hands

---

[1] *Textes Historiques*, II, 1314.

of the Weis, among whom Buddhism now began a flourishing career. So numerous had the monks become in 438 that the Wei Emperor's armies were depleted, and an edict was issued forbidding men under fifty to enter the monasteries. There was a more drastic prescription of Buddhism in 446, following upon an unpleasant shock which the Emperor had one day sustained at Ch'ang-an, where, strolling into a monastery, he had discovered not only a secret store of arms and ammunition, but also a hidden wine distillery and a subterranean harem.

The ban on Buddhism (which had been very incompletely obeyed) was removed by the next Emperor six years later, T'o-pa Tsun, the most devout of the Wei monarchs, who with tonsured head did penance for his father's sacrilege. In 475 a law was passed forbidding (upon religious grounds) the killing of horses or oxen. The north of China became a huge hive of clerics, an anticipation of modern Tibet.

THE ROCK SCULPTURES OF YÜN-KANG

I have said that in their Siberian home the Weis had worshipped the spirits of their ancestors in caves hewn out of the rock. When in 398 they established their capital at P'ing-ch'ēng, just within the northern frontier of China, they found (near by) cliffs of soft rock which afforded them an excellent opportunity of reproducing the cave-temples of their old home. It is probable that the famous rock-temples of Yün-kang were at first designed for the ancestral worship of the Wei Tartars, before their conversion to Buddhism. But even that savage old heathen T'o-pa Kuei, founder of the dynasty, had some tenderness for Buddhism. During his conquest of North China he spared the monasteries, and when he set up his capital at P'ing-ch'eng he issued a proclamation in which he speaks not, certainly, as a Buddhist, but as one favourable to the Buddhist Church.[1]

It was probably during the reign of his successor, T'o-pa Ssŭ, that the great Buddhist carvings at Yün-kang were begun. They will be illustrated and discussed by Mr. Ashton in his forthcoming work on Chinese sculpture; as will also the carvings at Lung-mēn, which were begun by the Weis when in 494 they removed their capital to Central China, and were carried on till the 8th century. This new capital was the seat of a vast cosmopolitan clericalism. In 512 there were more than 3000 foreign priests at Lo-yang, and more than 13,000 monasteries in the province of Honan.

[1] *Wei Shu*, 124, 4.

CHINESE PAINTING

TUN-HUANG (The Caves of the Thousand Buddhas)

Tun-huang was the last halting-place on the western frontiers of China for travellers who were about to cross the desert on their way to the great cities of Central Asia. Its territory had belonged till about 165 B.C. to the Yüeh-chih,[1] who were driven out of it by the Huns. Early in the 1st century B.C., in consequence of a series of victories over the Huns, the Chinese were able to extend their frontier to the edge of the desert. In 88 B.C. they established a garrison at Tun-huang and held the place intermittently until it became in 400 A.D. the capital of the Turkic "Western Liang" dynasty. In 421 it was annexed by another Turkic chieftain ruler of the "Northern Liang," who was in his turn deposed by the third Wei Emperor, T'o-pa T'ao, in 439.

About nine miles south-east of the town is a series of caves hollowed out of a cliff which rises above a dried torrent-bed. The walls of these caves are decorated with Buddhist frescoes; they contain altars presided over by Buddhist statues.[2] Numerous dedicatory inscriptions prove that the works which now exist belong to a period roughly extending from 450–1100 A.D.; but the origin of these rock-temples goes back to an even earlier period. From about 351 till 394 A.D. Tun-huang lay within the territory of the Previous Ch'ins, Tibetans of the stock called Ti, predecessors of the Latter Ch'ins whom I mentioned above as the patrons of Kumārajīva. In 366 a priest named Lo-tsun founded a rock-shrine in the Mo-kao Cave on the Hill of the Singing Sands[3] near Tun-huang. An inscription *Set up by the śramana Lo-tsun in the 2nd year of the period Chien-yüan, Ch'in dynasty*, was excavated in 1777, but subsequently lost sight of. The system of cave-temples was gradually extended "till it stretched westward as far as the Chiu Lung P'o (Nine Ridge Bank), and eastward as far as the San Wei Fēng (Peak of the Three Perils). In the Shēng Li period of T'ang (698–700) there were already more than 1000 caves."

[1] Identified as the speakers of the so-called "Tocharian" language, an Aryan speech once widely prevalent in the Tarim basin. For further references, see the index under 'Tun-huang' and 'Mo-kao.'

[2] See Stein, *Ruins of Desert Cathay*, 1912; and Pelliot, *Les Grottes de Touen-houang*, Paris, 1920–1922. For further references, see the index under 'Tun-huang' and 'Mo-kao.'

[3] About 8 miles S.E. of Tun-huang. This account of the foundation of the caves is taken from the *Li Chün Hsiu Kung-tē Chi* or "Record of the restoration of pious works, undertaken by the Lord Li," an inscription carved in 698 on the rock outside the original cave of Lo-tsun and reproduced in the *Hsi Yü Shui Tao Chi* (Vol. III), an early 19th-century treatise on the waterways of Eastern Turkestan.

Wei Paintings at the Caves.[1] Of the admirable Wei sculpture which is contained in these caves (for example, the Buddha in Cave 111) it is not my task to speak. The paintings, though of the highest importance historically, have not the unique place in art which is occupied by the *Life of Buddha* reliefs and some of the single Buddhas at Yün-kang.

They are crowded with too multifarious an exuberance of human and animal life; full of exquisite detail-grouping, they never achieve and seldom even aim at a united plastic scheme. The main cult-figures (Buddhas and Bodhisattvas), which depended for their efficacy on an exact conformity to Indian prototypes, retain their exotic luxuriance of outline. But the anecdotal scenes which crowd in upon them on every side are typically Chinese. Here are the landscape mannerisms of Ku K'ai-chih, the sprightly animals of the pre-T'ang painted vases, Confucian attitudes straight from the grave-reliefs of Shantung.

The principal exception is Cave 120 N, of which Professor Pelliot supplies some fifteen photographs. Here in most of the scenes we have a thoroughly Central Asian style—what for want of a better term we may call Turfanese. However, the crusader-like horsemen on the left wall, though their accoutrement has a wholly Occidental[2] air, are drawn in Chinese style; while the captives and foot-soldiers, apart from the fact that they wear their hair drawn back from the forehead in a way which seems to be typically Central Asian, are not at all exotic (Plate X).

To disentangle the various stylistic elements of which the early Tun-huang paintings are composed would be a most complicated and difficult task. It would necessarily involve a discussion of contemporary sculpture, and would, even in the field of painting, lead us far away from China. I have no doubt that these questions will be dealt with by M. Goloubew in his forthcoming work upon the art of Tun-huang.

THE SOUTH

Meanwhile the native dynasties ruled at Nanking. This period of the " Six Dynasties " marks a climax; it is the last phase of archaic China.

[1] Caves 18, 70, 120 N (slightly later), 130, 135, 139A, 140.

[2] Anachronistically, for such cavalry equipment did not become the fashion in Europe till the middle of the 13th century (Laking, *Arms and Armour*, III, 147). Similar horsemen are seen in the wall-painting of a tomb at Chi-an Hsien, Shēngking Province, Manchuria, excavated by the Japanese and published in *Chōsen Koseki Zufu*, Vol. I, Pl. 282. This species of equipment seems to have been used particularly by the Iranians. By means of it the Sarmatians defeated the Scythians and the Sassanians, the Parthians. It was borrowed by the Romans from the Alans, who were a Sarmatian tribe.

It was an age which (like our own) looked back upon the past. The culture of China had grown up spontaneously and instinctively. It now became self-conscious and introspective. The first anthologies are made; poets are classified and analysed. Liu Hsieh brings out his *Wēn Hsin Tiao Lung*, the earliest treatise on literature; Hsieh Ho (as we have seen) enunciates the Six Canons of painting.

Nor were these professors content merely to codify the literature of the past. They must make poetry of their own to exemplify their classifications and rules. But poetry must be beautiful; and, being persons of limited sensibility, they were never quite sure whether they had achieved this. Moreover, there was often much in their own careers that certainly was not beautiful,[1] and they were afraid that, unless they covered their productions with thick layers of loveliness, some of their own native villainy might protrude. So to make sure of their poems being beautiful and moving they filled them with such things as moonlight, springtime, flowers, and jade—which are indisputably beautiful; with partings, death, love lost, love unrequited—which are indisputably melancholy.

The Anthologies. The *Yü T'ai Hsin Yung* (New Songs of the Jade Terrace), compiled about the year 535 as a manual for the use of the Crown Prince by a minister of the Emperor Wu Ti, is a veritable corpus of prettiness and sentimentality. What is sentimentality? I wonder that this disease of the spirit has not been analysed and defined by modern psychologists. It certainly made its appearance in China, particularly in poetry, at a very early date; whereas in Europe it did not get a firm hold till the end of the 18th century. But though sentimentality had its birth in China, the Chinese cannot claim the credit of having exploited its possibilities to the utmost. This was reserved for its foster-mother, Japan, that great home and breeding-ground of *sensiblerie*.

The other great anthology of the time is the *Wēn Hsüan*, a great collection of prose and poetry brought together by the Emperor Wu Ti's short-lived son, Hsiao T'ung, about the year 530. It is an invaluable and at the same time an exasperating book. Precious, because so much of early Chinese literature survives only in its pages; irritating, because one soon becomes aware that the Prince's tastes were obviously the antithesis of one's own. " I have been reading the *Wēn Hsüan* on board ship," writes the 11th-century poet Su Tung-p'o, during one of his travels. " What a pity that both the arrangement and the selection are so in-

---

[1] As in that of the fourth Liang Emperor, Yüan Ti, who murdered his brother in order to secure the throne. He was a great manufacturer of sentimental verse.

competent. But the Liang dynasty ruled at a period when literary taste was at a low ebb ; and in Hsiao T'ung it reached its lowest point of all ! "[1]

Undoubtedly this trivial and elegant Court literature had its counterpart in painting and the decorative arts. But of Court painting very little is told us, and nothing remains. The fragments of sculpture which survive from the Liang tombs are in a traditional funerary style and probably bear little relation to the main art of the period. But of the Buddhist painting, particularly fresco painting, we may learn something from books.

The principal painter of the period is credited with the introduction into China of an Indian technique. The Weis in Northern China were in touch principally with Turkestan and the eastern provinces of Sassanian Persia ; the native dynasty in the south trafficked by sea with India, Cambodia, the Malay Islands ; and by land with Korea. In 535 the latter country asked for and obtained from China a present of " commentaries on various sūtras, particularly that of the Great Decease, the Book of Odes, doctors, painters, and professors." Korean Buddhist art is thus derived from Nanking ; it was transmitted to Japan. The Hōryūji frescoes are more Indian than those of Tun-huang, partly because they derive from the Buddhist art of Liang, which came by sea from India ; whereas the Wei art is derived from Central Asia and is only very indirectly Indian.

THE KOREAN TOMB-PAINTINGS

We have seen that in 535 the Liangs sent painters to the King of Korea. There still exist in Korea several tomb-paintings which are probably earlier than this date. They were discovered by the Japanese about 1905 and have since been published in the *Chōsen Koseki Zu-fu*, a series which is still incomplete.

At Baisanri, near the mouth of the Ta-tung River in Northern Korea, is the tomb of the " Four Gods." The four figures who squat stiffly in a row seem to be not " Gods," but probably the persons for whom the tomb was built. The larger figure is (according to Japanese interpretation) the father of the family. The three smaller ones are his wife and concubines. Above them is spread a primitive kind of canopy. On the right a figure advances leading a horse. On another wall is a hunting-scene somewhat in the technique of primitive cave-paintings. The fleeing deer, an extraordinary piece of impressionism, is obviously the rendering

[1] *Ch'ou-ch'ih Pi Chi*, I, 1.

of a single flash of vision. Much of the same method survives in the earliest frescoes at Tun-huang, though only in the side-scenes and narrative background, the imported cult-figures representing a wholly different stratum of art. The tomb is thought to date from about 400 A.D. Needless to say it represents a high degree of provincial[1] archaism. Probably it corresponds to the art of China proper in 400 B.C. rather than A.D. Buddhism, it may be observed, had entered Northern Korea from China in 372; but it did not till long afterwards become the accepted religion of the country.

A little further north is the Tomb of the Reliquary Gods, which is supposed to date from about 500. The frescoes show non-Buddhist cult-figures (the nature of which is still obscure) and fragments of cavalcades. The Tomb of the Twin Pillars which lies some ten miles to the north-east is said to date from about 510. On the walls of the tomb-passage are figures of ladies with (apparently) fur-trimmed jackets and pleated skirts. A horseman and an ox-cart are also discernible. On the north wall of the inner chamber, squatting on a dais, are the buried man and his wife, both immensely square and solid. On the east wall is a procession of ladies whose skirts and jackets seem to be made of some kind of ermine. They have (probably quite accidentally and fallaciously) the air of having stepped out of an early Persian miniature.

The Great Tomb at Gūkenri[2] close by dates from about 550 A.D. The magnificent, heraldically conceived dragon on the east wall of the funeral chamber recalls the recently discovered sculpture of the contemporary Liang tombs near Nanking (Plate XI.) On the north wall are painted the Black Warriors (the serpent and tortoise) twined in emblematic embrace. Above is an *apsara* or Buddhist angel, clearly derived (via China) from Indian art, but very much de-Indianized and adapted. In this tomb we see the results of the mission which in 535 brought back Buddhist painters from Nanking.

CHANG SĒNG-YU

Chang Sēng-yu was a successful official under the Southern Ch'i and Liang dynasties. Early in the 6th century he was made Governor of Wu-hsing in Kiangsu. The reigning Emperor Wu Ti was an ardent Buddhist. He built many temples at Nanking, and on solemn occasions

---

[1] If I may be allowed for a moment to treat Northern Korea as an outlying province of Chinese civilization. No wide ethnological gulf separates the Koreans from their northern Chinese neighbours.

[2] This is the Japanese pronunciation; the Korean is " U-hyön-ri."

took upon himself to mount the lectern and expound the scriptures. He devoted a long series of these séances to the Sūtras of the Great Decease and to the Mahāprajnāparamitā group. Many of the temples which he built or restored were decorated by Chang Sēng-yu. " In painting he used (for example, in the floral designs) a method of handling vermilion and verdigris which is said to be derived from India. Seen at a distance such work has the appearance of being carved in relief; but when more closely examined they turn out to be merely paintings."[1]

The use of shading to obtain the appearance of " relief " is quite foreign to Chinese art; but it is found in the Ajanta frescoes and in the wall-paintings of the Golden Hall at Hōryūji, to which I shall return in a later chapter.

He is also said to have been the first to use the " boneless " method of painting, that is to say, the immediate application of colour without the use of a preliminary basis of outline. This innovation, too, may have been derived from India, for something of the kind is found in the paintings of Cave 17 at Ajanta.

" Ku K'ai-chih and Lu T'an-wei," we read, " gave their angels, court-ladies, and heroines long, oval faces; Sēng-yu changed the fashion; his beauties were round-faced and plump."

From such scraps of information we can get very little idea of Chang's actual importance as an artist. It is possible, however, that we may one day know more of him, for the Ch'ien Lung Collection contained two of his works. The first was a hanging picture (about three feet high) of " Red-leaved Trees on Snowy Hills." The catalogue seems to regard it as genuine, but gives only the briefest particulars.

The second was an album, " Spirits of the Five Planets and Twenty-eight Constellations." It was once a long scroll, but was afterwards cut up into sections and mounted as an album. Each section had a long explicatory text. The *Kokka* (No. 259) reproduces a painting, " Washing the Elephant," which is supposed to be a copy by the 13th-century artist Ch'ien Hsüan of a painting by Chang Sēng-yu. Of paintings by him which once existed we have the titles of about twenty. The Emperor Hui Tsung (12th century) possessed sixteen, including the " Washing the Elephant " and the " Spirits of the Five Planets "; among them the " Sixteen

---

[1] Quoted by the *Shu Hua P'u* (XII, 24 recto) from the *Works* of Yang Shēn (1488–1529). The story probably has an earlier source; but I have looked for it in vain both in the *Liang Shu* (History of the Liang Dynasty) and the *Nan Shih* (History of the Southern Dynasties).

Arhats," " Vimalakīrti," " Mañjuśrī," " The Ten Famous Priests," and
the " Nine Stars."

We know from the *Ming Hua Chi* that before the great Buddhist per-
secution of 845 the Ting-shui Temple at Ch'ang-an contained three wall-
paintings of Indra by Chang Sēng-yu, all imported from other temples.
The T'ien-kung Temple at Lo-yang had two Bodhisattvas on wooden
panels, both brought from the south.

TS'AO CHUNG-TA

It was a custom in China at this time to give to foreigners, as their family
name, the name of the country from which they had migrated. Chung-ta's
family[1] had come from Ts'ao, a small kingdom near Samarkand, probably
dependent upon the Sassanian Empire. It lay south of the Zarafshan,
near the modern Ishtikhan.[2] " In this kingdom," says the *Sui Shu*
(History of the Sui Dynasty), " there are the gods called *Tek-sit*. The
various kingdoms that lie to the east of the Caspian Sea all honour them
and do them worship. Among these gods is one called the Golden Man.
His golden lotus-pedestal is fifteen feet wide, and he is high in proportion.
Each day they sacrifice to him five camels, ten horses, and a hundred sheep."
The religion here described has not been identified. Unknown heathen
cults of this kind, involving the use of statues, may have had a great
influence upon the development of Buddhist iconography.

Chung-ta rose to a high position at the Court of the Northern Ch'is.
He was the originator of an original style of figure-painting which found
many subsequent imitators and always remained distinct from the main
stream which culminated in Wu Tao-tzŭ. Kuo Jo-hsü[3] tells us in his
T'u Hua Chien Wēn Chih (I, 13) that Ts'ao's figures, with their clinging
draperies, looked as if they had just come out of the water ; while Wu's
looked as if they were being blown about by the wind. We might be
tempted to see in this distinctive treatment of drapery a result of Chung-ta's
Western origin ; but there may well have been nothing Persian in his
style, for he was a pupil of the Chinese painter Yüan Shēng.[4] Another

---

[1] The phrasing of the *Ming Hua Chi* indicates that it was not Chung-ta himself, but his
parents or ancestors, who were inhabitants of Ts'ao.

[2] See Chavannes, *Tou-kiue Occidentaux*, p. 139.

[3] Who flourished about 1060–1110 A.D. See *Shu Hua P'u*, XII, 12. The rival theory
that the Ts'ao style descended from Ts'ao Pu-hsing is almost certainly a misconception.

[4] So *Ming Hua Chi*, II, 1 verso. Elsewhere he is simply called a pupil of " Yüan," which
must mean Yüan Tzŭ-ang.

tradition, Jo-hsü tells us, derived the Ts'ao style from Ts'ao Pu-hsing and the Wu from an obscure 5th-century painter, Wu Lien. "The same distinction of Ts'ao and Wu schools existed in sculpture."

THE SUI DYNASTY

In 581 the Suis succeeded in reuniting China. Though they ruled for only thirty-seven years, the period was one of great historic importance. It saw, for example, the institution of the Literary Examinations, which, though exactly the same system prevails in England, has been commonly regarded here as the most whimsical of Chinese absurdities. From the year 595 onwards candidates for positions in the Public Service were tested in the composition of an obsolete type of poetry, the *fu*,[1] and were called upon to write various kinds of eulogy, inscription, and so forth, in prose. Hitherto a system of privilege and nomination had prevailed which worked well enough in the truncated Empire of the south; but now that China was again united into one huge dominion, such a system would have supplied neither the right quantity nor the right quality of official.

Another important innovation which is supposed to have taken place at this time was the invention of printing. A decree issued by the Emperor Wēn Ti in 593 has been thought to refer to the art of printing from wood-blocks. The passage was mistranslated by Julien in 1850, and his statements have misled all subsequent writers on the subject. The printing of secular books did not probably begin till the 9th century; but the British Museum possesses three *dhāranī* spells printed from wood-blocks in 764 A.D. by order of the Japanese Empress Shōtoku. It is probable that an art which was practised in Japan in the 8th century existed in China at a much earlier date. We have, I think, no actual evidence that it was invented in the 6th century; but such a date is not at all improbable. The priests who first used this art for the convenience of multiplying Buddhist spells may very well have kept it secret, suspecting that their clients would doubt the efficacy of machine-made charms.

The earliest woodcut picture known to exist is the frontispiece to the *Diamond Sūtra* of 868, discovered by Sir Aurel Stein at Tun-huang and now exhibited in the King's Library at the British Museum.[2] It will be more convenient to speak of the Sui painters in connection with the T'ang painters who were their pupils.

[1] See introduction to *The Temple and other Poems*.   [2] On the invention of wood-cuts, see my Note in the *New China Review*, 1919. Mr. T. F. Carter points out to me that though Julien forced the meaning of the passage, his inference was perhaps correct.

CHAPTER VIII
THE T'ANG DYNASTY

CHAPTER VIII

THE T'ANG DYNASTY

One may roughly divide the T'ang dynasty into three periods which cover the 7th, 8th, and 9th centuries respectively. The first one may call the period of Buddhist speculation; the second, of lyric poetry; the third, of Confucian reaction.

The Progress of Buddhism. Till the 4th century Chinese monasteries were inhabited chiefly by foreign monks. They were few in number and relatively small in size. During this early period that portion of the Buddhist scriptures known as Vinaya, or Monastic Rules, was not of much interest to Chinese Buddhists, and very little of it was translated. At the end of the 4th century the question of monastic discipline came to the fore, and in 399 a Chinese[1] monk, Fa-hsien, went to India to collect manuscripts of the Vinaya. He returned in 411 and spent the rest of his life translating these texts. A much more interesting phase of Buddhism began at Nanking in 529 with the arrival of the Zen patriarch Bodhidharma. I shall deal with his doctrines (which did not affect art until a much later date) in a separate chapter.

The third class of scriptures consists of the speculations which Indian thinkers wove round the original Sūtras—in fact, of Buddhist philosophy. For in the East, as in mediæval Europe, " thought for thought's sake " does not exist. Every philosopher is the servant of some Church; his task consists in pushing freedom of thought to the furthest point consistent with the articles of his faith. Orthodoxy may bend under the strain, but it must never break.

I have already mentioned Kumārajīva[2] as the translator of the Lotus and Vimalakīrti Sūtras. He also introduced into China the works of two of the four main schools of Buddhist philosophy, the Sautrāntika and the Śūnyavāda. The first, which may be called the Scriptural school, rejects those compromises whereby the earlier philosophers sought to mitigate Shākyamuni's absolute denial of the reality of phenomenal existence. In the *Satya Siddhi Śāstra* translated by Kumārajīva, every utterance of Buddha which might seem to touch on this point is quoted and analysed. The result is, of course, that a vast mass of inconsistency is exposed. The corollary of the Śāstra—namely, that we must accept the Sūtras blindly without trying to understand them, shows that this school had

---

[1] Like Kumārajīva he was a subject of the Tartar prince Fu Chien who ruled over N.W. China with his capital at Ch'ang-an.

[2] See above, pp. 40 and 78. He died at Ch'ang-an in 409 A.D.

91

not much importance as philosophy. Its chief utility was that it led to a close examination of the Sūtra texts.

But Kumārajīva's great service was his exposition of the Śūnyavāda or Nihilist doctrine of Nāgārjuna,[1] as contained in the famous Three Śāstras. After a pitiless exposure of the evasions and temporizings of his rivals, Nāgārjuna demonstrates that one position alone is impregnable—that of the Śūnyavādin or Nihilist who denies the existence of any reality whatsoever. The weakness of Nāgārjuna's teaching is that it does not explain our persistent delusion that things *do* exist. A new school[2] sprang up which was chiefly concerned in explaining why this illusion operates. Its greatest writer was Asanga, who lived at the end of the 4th century, but at the beginning of the 7th its doctrines were almost unknown in China.

In 629 the Chinese pilgrim Hsüan Tsang set out for India. His object was not to promote any particular doctrine or sect, but to collect a great corpus of the newer Buddhist philosophies. He brought back with him 657 books; of these he had translated 75 at the time of his death in 664. His translations may be divided into three groups. First, those expounding the Vijñānavāda, in particular the famous *Yogāchāra Śāstra*, said to have been revealed to Asanga by the Buddha of the Future, Maitreya.

Second, the Abhidharma of the Sarvāstivādins, who claim that, though the phenomenal world is constantly changing, it is yet composed of elements which have a real and fixed existence. The great exposition of this philosophy, which, strictly speaking, belongs to the Lesser Vehicle (Hīnayāna), is the *Kośaśāstra* of Asanga's brother Vasubandhu. This book, as arranged and translated by Hsüan Tsang, played an important part in the intellectual life of the T'ang dynasty and of mediæval Japan.

The third great task which Hsüan Tsang undertook was the editing and translation of the Mahāprajñāpāramitā Sūtras, a huge collection of scriptures arranged in 600 chapters. The " transcendent wisdom " (prajñāpāramitā) of this huge bible is the knowledge that—there is nothing to know, for nothing exists.

It might be urged that these translations and adaptations of Indian books are not of much relevance to the study of Chinese culture. This would, I think, be a mistake. Such men as Hsüan Tsang were not mere transcribers of alien thought any more than Mr. Eddington is a mere transcriber of the teaching of Einstein. It must be remembered, even in

---

[1] *Circa* 100 A.D.

[2] The Vijñānavāda or Yogāchārya, of which McGovern says that it " resulted in the formulation of a remarkably complete system of idealism " (*Mahāyāna Buddhism*, p. 23).

the case of translations, that Buddhist philosophy cannot, any more than Western philosophy, be translated without being understood. The number of Chinamen who shared Hsüan Tsang's interests was no doubt rather small. But if we are recording the intellectual progress of a people we are inevitably studying the activities of a few men. It is probable that those who read and understood the *Kośa Śāstra* were more numerous than those who to-day study the philosophy of Mr. George Moore.

Other Developments of Buddhism. T'ien-t'ai. Chih-k'ai, the founder of T'ien-t'ai or Synthetic Buddhism, was born in 538. At the age of eighteen he became a priest, and for twelve years devoted himself to the study of Buddhist theory, particularly to the teaching of the Zen sect. He then set up as a lecturer at Nanking and for eight years enjoyed great success.

Chih-k'ai was not only a speculative philosopher ; he was also a moralist. He saw that for the clergy Buddhism had become merely a rigorous course of intellectual training, involving the study of innumerable scriptures and treatises ; from this arduous and arid path the only escape was Zen or " Contemplative Buddhism," which to Chih-k'ai (who was no Yogi, but a man of vast practical piety and benevolence) was an intolerably narrow creed. For the laity there remained only the easy doctrines of the Amida School and a cult which differed little from pagan idolatry. Becoming dissatisfied with the work he was doing at Nanking, he retired to the T'ien-t'ai mountain in Che-kiang and worked out a popular and encyclopedic form of Buddhism,[1] based upon the teaching of the most all-embracing of Mahāyāna scriptures, the *Lotus of the Good Law*. In 585 he returned to Nanking and began to propagate his new creed. After a few years he retired to T'ien-t'ai with his disciples and founded there what became one of the greatest monastic establishments in the world. He died there in 597.

The Japanese followers of Chih-k'ai call him Shintan no Shaka, " The Shākyamuni of China," and with reason. He was a veritable second founder of the Buddhist faith. The moderate and comprehensive doctrine which he taught, with its lucid metaphysic and strong ethical emphasis, was exactly what the cultivated Chinese classes required. Yet even his enlightened doctrine, like every other phase of Buddhism, tended among the masses both of clergy and laity to degenerate into superstition. The special veneration for the Lotus Sūtra, which was the inspiration of Chih-k'ai's later teaching, turned, among his followers, into the actual

---

[1] For its philosophy see Eliot's *Hinduism and Buddhism*, III, 311.

worship of this book as a cult-object; and the belief that the mere repetition of the formula, " Praise to the Lotus Flower Sūtra of the Good Law," was an adequate means of salvation.

T'ien-t'ai Buddhism and Art.   The centre of T'ien-t'ai Buddhism was in the east; it left no mark of its influence upon the paintings of far-distant Tun-huang.   The huge monastic establishments of the sect suffered heavily during the destruction of 845 A.D., and of T'ien-t'ai art practically nothing survives.   The influence of the sect is seen in the large number of Lotus Book Mandalas (paintings which show Shākyamuni preaching the Lotus Sermon to legions of divinities upon the peak of the Sacred Hill), which we read of in works on T'ang art.   One such painting,[1] which is supposed to date from the 9th century, is now in the Museum of Fine Arts at Boston.

Tantric Buddhism.   In its most developed form (for example, in the Lamaism of Tibet) Tantric Buddhism is distinguished by three characteristics :

(1) The use of magic incantations, spells, and gestures.

(2) The encouragement of semi-religious, semi-erotic orgies, associated with the cult of the " female-emanations " (Śakti) of Buddhas.

(3) The cult of the gruesome.

This last began very early, for a picture of the Miracles of Manjuśrī[2] by Lu T'an-wei (5th century) showed a foreign priest holding in his hand a cup fashioned out of a human skull.   The use of spells must be at least as old as the Lotus Sūtra, which near the end has a whole chapter of them, such as :

ATTE TATTE NATTE VANATTE ANADE NĀDI KUNADI. SVĀHĀ. (Spell of Vaiśravana.)

Partly corrupted Sanskrit, partly mere jingle, these spells provided formulæ far more impressive and mysterious than the endless repetition of Amida's name or the recitation[3] of what was, after all, only the title of a book.   The Dhāranī (Spell) chapter was not regarded as a fanciful appendix to the Lotus Scripture, but rather as : *A ripe fruit forming when flower-time is over, Upon the Holy Tree of Law.*[4]

[1] Anesaki, *Buddhist Art*, Plate VI.
[2] Described in the *Hua Chien*, 14th century.
[3] " Praise to the Lotus Sūtra of the Good Law."
[4] Bishop Kwaishū, Japanese, 12th century.

In the remains discovered at Tun-huang the erotic element is, I think, entirely absent. The only *śakti* or female emanation known to the Chinese previous to the importation of Lamaism from Tibet seems to have been Tārā, the consort of Avalokiteśvara. A woodcut of Avalokiteśvara, dated 947, has an invocation to Tārā printed beneath it. The female form of Avalokiteśvara, so common in Chinese and Japanese mediæval art, was no doubt developed from his *śakti*[1]; but the gentle Madonnas of China have little in common with the scowling ogresses of Tibet.

Upon the Buddhist art of Central Asia (with which I am not here concerned) Tantrism left a much deeper mark; Grünwedel,[2] indeed, has credited the painters of Kucha with almost unbelievably sinister intentions.

THE MIDDLE PERIOD

The Emperor Ming Huang came to the throne in 712. His reign was preceded by the troublous times of the Empress Wu Hou, a murderous creature whose rule had prostrated China. Nor did her death end her power for evil, for she lived again in her daughter, who attempted to poison the young Emperor soon after he came to the throne.

Not simultaneously, but at different times during the first half of his reign Ming Huang carried through a series of reforms affecting every department of the State. He instituted schools throughout the Empire, founded the Literary College (Han-lin) and the Academy of Music, and reformed the Public Examinations.

Hitherto service in distant parts of China had been regarded as a punishment. The frontier provinces were looked upon as so many Botany Bays; refractory metropolitan officials were dumped into them as " Governors " or " Viceroys "; in reality they were exiled convicts. It is easy to see how disastrously such a system reacted upon the government of the Empire. Ming Huang persuaded men of reputation and ability to undertake these " pro-consular " posts and saw to it that it was made worth their while to do so.

Finally he instituted (though he himself was the first to violate them) a series of sumptuary laws. For a time the Imperial harem was much reduced in size and magnificence. We are told, indeed, that during the early years of his reign he took very little interest in it. He abolished

---

[1] And not, as used to be asserted, from the cult of some primitive Chinese Mother-goddess; for there is no evidence that such a cult ever existed in China.

[2] *Alt-Kutscha*, 1920.

capital punishment and issued an edict calling upon the governors of prisons to give better attention to the health and comfort of the inmates.

T'ANG POETRY

Most of the early T'ang poets imitated the rather insipid style of the Six Dynasties. Ch'ēn Tzŭ-ang[1] went further back, and in his famous *Hsien Yü*, a series of thirty-eight poems, imitated the gaunt severity of the *Yung Huai*, or " Songs from the Heart," a sequence of eighty-two poems written in the 3rd century by Yüan Chi. The *Hsien Yü* is in the old, free metre. But the new tone-pattern metres invented in the 6th century were being perfected by many contemporary poets. Li Po[2] used both mediums. Some of his finest work occurs in a series of Old Style poems which are strongly reminiscent both of the *Hsien Yü* and the *Yung Huai*. In these, as in almost all his poetry, Li Po develops to the highest imaginable pitch of intricacy the art of literary allusion. As out of several thousand poems which he wrote precisely those few have been translated which (not being allusive) are least typical of him, European readers are likely to think that the acrostic character of his poetry has been exaggerated—that all is very plain sailing. But the main reason why Li Po's poetry will never be known outside China is that its beauty is purely lyric. He depends on the exact use of particular words and cannot therefore be transferred to another language. What comes through in European versions and what has pleased so many Western readers is not the property of Li Po, but is inherited by him from earlier writers who have not yet been translated. Whatever appears whimsical, imaginative, " insouciant," in translations of Li Po's poems is almost invariably adapted from T'ao Ch'ien or some other of his predecessors. Whereas his consummate mastery of language, the quality which has made his name eternal, is (no doubt inevitably) not reflected in the slightest degree in the existing translations of his work.

Tu Fu. It was round the house of Prince Chi[3] rather than the palace of Ming Huang that cultivated society centred in the early years of the reign. This prince, the Emperor's brother, cared a great deal for art and learning, and not at all for birth and rank. Scholars, artists, poets, musicians all flocked to his house. Here were seen Tu Fu, the poet; the scholars Yen Ch'ao-yin, Liu Yen-ch'i, Chang Ē, Chēng Yu; and, greatest

---

[1] 656–698.   [2] 701–762.
[3] Called also Li Lung-fan and Hui-wēn T'ai-tzŭ.

figure of all in Ch'ang-an society, Li Kuei-nien, the director of the Imperial ballet. Here, too, and here alone, might be studied the masterpieces of calligraphy and painting which had belonged to the Sui and early T'ang Emperors.[1]

Tu Fu shared in the splendour of these golden days, but it is as the poet of *Les misères de la guerre*, the chronicler of ruin and disaster, that he is best remembered. The astonishing civilization of Ch'ang-an had crumbled at a touch. Imagine Versailles suddenly captured by Turks; the King, Madame de Maintenon, Monsieur, the Bastards, flying to the Breton coast; Le Brun, Couperin, Racine tramping destitute from town to town. Such was the fall of Ming Huang. Nor was it only the Tartars who sacked Ch'ang-an; the Tibetans and Uighurs hired by the Crown Prince to drive out the rebels proved even more destructive.

The poems of Li Po deal, as regards their content, so much in established clichés[2] that we get from reading them very little sense of personality. In the work of Tu Fu (who was perhaps not so pure an artist) we have the reflection of a grandeur, a zest, an emotional richness that have, I think, no parallel in any literature.

THE FALL OF MING HUANG

As the poets, painters, and musicians who graced Ming Huang's court were, by universal consent, the greatest whom China has known, so too were his war lords. Kao Hsien-chih carried Chinese arms beyond the Pamirs; the Khan of the Turks was deposed, the King of Samarkand sent tribute; kings of Kashmir and Gandhara became the vassals of China. Syrians, Turks, Persians thronged the capital. Christianity, Buddhism, Manichæism, Zoroastrianism flourished there side by side. For at this period Ch'ang-an was the capital of the world, as Rome was in the Middle Ages, and Paris is to-day. Later, China was to become not the centre of the great world, but a world by herself, apart.

Huge military disasters preceded the revolution which I am about to describe. But it was the Emperor's reckless personal conduct which precipitated the catastrophe.

In 745 he met Lady Yang, who for ten years had been the concubine of his eighteenth son, Prince Shou. She was twenty-seven; he was sixty. She was fat, wore false side-locks and an outrageous yellow skirt, was

---

[1] Stolen from the Imperial Palace in 701 by the picture-restorer Chang I-chih.
[2] This is, of course, not apparent in translations.

obstinate, capricious, and overbearing. The Emperor fell in love with her, called her " his priestess, the Great Pure One,"[1] and soon installed her in the Palace, with the official title Yang Kuei-fei (Exalted Princess Yang).

It soon became apparent that he had not fallen under the domination of a single woman, but of a whole clan. Kuei-fei's three sisters were raised to the peerage. Her cousins were given important posts. They built themselves vast palaces, competing in lavishness and splendour. The servants of each of the five Yang households had a different coloured livery. When the Emperor visited his Summer Palace, the retinues of the " five households " joined in his procession, their liveries weaving an embroidery " gay as a valley full of flowers." Yang Kuo-chung, a second-cousin, led the throng displaying the banner of Chien-nan, the district of which he had been made honorary Governor. Fallen bracelets, slippers, jewels, littered the road ; a heavy scent of perfume hung for days over the country-side.

An Lu-shan. His father was a Tartar ; of the tribe from whom the Manchus are supposed to be in part descended. His mother was a Turkic witch-woman. Being " a great reader of men's thoughts and the master of many dialects, Turkic, Tartar, and Chinese," he was made an intendant of markets, but was caught stealing a sheep. The Governor of the district (in north-eastern China) condemned him to death. " Sir," cried An Lu-shan, " if you would crush your enemies, you had best spare me." The Governor liked his boldness, and, seeing that he was a fine-looking, sturdy fellow, set him free. Lu-shan knew every hill and stream in the district, and was often used by the Chinese as a guide in their campaigns upon the northern frontier. Once he was given five horsemen to command, and with their aid captured twenty Tartars. Soon he became the captain of a squadron.

By flattering and bribing an Imperial inspector who was visiting the province, Lu-shan obtained the great object of his ambition—that his name should be known to the Emperor. In 742, having already become Governor of his native province, he was summoned to Court and soon showed that he was as much at home in the mazes of Court intrigue as he had been in the twisting bypaths of Yin-shan.

Yang Kuei-fei adopted him as her child ; the Emperor soon treated him as an equal. His immense corpulency, which in early life he had corrected

---

[1] A Taoist title (T'ai-chēn). Since 736 the Emperor had been dabbling in Taoist mysticism and magic.

by fasting, was an asset at Court. Fat men are supposed to be good-natured and simple. Whilst parading an affable obesity Lu-shan was engaged in a multiplicity of sinister schemes.

In the autumn of 751 a great fire destroyed the equipment of 370,000 Imperial troops; Lu-shan's armies in the north, which were supplied by a separate arsenal, were unaffected. In the spring of 755 (he was now at the head of his armies) he wrote to the Emperor asking him to dismiss thirty-two Chinese generals and replace them by Tartars; the request was granted. In the autumn he announced that he was sending three thousand Tartar horses with two native grooms each as a present to the Emperor. At last Ming Huang's suspicions were aroused; what Lu-shan proposed was nothing less than a cavalry reconnaissance of the route between his province and the capital. A messenger was despatched with a letter entreating him to postpone the gift. Lu-shan received the letter without rising from the couch where he lay. " Tell the Son of Heaven," he said, " that he and I will soon meet."

It is not my intention to describe the campaign by which the rebels, rapidly mastering the provinces of Honan and Shansi, marched westwards to Ch'ang-an. One evening in July, 756, the Emperor looked in vain for the fire-signals, which were discharged each evening at a distance of six miles from the capital. He sent in panic for Yang Kuo-chung, who advised him to fly immediately to the south. He left the city accompanied only by Yang Kuei-fei, her brothers and sisters, and some few members of his own family. They reached Hsien-yang just before midday. The Emperor had not yet eaten; a peasant brought him a dish of rice, beans, and corn, for no one in the panic-stricken party had thought to bring provisions for the journey. The Imperial grand-children scrambled for a share of the food. At midnight they reached Chin-ch'ēng (The Golden City). The inhabitants had fled carrying everything with them; at the inn not even a lamp had been left behind. The fugitives made pillows of straw and lay down together in the dark, " high and humble, shoulder to shoulder."

Next day they reached the inn at Ma-wei. The soldiers of the escort were tired and hungry. A rumour had spread among them that Yang Kuei-fei's brother, Yang Kuo-chung, was in secret correspondence with the rebels. A messenger was sent to warn the Crown Prince, but before he returned it chanced that Kuo-chung himself came down the street on horseback. Some Tibetan envoys who were stranded in this deserted town pressed round him begging for food. " Traitor ! " cried the Chinese troops, " he is plotting with foreigners." Instantly they fell upon him and slew him.

The troops next demanded the death of Kuei-fei herself. The Emperor promised that " he would treat her as justice demanded." He went back into the inn and stood a long while with bowed head, leaning upon his staff. At last Wei Ē, the Registrar of Ch'ang-an, stepped forward and, beating his head upon the floor, besought the Emperor not to exasperate the soldiers by delay. " Kuei-fei," he answered, " lived hidden away in the Palace. What could she know of treason and plots ? " " That is true," replied the eunuch Kao Li-shih, another member of the Imperial clique, " but so long as she is by Your Majesty's side the soldiers will be hostile and your own life in danger." " Take her," said the Emperor, and the eunuch dragged her to a wayside shrine, where he throttled her with a rope. Later, the body was thrown into a hole by the roadside, wrapped in the purple hangings of the Imperial coach.

Next day the Emperor continued his journey to Ssechuan. This flight figures in Court poetry of the time as an Imperial Pleasure Tour. " Six Dragon-steeds draw thee to the West," writes Li Po, " while the multitudes rejoice. Nor is thy glory diminished ; for at the Presence this Southern City[1] is changed into thine own Ch'ang-an."

Meanwhile the rebels did not prosper. Lu-shan had declared himself Emperor of the Yen dynasty, but for many months his sight had been failing, and he now lay chafing in his tent, quite blind, and irritable to the verge of madness. His fettered energy found its outlet in orgies of cruelty. On the most trivial pretexts even his favourites were pitilessly lashed. A eunuch who had suffered more than any conspired with an officer of the guard to place upon the " throne " Lu-shan's feeble-minded son, An Ch'ing-hsü. The eunuch entered his master's tent by night and plunged a sword through the huge and helpless frame. Lu-shan stretched out his hand to grasp the dagger that lay always at his pillow-side. It was not there. " It is a friend has slain me," he cried, and soon expired.

The menace was over. The Imperial army, reinforced by foreign troops from Turkestan, rapidly recovered the lost cities. The ex-Emperor (he had abdicated in favour of his son) returned to his old capital. He settled by choice in apartments upon the edge of the Imperial Precincts. Twice a day he stood in tears in front of Kuei-fei's portrait. The pupils of the

---

[1] Ch'ēng-tu, capital of Ssechuan.

Pear-tree Garden[1] once more delighted their instructor. Much of his time was spent in receiving those small marks of sympathy which a people delights in extending to the dowagered or deposed. He would sit for hours on a tower above the road. From time to time the passers-by would notice him and cheer; then, gratified, he would distribute small largesses of wine and food. But at last even these pleasures were taken from him. It was thought that he was "courting the mob," and on the plea that his apartments were damp, he was removed to the Inner Palace, where he died two years later at the age of seventy-eight.

LATE T'ANG (The Restoration)

At the beginning of the 9th century there were two political parties at Ch'ang-an. The first, whom we will call the Liberals, realized that China was no longer the sole great Empire of the East. They were in favour of alliance rather than wars, and turned naturally to the Uighurs, who alone at this time were able to resist the growing power of the Arabs. This involved the admission of Uighur settlers into China and tolerance towards the Manichæan[2] religion. The Liberal statesmen, though few of them were exclusively Buddhist in their beliefs, tended to support the eclectic doctrine of the T'ien-t'ai Sect, including the theory that Truth has various aspects, some of which can only be apprehended by a chosen few. The Conservatives, on the other hand, wished to restore the China of pre-Buddhist times. It was not becoming, they held, that China should hold relations with the outside world except as a conqueror. Buddhism, a religion derived from nations who ought to be the vassals, not the teachers of China, must be abolished; and with it Christianity, Zoroastrianism, and the religion of Mani. The leader of the Conservative party was the famous writer Han Yü (768–824), whose anti-Buddhist tract has many times been translated.[3] In it he wisely refrains from attempting to refute the philosophical tenets of Buddhism; he merely appeals to the national prejudices of the Chinese. The Emperor Hsien Tsung, to whom this essay was addressed, replied by banishing its author to the marshes of Kuang-tung.

The whole thesis of Han Yü was that the original system of government and personal conduct, perfect in every particular, which was established

[1] A name given to the Academy of Music. Ming Huang, himself a prolific composer, used to teach there.

[2] See *Un Traité Manichéen retrouvé en Chine*, by Chavannes and Pelliot, Paris, 1913

[3] E.g. Giles, *History of Chinese Literature*, p. 200.

by the legendary Emperors Yao and Shun, had slowly succumbed to the corrosions of mysticism and heresy. To prove this theory, he laid the foundations of the great historical work known as the Mirror of History. It might more fitly be called a Mirror of Conservatism.

Han Yü's arguments are weak, but his style is admirable and his sincerity disarming. The abuses to which he called attention (above all, to the economic evils of wholesale monasticism) were very real. His protests lived after him and were undoubtedly instrumental in obtaining the suppression of the " inspired religions " which took place twenty years after his death.

At the beginning of the year 815 a revolution broke out in the provinces, which, it seems fairly clear, was secretly supported by the Conservatives at the capital. In the summer the Liberal Prime Minister, Wu Yüan-hēng, was assassinated by emissaries of the Conservative " Fascisti." So strong was the anti-governmental movement at the capital that (at least, in the view of Wu Yüan-hēng's friends) no adequate steps were taken to arrest the assassins. It was at this point that Po Chü-i,[1] already the most popular writer of his day, addressed to the Throne his memorial " Upon the Murder of the Prime Minister," demanding that the crime should be investigated and the " Fascisti " energetically crushed. The Emperor, now surrounded by Conservatives, instantly banished Po Chü-i to the south.

The poetry of Po Chü-i. Probably no other Chinese poet is so well known to European readers, for about two hundred of his poems have been translated. Moreover, he is the most translatable of poets, for his effects depend rather on the general structure of his poems—on the sequence of thoughts and images—than on any magic of individual words and phrases. His earliest poems, written between the ages of sixteen and nineteen, are completely in the style of the previous century. It is by one of these that he is represented in Giles's *Chinese Poetry.* As well might Shelley be represented in an anthology by one of the poems from *Victor and Cazire.*

In 806 he suddenly leapt to fame through the publication of his *Everlasting Wrong,* an imitation of the popular narrative ballads which were then current. It is the story of Ming Huang's fall, gracefully but not very movingly told. In 809, inspired by the " social reform " poems of Tu Fu, he began to write his *Satires,* and, in the following year, the similar *Songs of Ch'in.*

Gradually, through all these phases, he moved towards a style such as

---

[1] 772–846. See 170 *Chinese Poems, More Translations,* and *The Temple.*

never existed in China—has, indeed, been achieved by no other poet in the world—a perfect instrument of self-revelation. Henceforward the unique subject of his poems is himself, his sorrows, consolations, exasperations; his laziness, his tenderness. Here is the portrait of a whole life with all its stages from early manhood to great old age. To have read this autobiography is to have lived another life besides one's own. The appeal of his poems is not in any way exotic. There is no conventional eastern background, no aroma of the Willow Pattern. They deal with what is common to all human life, with what makes the life of any man, if chance enables us to see it as a connected whole, so profoundly moving a spectacle—I mean the gradual processes of growth and decay, the slow pilgrimage through youth and maturity to feebleness and death.

Such a theme could hardly fail to interest us, even if it were handled with only moderate artistic skill. But Po Chü-i has an astonishing and unparalleled power of turning everything into poetry, a power which hardly ever fails him in all his four thousand poems.

The Triumph of the Conservatives. In 845, a year before Po Chü'-i's death, the foreign religions received their quietus. The Manichæans, no longer politically powerful, had been dealt with two years before. Now all the Christian and Zoroastrian clergy, to the number of 2000, were secularized. Nearly 5000 large Buddhist monasteries were destroyed, and 40,000 local temples; while 260,500 Buddhist priests and nuns were restored to secular life. The figures here given represent rather what the Government aimed at than what it actually effected. But, in any case, the destruction of works of art was tremendous, and was greatest in the neighbourhood of Ch'ang-an, precisely in those temples whose walls were decorated by the great Buddhist painters of the 8th century. After this cataclysm frescoes by Wu Tao-tzǔ, once so numerous, became of the utmost rarity. In many cases the abandoned monasteries were restored in the 10th century; but by then the wall-paintings and other works of art, left for centuries in roofless and half-demolished buildings, had completely perished.

CHAPTER IX
THE T'ANG PAINTERS

THE T'ANG PAINTERS

BUDDHIST ART; WU TAO-TZŬ AND HIS FOLLOWERS

Ever since the introduction of Buddhism a large number of foreign priests had lived in China. Among them must have been many painters. I have mentioned a tradition that Ts'ao Pu-hsing took lessons from the Sogdian priest Sēng-hui. Two foreign priests, Chi-ti-chü and Mārābodhi, are mentioned as having painted in the first half of the 6th century; in the second half, an Indian named Śākyabuddha, renowned for his visions and austerities, served first the declining Weis and then the Sui Emperor. He painted a picture showing the customs of Fu-lin Country—that is to say, of the Byzantine Empire; and one of foreign animals.

Another Indian arrived during the reign of Wēn Ti (589–605). He had come to make a pilgrimage to all the Aśokan stupas[1] in China. "When he got to the Great Stone Temple near Ch'ēng-tu he suddenly looked up and saw in the sky the forms of twelve heavenly beings. He therefore drew them exactly as they appeared to him and then carved them in wood." His name is given in Chinese as *Tan-mo-cho-ch'a*. I am inclined to think that the two last characters require slight emendation and that we should call him Dharmagupta.

Another foreign painter of the Sui dynasty was Wei-ch'ih Po-chih-na, a member of the Khotanese royal family. His " Six Foreign Nations," " Exotic Trees," and " Brahmans " are mentioned. The *Ming Hua Chi* gives a long list of wall-paintings in temples at Ch'ang-an and Lo-yang which were painted by " Wei-ch'ih."[2] Many of these may well have been by his more famous son Wei-ch'ih I-sēng, who was brought up in Khotan and sent by the king of that country to the Chinese Court about the year 630, with high recommendations of his skill in painting. His elder brother Chia-sēng, apparently also a painter, remained in Khotan. The *Ming Hua Chi* tells us that the father's handling was free and full of character; the son's brushwork was tight and forceful, " like bent ironwork or twisted string." From the *Hua Chien* we learn that he laid on his colours very thick, so that they stood out upon the silk, but not in such a way as to obscure the individual brush-strokes.

[1] Pagodas supposed to have been built by the Indian King Aśoka (4th and 3rd centuries B.C.), the great patron of Buddhism. He is said with the aid of demons to have built 84,000 temples in a single night. The connection of Chinese temples with his name is of course purely mythological.

[2] " Wei-ch'ih " appears to stand for Vijaya, which was the Sanskrit name of the family; or perhaps for Visha, the Khotanese form?

At the Tz'ŭ-ēn Temple (Ch'ang-an) he painted divinities, flowers in chiaroscuro, and a Thousand-eyed Thousand-armed Avalokiteśvara " of indescribable delicacy and fineness." At another temple he painted " Buddha subduing the Demons." A 16th-century writer[1] compares these chiaroscuro or " perspective " flowers to those painted by Chang Sēng-yu in the I-shēng Temple at Nanking, which " at a distance deceive the eye into believing that they are in relief, but when looked at close turn out to be flush with the wall." (Such childish *trompe-œil* never fail to delight. There used to be some fine specimens at Dryden Hall in Northamptonshire.)

The collection of the Sung Emperor Hui Tsung contained eight pictures by Wei-ch'ih I-sēng, including an Avalokiteśvara, a Maitreya, and two Vidyarājas. A ninth picture was acquired by Hui Tsung after the completion of his Hsüan Ho Catalogue—the Devarāja or Heavenly King. It is the subject of a long notice in the *Shu Hua Fang*, and of an interesting article by Herbert Mueller[2] in the *Ostasiatische Zeitschrift*; it formerly belonged to the Viceroy Tuan Fang. The king, who is probably Vaiśravana, the Deva of the North, is seated on a throne with attendant figures surrounding him. His feet are upon an oval mat; above his head is a canopy with streamers flying in the wind. Below, a gipsyish-looking individual with a dark beard is playing on a lute; at his side a woman is beating heavy wooden clappers; while in front of them a girl with bare braceleted arms is dancing on an oval carpet.

This figure is almost identical with that of the dancer in Mr. Berenson's roll, which almost certainly preserves the design of a T'ang picture. When, further, we read[3] that in the 13th century Chao Tu-ch'ēng possessed a painting by Wei-ch'ih I-sēng entitled " Dancing-girls of Kucha," it seems probable that Mr. Berenson's picture, which shows many affinities to Tuan Fang's Devarāja, is in some way connected with Wei-ch'ih I-sēng. It may even be identical with the " Dancing-girls " which belonged to Chao Tu-ch'ēng. The dancers in both pictures are wholly un-Chinese, both in costume and attitude. The type occurs in several of the Stein paintings.

The *Ming Hua Chi* mentions a number of paintings by Wei-ch'ih on temple walls at Ch'ang-an and Lo-yang; it is not clear whether they were painted by the father or the son. They include a Vasu (the St. Simeon

[1] Yang Shēn in the *Yang Shēng-an Chi*. See above, p. 85.

[2] Who reproduces it from an illustration in the second number of the Chinese art-journal *Chung Kuo Ming Hua Chi.*, Ost. Zeit., IX, 300.

[3] The *Yün Yen Huo Yen Lu*, a list of pictures seen by the 13th-century connoisseur Chou Mi.

of the Buddhist gospel) and a " greyhound and falcon." The latter probably appeared as accessories in one of the frescoes mentioned. The Wei-ch'ihs stand slightly apart from the main stream of early T'ang painting. " Their men and divinities, birds and flowers, are all outlandish, lack the dignity and restraint of Chinese art."[1]

The *Hua Chien* (14th century) mentions that the Korean type of Avalokiteśvara is derived from Wei-ch'ih I-sēng, and carries his minute and delicate style of workmanship to an extreme.

YEN LI-TĒ AND YEN LI-PĒN

Yen Li-tē was a pupil of his father, Yen Pi, and of the Sui artist Chan Tzŭ-ch'ien, whom the *Hua Chien* calls " the father of T'ang painting."

Tzŭ-ch'ien, who was active during the whole of the second half of the 6th century, painted a large number of frescoes in the temples of the two capitals. " In the landscape backgrounds of architectural paintings he achieved an effect of recession," experimented, that is to say, in perspective. It is noteworthy that he painted a portrait in black-and-white. His pupil Yen Li-tē was promoted, upon the accession of the T'ang dynasty, to high official rank, ultimately becoming Grand Architect and President of the Board of Works. His paintings (eight of them were preserved in the Imperial collections of the 12th century) included " The Seven Planets," " The Journeying of Vaiśravana," " Wang Hsi-chih writing," and " Illustrations to the thought of Shēn Yo's[2] poem upon the Wild Geese of the Lake." In the last we have the beginning of what became an important phase of Chinese painting—the attempt to express pictorially, not by concrete illustration but by subtle suggestion, the mood or, as the Japanese say, the *omomuki*, of a lyric poem. Shēn Yo's poem is as follows :

> *Where bright waters flood the Spring shore*
> *A journeying flock swerves with bended wing ;*
> *They sip the wavelets, tug the yielding weeds,*
> *Their folded wings flaked with icy dew,*
> *A-flock they sail, pushing the quiet stream,*
> *Or singly each his own gleam pursues.*
> *Now almost earthward they trail a dipping flight ;*
> *Now upward quavering tumbled legions rise.*
> *Each rushing wing skims the rippled lake ;*
> *At one swoop they are gone to their native land.*

[1] Chu Ching-hsüan in the *T'ang Ch'ao Ming Hua Lu.* See p. 117 (note 1).
[2] 441–513 A.D. The first writer to formulate definite rules of tone-pattern in Chinese verse.

One of Yen Li-tē's last pictures represented the departure of Princess Wēn-ch'ēng for Tibet. This lady, daughter[1] of the Emperor T'ai Tsung, was sent in 641 to marry the King of Tibet, who two years before had married a Nepalese princess. Both his wives were fervent Buddhists, and the rapid development of Buddhism during his reign was probably due to their influence.

In 647 Li-tē superintended the restoration of one of the Emperor's summer palaces near Ch'ang-an. His death must have taken place soon afterwards.

YEN LI-PĒN

Yen Li-pēn was a younger brother of Li-tē. He was probably born about 600 A.D. He seems to have worked in conjunction with his father at the task of portraying the hosts of foreign envoys who flocked to the Chinese Court at the beginning of T'ai Tsung's reign. Of the forty-two pictures by him that the Imperial collection contained in the 12th century, the larger part is Taoist or Buddhist. In 626 he was employed by the Emperor to paint portraits of eighteen famous contemporary scholars. In 635 the people of Sogdia sent a lion as tribute; the official painting of it was made by Li-pēn. In 636, upon the occasion of the Empress's death, T'ai Tsung began to design the Chao Ling, his family tomb. Part of the decoration was to be a series of reliefs representing the six horses who had served him best in war. Of these six reliefs two are now in the Museum of Philadelphia.

The *Ming Hua Chi* tells us that in the 9th century Li-pēn's " Chao Ling series-of-images picture "[2] was still preserved. It is not quite clear what this means, but it seems to suggest (as was in any case highly probable, in view of his position at Court) that Yen Li-pēn was connected with the designing of the Chao Ling reliefs.[3] In 643 he was employed to paint the portraits of twenty-four famous men of the time for the Ling Yen Ko, a kind of National Portrait Gallery instituted by the Emperor T'ai Tsung

The Ch'ien Lung Collection contained three long rolls attributed to Li-pēn himself, and two copies. The first was " Hsiao Hui stealing the Lan T'ing Scroll." The story which this picture illustrated has already

---

[1] So T'ai Tsung told the Tibetans; but she is not given in the official list of his daughters in the *T'ang Shu*. The painting is mentioned in *Shu Hua Pu*, 95, 1.

[2] Chao Ling Lieh Hsiang T'u.

[3] Yen Li-tē, the elder brother, was buried in the Chao Ling mausoleum, see *Ch'ang-an Ch'ih*, XVI, 14 recto. For a further discussion of the reliefs, see *Burlington Magazine*, 1923, p. 117 (September).

been told on p. 70. The second was a set of illustrations to the *Book of Filial Piety*; the third a *Gathering of Tributary Princes*. The same collection contained a painting of " Tribute-bearers from Various Lands," in twenty-five parts, attributed by some to Yen Li-pēn, by others to Yen Li-tē. A scroll representing a group of scholars collating classic texts under the superintendence of the Emperor of Northern Ch'i was one of Li-pēn's most famous pictures. A copy of it was for sale in New York a few years ago.

In 1917 a reproduction of a picture attributed to Li-pēn was published by the Shanghai Commercial Press. The original was at that time, and may still be, in the possession of a Mr. Lin. The painting represents thirteen famous Emperors, beginning with the Han dynasty and going down to the last Emperor of Sui. At the end of the painting (which appears from the reproduction to be a coloured roll on silk) are several inscriptions. The most important of these was composed by Chou Pi-ta, a well-known scholar, in 1188. It was published in his works, the *P'ing Yüan Chi*, and is here probably copied by a comparatively recent hand, the original inscription having been lost. Chou says :

"*My brother Tzŭ-chung, wishing me to see the picture, acquired it for 500,000 cash. When I began to unroll it I found it to be in so damaged a condition that I dared not proceed. So I gave it immediately to a mounter named Li Chin, who undertook to repair it for 40,000 cash. When he had done his work I examined it and came to the following conclusion : of the thirteen Emperors, Hsüan Ti of the Ch'ēn dynasty is admirably drawn, and so are his two ministers, two fan-holders, and attendants, and four litter-bearers. Moreover, the silk in this part is particularly worn out. I have no doubt that this portion is the work of Yen Li-pēn. The rest of the picture appears to me to be a copy.*"

It is this part of the picture that I have chosen for reproduction. The Emperor Hsüan, 4th Emperor of the Ch'ēn dynasty, reigned from 569 till 582 A.D. The inscription in the upper corner of the picture says : " The Emperor Hsüan's personal name was Hsü. He reigned fourteen years. He showed a deep reverence for Buddha's Law and commanded his courtiers to read the Sūtras to him every day " (Pl. XII).

One of his most celebrated pictures, the " Visit of Manjuśrī to Vimala-kīrti," was still in existence at the beginning of the 17th century. The same subject is treated in one of the frescoes at Tun-huang.[1] The figure of Vimalakīrti strongly recalls some of the Emperors in the scroll I have

[1] Pelliot, Vol. I, Pl. XI.

been discussing, and one may guess that the fresco is at least an echo of Yen Li-pēn's prototype.

WU TAO-TZŬ

Wu Tao-tzŭ was born at Yang-chai in Honan about 700. He lost his parents while he was still a boy, and his youth was spent in great poverty. At a very early age he showed a marvellous capacity for painting and worked so rapidly that " the neighbourhood of Lo-yang soon teemed with his pictures." We next find him holding a small municipal post at Hsia-ch'iu, near Yen-chou in Shantung; but of the circumstances which carried him so far from his home we know nothing at all. His fame having reached the Emperor's ears, he was summoned to Ch'ang-an and appointed *Nei-chiao Po-shih*. The duty of these officials, as defined in the T'ang History,[1] was " to teach the Court ladies writing, arithmetic, and the fine arts generally." From this agreeable position he was promoted to be " Companion to Prince Ning."[2] It is said that he took lessons in calligraphy from Ho Chih-chang (the patron of Li Po), and Chang Hsü (another of the " Eight Immortals of the Wine-cup "), but was dissatisfied with his progress and returned to painting.

In his early years he made a close study of his classical predecessors, particularly of Ku K'ai-chih and Chang Sēng-yu. Of his copies of Ku K'ai-chih, the *Hua Chien* (14th century) says : " In style and general arrangement there is a considerable resemblance to the originals. In the periods Hsüan Ho[3] and Shao Hsing[4] they were actually mistaken for originals and classified as genuine works as Ku. But anyone who takes the trouble to look at them can see the difference."[5] This passage suggests (and other considerations point to the same conclusion) that the Emperor Hui Tsung was not a very discriminating collector. For I think it is obviously to the Imperial collections of these two epochs that the writer, T'ang Hou, refers. It must have been between 720 and 730 that the old minister Wei Tzŭ-li,[6] who had been President of the Board of War in 708, took Wu Tao-tzŭ on to his staff. It was probably Prince Ning who introduced the painter to the statesman, for it was Prince Ning who saved Wei from death during the revolution that put an end to the usurping reign of the Empress Wu Hou, and we have already seen that Wu Tao-tzŭ held a post in this prince's retinue.

---

[1] XLVIII, 10 recto.
[2] Brother of the Emperor; died in 731 A.D.
[3] 1119–1126.
[4] 1131–1163.
[5] *Shu Hua P'u*, 90, 7. See above, p. 58.
[6] *T'ang History*, CXVI, 5.

He travelled with his new patron along the Ch'ang-an–Ch'eng-tu road and painted its stupendously rugged scenery,[1] " creating " (as the *Ming Hua Chi* informs us) " a new style of landscape-painting." But in what did the innovation consist? We are not told. Two landscapes preserved in the Kōtō-in, Daitokuji, Kyōto, have long been attributed to Wu Tao-tzŭ ; but in the absence of documentary evidence such temple-attributions are worth nothing.[2]

We do not know how or when Wu Tao-tzŭ died. The Taoists have annexed him as one of their divinities and tell us that he disappeared into one of his own pictures. The story is, at any rate, as old as the 17th century, for it is told in the *Shu Hua Fang*. The definite facts which we know about his life connect him with the early part of Ming Huang's reign. The story of his competition with Li Ssŭ-hsün during the T'ien Pao era (742–756) is obviously apocryphal, for Li died, at the latest, in 720.

The great work of Wu Tao-tzŭ's life was the decoration of the temple walls at Ch'ang-an and Lo-yang. He is said to have painted three hundred frescoes—a sufficient *opus* for any painter. Most of these temples fell into dilapidation after the Buddhist proscription of 845. In the 11th century Wu's frescoes were already of the utmost rarity. The Wu-chēn Ssŭ[3] on Wang Shun Hill, about twenty miles south-east of Ch'ang-an, was famous for its wall-painting by Wu Tao-tzŭ, which was " fresh as the day it was painted " when Po Chü-i saw it in 814. But when a Sung poet, Su Shun-ch'in, visited the temple about 1040, the works of art described by Po Chü-i had all vanished.

The poet Su Tung-p'o, himself a painter and accomplished writer upon art, stated in 1085 that he knew only one or two genuine Wu Tao-tzŭs.[4] One of these, a fresco at the Lung-hsing Ssŭ, at Ju-chou in the province of Honan, was restored by Tung-p'o's brother, Tzŭ-yu.[5] It is described as being in a minute and delicate style, so that it was probably an early work.

[1] For a description of this road, see Li Po's poem *Shu Tao Nan* which has been many times translated, e.g. in my pamphlet *Li Po*, Luzac, 1919.

[2] Some dim adumbration of Wu's landscape style may perhaps be seen in the " Snowy Mountains " reproduced on Plate XIII ; the picture is attributed to Yang Fei, an imitator of Wu's style who seems to have lived towards the end of the 8th century.

[3] For a description of this temple, see my *The Temple and other Poems*. Allen and Unwin, 1923.

[4] *Shu Hua Fang*, IV, 11. *Shu Hua P'u*, 81, 18.

[5] *Tung-p'o Shih Ch'ao*, p. 74.

Mi Fei,[1] writing at about the same time, says that, " though his head is white," he has only been able to discover four genuine Wu Tao-tzŭs : (1) Buddha with Attendants, belonging to Su Tung-p‘o. (2) A boldly and rapidly executed pair of Devarājas " painted with brush-strokes coarse as cabbage-stalks," belonging to a certain Wang Fang. (3) The " Heavenly Skiff " (*T‘ien P‘ēng*), belonging to Chao Ta-nien. (4) The Mahākaruna Avalokiteśvara, belonging to Chou T‘ung.

As typical of " the sort of Wu's which are collected by the members of exalted families," he mentions a Devarāja belonging to his friend Li Lung-mien, the greatest painter of the Sung dynasty. " It is pretty," he says, " and delicately drawn ; but it lacks vigour and style, and is probably the work of some pupil or imitator. . . . Whenever people get hold of a Buddhist painting, they call it a Wu Tao-tzŭ. His pictures exercised so strong an influence over contemporary painters that one finds his types everywhere and it is easy to be misled." When Mi Fei speaks of the spurious Wu Tao-tzŭs amassed by " exalted families," it is, I think, beyond doubt that he is referring discreetly to the ninety-three pictures by Wu which figure in the catalogue of the Emperor Hui Tsung's collection, which must have been compiled soon after Mi Fei wrote these sceptical comments.

It may at first sight seem strange that about three hundred years after an artist's death there should be any doubt as to whether nearly a hundred, or only two or three of his paintings have survived. It should be remembered, however, that a somewhat similar position exists to-day with regard to Rembrandt's etchings ; some writers admitting less than eighty as genuine, while others accept over three hundred.

There is no reason to doubt that the Emperor Hui Tsung was an accomplished painter, and it is certain that he was an enthusiastic collector. But, as modern instances show, both these qualities may be combined with a complete lack of critical judgment.

The vast collection of the 18th-century Emperor Ch‘ien Lung contained only one picture ascribed to Wu Tao-tzŭ, a large kakemono of demons, protectors of the Faith, illustrating the *Fo-shuo Hu Chu T‘ung-tzŭ Ching*.[2] Of actually surviving works which may reproduce designs by Wu Tao-tzŭ the most important is the Shākyamuni Trinity of the Tōfukuji, Kyōto.[3] Its bold calligraphic line-work corresponds to what we are told of Wu's

---

[1] Strictly, Mi Fu ; but Fei is too familiar to discard. He lived 1051–1107. See *Shu Hua Fang, loc. cit.*

[2] Nanjio 488. Trip, XII, 5.   [3] See *Shimbi Taikwan*, Vol. I.

mature style, but there is no reason to suppose that this Trinity is more than a vague echo of a type created by Wu. There is a type of Standing Avalokiteśvara with high rectangular tiara, accompanied by acolytes, which seems to be founded upon a design by Wu Tao-tzŭ. Most of the existing versions of this picture are either rubbings from incised stones or else paintings copied from such rubbings. One such Avalokiteśvara is reproduced on page 214 of Ferguson's *Outlines of Chinese Art*. A painting slightly different, but connected with the other, is in the Freer Collection. Fenollosa, who reproduced it opposite page 132 of his *Epochs*, considered the fish-basket, which in this version the goddess carries on her right arm, to be a later addition. The British Museum possesses a painting of an Arhat leaning on a staff by the 18th-century artist Li Kēn. It is labelled " after Wu Tao-tzŭ." It would be surprising if this picture were based upon a T'ang design, for the whole pose and style of the figure argue against such an origin. But seeing that we know nothing of Wu Tao-tzŭ's art beyond what we can read in books, it would be rash to assert that this picture has no connection whatever with an original by him. The Museum also possesses a rubbing of an incised stone which is in the Municipal Office (*Fu shu*) at Ch'ēng-tu, the capital of Ssechuan. The subject is " The Dark Warriors," i.e. the Tortoise and the Serpent, who together form the symbol of the North (Plate XIV).

There is a special connection between the city of Ch'ēng-tu and the tortoise, for at the time when the place was first built the city walls refused to stand upright till the builders founded them upon the orbit indicated by a wise tortoise. When the walls were successfully finished they surrounded them by a huge moat, into which the tortoise dived. It seldom shows itself, but still lives on, the secret genius of the town. It appeared, says the observant traveller Wang Shih-chēng[1] in 1673, " large as a horse and followed by an innumerable retinue of smaller tortoises." Wang Shih-chēn mentions the stone incised with Wu Tao-tzŭ's design, and appends this inevitable story : " Every day at noon a huge crowd of serpents and tortoises used to collect near the incised stone and even on neighbouring roofs and trees. This incommoded a certain Mei Lang-chung, who had become Governor of the town and had to transact his business in the office where the stone was kept. He therefore gouged out the eyes of the Serpent and Tortoise, thus destroying their magic power. Henceforward all rubbings of the stone were stamped with the Governor's seal as a protection against evil influences." Old Ch'ēng-tu (as opposed to the Manchu

[1] 1634–1711.

quarter) is still called Tortoise Town. Such stories (and they are told in connection with the works of almost every Chinese painter) belong to folk-lore rather than to art-history. I have in general omitted them, because a sufficient number of them has already been told in Giles's *Chinese Pictorial Art*.

According to Chinese legend, all tortoises are female. They are fertilized by union with the snake. The snake and tortoise together form the symbol of the northern division of the firmament.[1] Wu Tao-tzŭ, like many of his predecessors, was a good deal occupied with such astronomical illus-trations. The catalogue of Hui Tsung's collection includes at least thirteen star-paintings by him, among them " The Twenty-eight Lunar Asterisms," " The Five Planets," and several single planets and stars.

The pose of the two creatures (which makes a fine pattern) was probably standardized long before Wu Tao-tzŭ's time. The rubbing therefore tells us very little about what was individual in Wu's representation of the subject. The famous incised portrait of Confucius at Ch'ü-fou, also attributed to Wu, is even less informative. At the P'u-mēn-ssŭ, near Fēng-hsiang, the same traveller, Wang Shih-shēn,[2] saw in 1695 a painting by Wu Tao-tzŭ called " The Fool." The context suggests that this, too, was a stone-incision. I have not met with any rubbing of it.

WU TAO-TZŬ'S STYLE

If, in our attempt to reconstruct Wu's style, we turn from existing works of art to literary evidence, we do not fare much better than before. It is clear, at any rate, that he was an extreme realist, for Su Tung-p'o writes : " Wu Tao-tzŭ's figures might have been drawn from lantern-shadows on the wall.[3] They seem to walk out of the picture and back into it ; they project, can be seen from each side. The flat planes and tilted angles fit into one another as though by a natural geometric law."[4]

The second characteristic which all writers are agreed upon is the tradi-tional character of his art. " His originality never led him to violate the classical canons," says Su Tung-p'o more than once. What seems most to have struck his contemporaries was his extraordinary fertility of imagina-tion and technical facility. We have already seen that he painted over

[1] The Chinese astronomers divide the sky into five spheres or " Palaces."
[2] *Ch'in Shu I Ch'ēng Chi*, p. 8. Reprinted in the *Fang Hu Chai* series of geographical works.
[3] It was a favourite pastime of the Chinese to make such shadow-portraits.
[4] *Shu Hua P'u*, 81, 17.

three hundred frescoes in the temples of Ch'ang-an and Lo-yang. The ease and rapidity with which he worked startled those who watched him. The following story, told by Chu Ching-hsüan,[1] is worth giving, though it has been partially translated before: " When at the beginning of the Yüan Ho period (806–821) I was up for my examinations I lodged at the Lung-hsing Temple. Here I found a man who was more than eighty years old, who told me that when Wu Tao-tzŭ was going to put in the haloes of some figures he had painted at the Hsing-shan Temple, the whole of Ch'ang-an—merchants, shopkeepers, young and old, high and low—crowded to see him do it, encircling him with a dense human wall. He executed the haloes with so violent a rush and swirl that it seemed as though a whirlwind possessed his hand, and all who saw it cried that some god was helping him."[2]

Tung Yu[3] speaks, like Su Tung-p'o, of the three-dimensional realism of Wu's pictures. " They are like sculpture," he says ; " when he paints a face, the cheek-bones project, the nose is fleshy, the eyes hollow, the cheeks dimpled. But these effects are not got by heavy ink shading. The shape of the features seems to have come spontaneously, yet inevitably. If a sculptor tried to follow this method, his planes would become confused ; we should not know where was the nose, the eye, the forehead, the cheek ; all would be inextricably confused. Yang Hui-chih and Wu Tao-tzŭ both came into prominence during the K'ai-yuan period (713–742) ; but Yang, finding that he made no progress, took to sculpture, which he thought was an easier craft. . . .

" Wu Tao-tzŭ's figures remind one of sculpture. One can see them sideways and all round. His line-work consists of minute curves like rolled copper wire ; however thickly his red or white paint is laid on, the structure of the forms and modelling of the flesh are never obscured."

Besides this sculpturesque quality, all writers attribute to him a certain grandiose quality of design, an ease and bigness similar to the *grand souffle* of Tu Fu's verse. Even his smallest figures are said to have had this generous and imposing character of line. T'ang Hou tells us in the *Hua Chien* that in Wu's early years his linework was very minute ; " in his middle period the brush-strokes were coarse as cabbage-stalks. His figures stand out in relief ; they seem actually to live and move. His method of

---

[1] Who lived in the 9th century and not (as Hirth suggests on p. 125 of his *Scraps*) *circa* 1000.

[2] *Shu Hua P'u*, 46, 16.

[3] A writer of the 12th century. See *Shu Hua P'u*, 81, 19.

colouring was to tint his dry-ink under-drawings with a light transparent wash, applying it in the most rapid and cursory way. Yet, as though by magic, the colours stood out brilliantly on the silk."

The author of the *Hua Chien* lived in the 14th century. He is no doubt quoting earlier descriptions of Wu's style. But we must remember that already in the 11th century connoisseurs of great eminence, such as Su Tung-p'o and Mi Fei, believed that practically the whole of Wu's *œuvre* was irrevocably lost.

In what exactly did Wu's genius consist? One feels that what one learns of him from Chinese texts applies rather to the whole of 8th-century Buddhist painting than to Wu Tao-tzŭ in particular. The same difficulty would arise if one were trying to describe the style of Bach. All that can be put into words concerning him applies equally to pupils, minor relatives, and a score of contemporary Kapellmeister. Yet we know when we hear it that Bach's music has an indefinable quality which separates it entirely from all else that was written in his century. I feel intuitively that Wu Tao-tzŭ resembled Bach in this respect, and that when we are told that he used this or that kind of colour or line, we are learning no more of the essential Wu Tao-tzŭ than we should learn about Bach if we were told merely that he wrote cantatas and fugues. We know little of Wu. But we at least know far more of him than of Apelles, about whose style and merits the connoisseurs of the 18th century were wont to speak with an air of confident familiarity.

WU TAO-TZŬ'S PUPILS

The most important of Wu's pupils was Lu Lĕng-ch'ieh, famous for his paintings of Lohan.[1] The Lohan were the original disciples of Shākyamuni. In a wider sense a Lohan is an ascetic ripe for annihilation,[2] one who is about to escape from the Wheel of Life and Death, whose present incarnation is an ante-chamber to Nirvāna. In the theology of Chinese Buddhism he is to a great extent replaced by the Bodhisattva, who is preoccupied not only with his own salvation, but also by the desire to help mankind.

But though the Lohan disappear from the theology of the North they continue to play an important part in popular superstition and in art. The Sixteen Lohan are frequently depicted, as also the Eighteen and Five

[1] "Worthy Ones," Sanskrit *Arhan*; Japanese *Rakan*.
[2] Buddhists object to this term. I do not here use it in any technical sense.

118

Hundred. Lu Lēng-ch'ieh's most famous picture, versions of which were still extant in the Ming dynasty, was " The Sixteen Lohan crossing the Sea." They were invited to dine with the Dragon King who lives in the middle of the ocean. They are shown crossing the waves in coracles made of leaves, upon the backs of toads, tortoises, dragons, deer, and fabulous sea-monsters. The whole conception is strongly coloured by Taoist mythology.

The *Shu Hua Fang* gives a description of Lu Lēng-ch'ieh's picture, which corresponds closely to numerous modern versions of the subject. It is probable that Lu painted various sets of Lohan, some in colours and some in black-and-white. The Emperor Hui Tsung's collection contained several of these sets. There is no reason to suppose that the fanciful, semi-Taoist treatment of the Lohan legend began with Lu Lēng-ch'ieh, who does not seem to be regarded as at all an original artist. The *Shu Hua Fang* (IV, 22) quotes a statement that the conception goes back as far as the 4th century.[1] The Hui Tsung collection contained " Sixteen Lohans " by Chang Sēng-yu, who lived in the first half of the 6th century. Lu Lēng-ch'ieh followed Ming Huang into exile and obtained great notoriety in Ssechuan. The story of his death (if we are to place any confidence in it) is of some importance; for it establishes the fact that Wu Tao-tzŭ survived the revolution of 756–758. The story is that Lu spent his whole strength in a frenzied effort to paint a fresco which should rival one recently painted by Wu. Within a month he died exhausted. Since this took place at Ch'ang-an, it must have happened after Lu's return from the West. This story is not very convincing; nor is the legend that when Wu Tao-tzŭ was old he hired assassins to do away with a young rival, the painter Huang-fu Chēn.

WU'S INFLUENCE UPON SCULPTURE

We have seen that Wu's fellow-student, Yang Hui-chih, afterwards became a sculptor. A pupil of Wu's, Chang Ai-ērh, took the same course. Sculpture seems, indeed, from the 6th century onwards to have been the refuge of unsuccessful painters. The sculptors Han Po-t'ung (6th century) and Tou Hung-kuo and Mao P'o-lo (7th century) all began as painters. So in the 8th century did Yüan Tung-chien and Sun Jēn-kuei; and in the 9th, Chin Chung-i.

[1] Tai K'uei (d. 395 A.D.) painted a picture of " Lohan of the Five Regions of India." (*Ming Hua Chi*, V, 16.)

LATER BUDDHIST PAINTING

During the last quarter of the 9th century there was a revival of Buddhism (it had been suppressed in 845), and many temples were restored and re-decorated. In this revival a large number of comparatively unimportant artists took part.

Chang Nan-pēn flourished about 870–890. He terrified his contemporaries by the realism of his flaming Vidyarājas, angry emanations by the projection of which a Buddha keeps at bay the demons and ogres which beset the Faith. It is, indeed, as a painter of fire that he is remembered. His masterpiece was a Pratyeka Buddha clad in flames.

CHAPTER X
THE TUN-HUANG PAINTINGS

CHAPTER X
THE TUN-HUANG PAINTINGS
(T'ANG DYNASTY)

I have already discussed the 5th- and 6th-century paintings at Tun-huang. But certain problems connected with them (which I must mention, but am not qualified to solve) have been deferred to this chapter.

The term "Gandharan" has been very freely used in connection both with the sculpture of the Weis and with the frescoes and silk-paintings of Tun-huang. The monuments of Gandhara cannot be dated with certainty, but they seem to belong principally to the period of the Kushanas. It is by no means certain that Kanishka was not a Buddhist long before he conquered Gandhara, and in any case he may well have brought an art with him into India.[1] For his father had conquered Parthia, where a provincial form of Græco-Roman art had long prevailed. There are many scenes in the Yün-kang reliefs which remind one much more of late provincial Roman art than of anything Greek or Indian. For example, the scenes from the Life of Buddha[2] strangely recall the Antinoë[3] room at the Musée Guimet.

Certain figures (e.g. the "Bacchus") are of obviously Western origin; but I see no evidence that they are directly derived from the Græco-Indian art of a particular region. May not Buddhist art have flourished simultaneously in Central Asia and North-western India, under Kanishka's patronage in both cases? And may not Central Asia have influenced India quite as much as India influenced Central Asia?

These are questions which I put quite tentatively. They only concern the subject of painting in a minor degree, and I must not here linger over them. There is at least one picture in the Stein Collection which definitely reproduced Gandharan models. This is a large silk painting in rather fragmentary condition which represents statues worshipped in the artist's day at certain important shrines in India. The picture is simply an illustrated catalogue; it makes no attempt to be a work of art, and therefore need not detain us.

Earlier T'ang Frescoes. I have already spoken of what I have provisionally called "Turfanese" influence in some of the earlier frescoes. In the

---

[1] I cannot agree with M. Foucher who says (*Beginnings of Buddhist Art*, p. 128), "The Turk Kanishka had no direct influence on Indo-Greek art."

[2] They do not come out very clearly in Chavannes's plates. To me they seem the most beautiful of all Chinese sculptures.

[3] A city in Egypt founded by Hadrian about 130 A.D.

7th century, with the expansion of T'ang power in the west, Tun-huang became more definitely a Chinese city. On the whole, except for the exotic element which is necessarily found in the actual cult-figures (Buddhas and Bodhisattvas), the earlier T'ang frescoes are remarkably Chinese.

A painting in the first cave (Plate XVIII) represents the Visit of Mañjuśrī to Vimalakīrti. The recluse, sitting in an attitude of royal ease on his high canopied dais, has the air of a Chinese Emperor rather than a saintly invalid. He so strongly resembles the emperors in Yen Li-pēn's scroll,[1] that I at first imagined this fresco to date from the 7th century. Professor Pelliot tells me that it more probably belongs to the end of the 9th. However, " The Visit to Vimalakīrti " was one of Li-pēn's most famous pictures, and some reminiscence of it may lurk in the Tun-huang wall-painting. The right wall of Cave 70 shows " The Fight for Buddha's Relics." In the background is a Chinese walled city, which I take to be meant for Kuśinagara. The two rows of warriors represent, I suppose, the armies of Kuśinagara and Magadha. Ajātaśatru, King of Magadha, advances in the foreground, a noble figure in full Confucian garb. The Governor of Kuśinagara, in whose keeping the relics lie, is seen on horseback before the city gate, supported by a group of elders. The composition as it stands is somewhat stiff ; but the painting, which is in any case an extremely lively and entertaining work, is unfinished and was suspended at an unfortunate moment (Plate XVII).

The " Procession of the Donor " (Cave 17 b) has attracted the attention of all who have examined M. Pelliot's *Grottes de Touen-houang*.[2] Here, it has been said, is the clue to the origin of the Tosa school of Japan ; and the rhythmic cavalcades of Sumiyoshi Keion have been regarded as the offspring of this statuesque frieze. It should, however, be remembered that Keion (and those who have compared this fresco to Tosa art have, I think, always had Keion in mind) lived nearly five hundred years after this Tun-huang wall was painted. Moreover, the resemblance is one of subject rather than treatment. Keion's horsemen are in motion ; they swerve, they undulate ; every line betrays an eager straining. The cavalcade of Tun-huang is monumental ; movement has been crystallized into statuary. The great pennoned flags point like fingers of stone ; the lances rise like spires (Plate XVI).

And long before the time of Keion, Japan had developed a style of painting which, whatever may have been its ultimate origin, had already become utterly distinct from any art which had ever existed. A

[1] See above, p. 111.   [2] See also Stein's *Serindia*, Vol. II, Fig. 232.

superficial observer might collocate Keion with the frieze of Tun-huang ; but for the Genji scroll of Takayoshi[1] no parallel could be found.

THE HŌRYŪJI WALL-PAINTINGS

The wall-paintings in the Golden Hall of the Hōryūji Temple at Nara, though there is no proof that they are actually the work of a Chinese painter, stand in such close relation to early T'ang art that I must mention them briefly here. The first Europeans who noticed them were struck by their " Indian " character and compared them to the Ajanta frescoes. I think that Fenollosa was right in pointing out that the resemblance is only of a very general character. It now seems to be established that they were painted about 712 A.D., possibly (as local tradition asserts) by a Korean, but in any case in a style quite typical of Chinese Buddhist art in the 7th century. The principal paintings consist of four groups of deities representing the Spheres of the Four Buddhas Shākyamuni, Amida, Ratnasambhava, and Bhaishajyaguru. The last is the best preserved. The Buddha of Healing sits not cross-legged, but in European fashion, with his legs held wide apart in a solid, uncompromising attitude. He is attended by Bodhisattvas, priests, and Kings of Heaven. Shākyamuni is supported only by two Bodhisattvas and a few attendant angels ; Amida by Avalokiteśvara, Mahāsthāmaprāpta and priests. The Ratnasambhava group, painted on the East wall, is much defaced. It is probable that in these frescoes we have an echo of the art of such Buddhist painters as Wei-chih I-sēng and Yen Li-pēn.

THE STEIN COLLECTION

It is unfortunate that the paintings on silk from Tun-huang belong to a comparatively late and decadent period. The earliest dated picture is the " Four Forms of Avalokiteśvara," 864 A.D.[2] ; the latest is " Avalokiteśvara with attendants and donors,"[3] dated 983. It is not likely that the collection contains many paintings either much earlier or much later than these two. I have no intention of making here a detailed study of these pictures in relation to their subjects. A beginning in that direction was made by Petrucci in his Appendix to *Serindia*, which deals with the " Mandalas "[4] or groups of divinities.

---

[1] *Circa* 1100. See *Kokka*, 17, 18, 306. Keion flourished *circa* 1200.
[2] Stein and Binyon, *The Thousand Buddhas*, Pl. XVI. [3] *Serindia*, Pl. LXVI.
[4] Petrucci, like the Japanese, calls by this name any group of divinities ranged round a central cult-figure. He also seems to use the term " Paradise " as a synonym to Mandala.

Paradises. I have spoken before of the timeless, spiritual Buddha Amida and of his Western Paradise. The painters of Tun-huang, still pious Amidists at a time when new doctrines had probably begun to leave their mark on Buddhist art in other parts of China, were never weary of depicting this Paradise. And not content, like the Wei sculptors, to symbolize the Land of Bliss by an angel, a palace roof, and a tree or two, they attempted to make their pictures complete diagrams of heaven, with all its appurtenances and inhabitants. The result is something like those commemorative group-paintings that used to be published as supplements to our illustrated journals ("Lord Salisbury's First Parliament, with key"). Unfortunately the Tun-huang painters, though they labelled some of the principal deities, supplied no key; so that, although we recognize without much difficulty the faces of "Front Bench" divinities, we are often somewhat in the dark about the rank and file.

Not content with crowding every species of architectural and floral detail into their main design, the Paradise-painters framed it with miniature side-scenes, illustrating sūtras connected with the central cult-figure. One of the best Paradises is a large silk-painting (5 ft. $9\frac{1}{2}$ in. × 4 ft.) which is reproduced on Plate VI of the *Thousand Buddhas*. Chavannes describes it as "Paradise of Shākyamuni or Amitābha" (Amida). I do not think that, strictly speaking, there is any Paradise over which Shākyamuni presides. But the Buddhists of this school seem to have taken the view that Shākyamuni after his decease *turned into* Amida. The following couplet is often quoted by the Japanese Nō Plays :

Once on the Vulture Peak he preached the Lotus Law ;
Now in the Western Land he is called Amida.[1]

It is quoted from the "Liturgies of Avalokiteśvara" (*Kuan-yin Ch'an-fa*), of which one version was compiled for the Emperor Wu of Liang early in the 6th century, and another about 1000 A.D. Whatever may be the date of this couplet, I think it certainly expresses the view of the Tun-huang artists.

At the top of the Paradise to which I have referred is "a valance of orange drapery set in a black-flowered band." Next come four small Buddhas who appear above the roof of an elaborate palace which is built round a courtyard. Below sits the Buddha flanked by a host of Bodhisattvas and disciples, his right hand raised in *vitarka-mudrā*, the mystic gesture of discussion. In front the Heavenly Dancer (who occupies an important place in all Paradise paintings) performs on a separate terrace.

[1] For a slightly different version, see above, p. 23.

Musicians, six on each side, accompany her movements—with harp, flute, pipe, clappers, and mouth-organs.

The picture is framed by miniature side-scenes. Those on the left represent (1) The Story of the One-horned Rishi; (2) The Two Brothers; those on the right, the story of the Wicked Minister Rāhula. The first of these stories (only the preliminaries of which are here illustrated) occurs in the *Mahābhārata* and is the subject of the well-known Nō-play, *Ikkaku Sennin*,[1] so there is no need to tell it here. The story of the Two Brothers[2] is as follows: The Good Brother, pitying the distress of the poor, determines to relieve their suffering by procuring and selling on their behalf the famous jewel that is kept in the Sea-dragon's palace. He searches the city of Benares for a pilot to guide him across the sea, but in all the town there is not one to be found. At last he hears of a sailor who in bygone years had steered many ocean ships. He finds this man's lodging; but the pilot, alas! is eighty years old, and blind. He consents to guide the ship by question and answer. Thus, they come to a shore where the sands are of silver dust, and the pilot questions them, asking whether " the Mountain of Silver is yet in sight, and upon which side it lies?" So they steer as he bids them, till they come to the Palace of the Dragon King. The Good Brother returns to India with the jewel; the Wicked Brother steals it from him while he is asleep. . . . This is not nearly the end of the story, but the latter part is not, I think, illustrated in any of the paintings which I am discussing.

Next comes the story of the Wicked Minister Rāhula, who kills the King of Benares and his five sons. The sixth escapes with his wife and child. They travel for many days through inhospitable deserts, till all their provisions are exhausted. The Prince is about to slay and eat the Princess, when the child intervenes, offering his own flesh. They continue their journey, eating the infant piecemeal, till nothing but his bones are left. Then, of course, he is miraculously restored to life. This rather absurd story was immensely popular.

Many of the Paradises have side-scenes illustrating the legend of Queen Vaidehi, as told in the *Amitāyurdhyāna Sūtra*,[3] one of the three favourite scriptures of the Amidists.

The wicked Prince Ajātaśatru locks up his father, King Bimbisāra, behind

[1] See *Nō-plays of Japan*, p. 288.
[2] See Chavannes, *Contes et Legéndes du Bouddhisme Chinois*, p. 23.
[3] Translated into Chinese by Kāladasha in 424 A.D. See *Sacred Books of the East*, Vol. 49, p. 161.

seven doors, with the intention of letting him starve to death. But Queen Vaidehi manages to convey food to him. After a time Ajātaśatru discovers to his astonishment that his father is still alive, and soon learns from his men-at-arms that the Queen is to blame. He seizes his sword and rushes upon her, but is restrained by a wise Minister who reminds him that, although the Vedas, Śāstras, and Sūtras record eighteen thousand cases of wicked princes who have slain their fathers, there is not known to history any example of a prince who slew his mother. "Then the Prince repented, threw down his sword, and did his mother no hurt. But he bade the officers of his Palace shut her fast into the inner rooms; and there he kept her."

The Queen, in great despondency, prayed to Shākyamuni that he would appear to her and comfort her. When she raised her head from prayer, there was the Blessed One, all golden and shining, with Maudgalyāyana on his left and Ānanda on his right; while above them hovered the gods Indra and Brahma with all the host of Heaven, scattering flower-blossoms through the air. It was then that Shākyamuni imparted to the Queen the secret of the "Sixteen Meditations," by the use of which even those who dwell amidst the sorrows of Jambudvīpa may at any time behold Amida in his Paradise. The first meditation must be upon the idea of the setting sun, "to which all things that have sight are wont to turn their eyes." The second meditation is upon water; the third, upon the Floor of the Paradise; the fourth, upon its trees; the fifth, upon its Lotus Ponds. In the sixth the preceding elements are combined; it is called the General Vision.

Gradually the splendours of Heaven are disclosed, till in the Sixteenth Vision Amida and all his golden host appear. In a closing passage Shākyamuni promises to all who repeat ten times the words "Praise to Amida the Buddha," absolution for the sins committed during eighty millions æons of Birth and Death. And to all who shall practise this Samādhi of the Sixteen Meditations he promises that they shall with their own eyes behold Amida Buddha and the twin Great Ones, Avalokiteśvara and Mahāsthāmaprāpta.

The most beautiful of the "Paradises" in the Stein Collection represents not the Western Land of Amida, but the Eastern Paradise of Bhaishajyaguru, Buddha of Healing. The cult of this Buddha seems to have been introduced into China much later[1] than that of Amida. His Eastern Heaven is simply a counterpart of Amida's Western Land. The

[1] The principal scripture was translated c. 700 A.D.

picture[1] is in a fragmentary condition, and it is very difficult to grasp its general design. What astonishes one is the delicacy and beauty of each successive group of figures, trees, or buildings upon which the eye falls. Most lovely of all are the side-wings of the Heavenly Palace and the curious flat-leaved trees that grow in front of them. Here the slaty-blue of the roofs contrasts exquisitely with the cool green of the leaves; while below flash the red skirts and rainbow-haloes of the two Lesser Buddhas.

A much less crowded and complicated design is that of the " Amida with Attendants and Monks."[2] It is a curiously symmetrical composition. The figures have a fullness of feature that is almost Semitic. Technically the picture is of some interest owing to the fact that the modelling of the flesh is brought out by the use of high lights, a practice quite foreign to Chinese painting, as also, I think, to such Indian wall-painting as has survived (Plate XXI).

Of the pictures representing single deities, the best is perhaps the " Avalokiteśvara with the Willow Spray."[3] In actual handling it is in places rather weak, but it is certainly the reproduction of a model superb both in colour and design. The contrasts of orange-red and olive-green (used with such good effect in many of the Avalokiteśvara paintings) are here particularly beautiful (Plate XXII).

Stories such as that of the Good and Bad Brothers are supposed to narrate incidents which befell the Buddha in his previous incarnations. The Indians call them *Jātakas*, or " Birth Stories." But Buddhist art, from the Gandhara reliefs onwards, has delighted to illustrate not only the episodes of Buddha's former incarnations, but also his life as Shākyamuni; and the Stein Collection contains a whole series of such scenes, painted on silk banners. They are completely Chinese in style, and throw a good deal of light on contemporary secular painting.

The most important banner in the collection is unfortunately incomplete.[4] The upper scene shows Buddha's horse Kanthaka and his groom Chhandaka. It is the moment at which he finally renounces his princely life. Horse and groom kneel before him in an attitude of profound despondency. Below, Buddha[5] is seated on a ledge of rock above a deep ravine. Pink-flowering fruit-trees are in bloom upon the opposite bank. The heads of Kanthaka and the groom are just visible. The rest of the scene is lost.

[1] See *Serindia*, Pl. LVII, and *Thousand Buddhas*, Pls. I and II. The picture measures 6 ft. 9 ins. by 5 ft. 7 ins. (My Plate XX.)

[2] *Thousand Buddhas*, Pl. X.   [3] *Ibid.*, Pl. XXI.   [4] *Serindia*, Pl. LXXVI shows Scene 3.

[5] I am calling him so for convenience. He was at this time still Prince Siddartha.

A second fragment of the same banner shows the mounted messengers of Buddha's father riding through the mountains in search for the lost Prince. They wear black caps with long streamers ; one is dressed in bright yellow, another in blue, another in red, another in green, another in terra-cotta. On the hill-side in the foreground is a group of weeping-willows, and at the bottom of the picture are flowering trees and pink-flowered plants growing in the grass. This is the one painting in the collection which appears to have come from the hand of a great artist (Plate XXIII).

Another banner,[1] remarkable for the romantic treatment of its landscape settings, begins with the same subject as the last. Here, however, the Farewell takes place under a huge precipice tufted with highly stylized trees. In the background are desolate grey-blue mountains and coiling wreaths of cloud. The second scene takes place on a platform of rock beneath high cliffs which are backed by a melodramatic storm-sky. On the left sits Buddha in the act of removing his three-pronged tiara. In the centre, the Heavenly Hairdresser advances holding a razor in his hand ; while the god Indra stands behind him with hands pressed together in sign of adoration. Chapter XVIII of the *Abhiniskramana Sūtra*[2] tells how Buddha, in preparation for the period of his Austerities, lopped off his hair with his sword. At this moment Indra appeared from Heaven with a host of devas and caught the severed locks before they fell to the ground. One of the devas, magically assuming the guise of a hairdresser, then stepped forward, holding an exquisitely sharp razor in his hand.

Buddha. Do you feel equal to shaving my head ?

Hairdresser. To be sure I do, and skilfully at that.

Buddha. Well, try your hand and we shall see.

The five little figures who kneel in the foreground must, I suppose, be the five Brahmans whom Buddha afterwards secured as his first five converts. The whole scene, highly florid and sumptuous in the original versions of the story, is admirably simplified and secularized by the sober hand of the Chinese painter. Even Indra, the Lord of Heaven, who in Indian art is invested with all the barbarous majesty of an Asiatic potentate, is here merely a rather " décolleté " Chinaman.[3] In the bottom scene the Buddha (now a *Muni* or ascetic) is seated, naked to the waist, on a low rock upon the bare hillock. His head is crowned with a pile of leaves. The hills and rocks are shaded to indicate contour. The outline, though

---

[1] *Serindia*, Pl. LXXV, 75, 1 ft. by 7¼ in. (My Plate XXIV).

[2] Translated by Jinagupta *c*. 600 A.D. Tripitaka XIV, 8 and 9.

[3] I do not see who else but Indra can be meant. The figure looks more like a Bodhisattva.

there is a tendency towards uniform thickness in each object represented, has the beginnings of that supple calligraphic quality which the Sung painters developed. Here, in embryo, are the very rocks of Hsia Kuei, of Kanō Motonobu.

Violence can only be subdued by violence; and the gentle Bodhisattvas of the Stein Collection have some ferocious and horrifying neighbours, powers that to conquer Evil assume the guise of Evil. Such is the Three-headed Bodhisattva[1] reproduced on Plate XXV. It is said that this terrifying shape is assumed by the Bodhisattva Samantabhadra to curb the insolence of demons. In his head-dress he wears a small medallion of Amida, his " Dhyāni " Buddha. In the foreground a swine-headed devil is seen fleeing in consternation. On his breast are two (highly conventionalized) skulls, reminders that even in the mild religion of Tun-huang the cult of the gruesome was not wholly neglected. He is indeed a near approach to the sinister deities of Tartary and Tibet.

THE PIETY OF TUN-HUANG

Salmony in his *Europa-Ostasien*[2] has shown that the rise and fall of religious art follows a fixed path. The early stages reflect the primitive intensity of the new belief (for example, the tympanon of St. Pierre de Moissac or the carvings of Yün-kang). Then comes the period of " fruition "; the strangeness of the gods is softened and humanized, for they, once mysterious, have become familiars in Church and household. Such is the art of Lung-mēn.

Last comes what Salmony calls " Die Ausbreitung." The artist is no longer struggling to express a religious emotion in plastic terms. He is concerned only with the rendering of a particular set of bodily forms. At Tun-huang all these stages may be seen, but in the earlier paintings of the Stein Collection it is the second which prevails. The Buddhism of Tun-huang is " mediæval." Amida is Christ; the Bodhisattvas, his Saints. To the Mahāyāna doctors who propagated it the doctrine of Amida's Paradise may have been no more than a metaphysical allegory; but to the common people it was a plain promise of just such a Heaven as that to which the mediæval Christian aspired. Bright lights, music, rich food and drinks, the vision of beings superior to oneself—are not these the eternal aspirations of the Western *plebs* ?

[1] Called Vajrapāni Bodhisattva or Vajra Vidyarāja Bodhisattva, but these names perhaps belong more properly to a later phase when he is in the service not of Amida, but of the Sun Buddha Vairochana.　　　　[2] Kiepenhauer, Potsdam, 1922.

Just as in the pictures, the side-scenes bring us into closer touch with the artists than do the main cult-figures, so too in the religious literature of the Caves it is not the formal Scriptures, paraphrased from the Sanskrit, which reveal to us the spirit of those who worshipped there. We learn far more from the few fragments of popular literature which have been found.

There is among the Stein MSS. a Life of Buddha in ballad form.[1] It has not in spirit the remotest connection with those highly ornamental Sanskrit " Lives " which, though impressive in the intoxicating sonority of the original, become so tedious when translated into Chinese. The contrast between this gaunt, popular literature and the sumptuous prolixity of the Sūtras has an exact parallel in the contrast, say, between the " Life Scenes " carved at Yün-kang and those of Amarāvatī. The same MS. contains a ballad in ten stanzas on the transcience of human life :

> *Look upon the life of man, how fast his hours slide by,*
> *His seasons fly.*
> *His days, like the swift top that seems asleep,*
> *Their secret motions keep.*
> *Whose wholesome youth and beauty while he knows it not*
> *Already rot.*
> *Who while with Magic Wheel he holds the world in sway*
> *Doth still decay.*

In the stanzas which follow, sages, patriarchs, warriors, and courtesans are put in mind of their mortality. Yet the Scriptures teach us of another land, telling us it is of fairer aspect than this earth—Sukhāvatī, the Blessed Land of Amida.

> *Then soon, then now set out upon your way,*
> *Make no delay,*
> *But thither quickly go,*
> *Where (doubt it not, for it is surely so)*
> *Nought shall decay.*

These songs, judging from the appearance of the MS., were written early in the 9th century. They and other relics of the Caves in which the mind of the Tun-huang Buddhists has expressed itself freely, show us a state of feeling akin to that of Europe in the 13th and 14th centuries. This spirit and much of the material environment that went with it[2] travelled slowly westward. Tun-huang was a little bit old-fashioned in its beliefs, as became a remote provincial town.

[1] Its number in the collection is S. 2204.   [2] E.g. the armour.

THE TUN-HUANG PAINTINGS

THE TUN-HUANG PAINTINGS, AN ARCHAIC PROVINCIAL SCHOOL

Style. The boisterous, calligraphic outline, the billowing draperies, the breadth and freedom of style which all writers ascribe to Wu Tao-tzŭ and his followers are not to be found at Tun-huang. The school of Tun-huang is probably an independent offshoot of the Northern 6th-century school founded by Chung-ta the Sogdian.

Subject. The subjects of the Stein paintings (9th and 10th centuries) belong to a phase of Buddhist iconography which had become quite out of date in Central China. Amida and his Paradise dominate this local and highly Conservative school; at Ch'ang-an we find on the one hand creations of the Magic Sect such as the Five Mysterious Buddhas,[1] and terrifying Tantric apparitions such as the Five Vidyarājas[2]; in the other, new matronly forms of Avalokiteśvara (By Moonlight, Clad in White Robes, etc.), and a continual swarm of Lohan. Among the ninety-three pictures in the Hui Tsung Collection which were attributed to Wu Tao-tzŭ only one represented Amida, and he does not seem ever to have painted a Western Paradise; whereas in the Stein Collection we find Amida at every turn, but no " Sixteen Lohans," no Vidyarājas,[3] no magic Quintads. The Buddhism reflected in the silk-paintings from Tun-huang is, in fact, several hundred years behind the times. Its iconography is that of the 7th century, which was dominated by Amida, just as the 5th was dominated by Maitreya and the 6th by Shākyamuni.

THE KWAKO GENZAI INGWA KYŌ

In connection with the Life of Buddha scenes in the Stein Collection it is interesting to examine the famous Japanese illustrations to the *Ingwa Kyō*,[4] copied from a Chinese original. These consisted originally of four scrolls[5] with pictures at the top, and the text of the Sūtra at the bottom.

[1] Japanese *Gohimitsu Nyorai*. See *Shimbi Taikwan*, I.

[2] Japanese *Myō-ō*.

[3] Unless the three-headed deity reproduced in Plate 25 be one.

[4] In Sanskrit *Atīta-pratyut-panna-hetuphala Sūtra*, No. 666 of Nanjio's Catalogue. The story of the previous Buddha Samantaprabha and his prediction to the hermit Sumati of the coming of Shākyamuni, followed by the Life of the historic Buddha. Translated from the Sanskrit *c.* 440 A.D.

[5] The first part of Scroll I belongs to the Jōbon Kendaiji, Kyōto; the third scroll to the Hō-on-in, Daigo; both are now in the Imperial Museum, Kyōto. The second part of the fourth scroll is in the School of Fine Arts, Tōkyō.

There is evidence that the second scroll (now lost) bore a colophon with the date 735, and it is generally accepted that this is the date at which the illustrations were copied. The Chinese original probably dated from about the 6th century. As regards general treatment, there is a very close kinship between the Life scenes in the scrolls and those in the Stein banners. The costumes in the former (they are, of course, entirely Chinese) point to an earlier fashion, particularly in head-dresses, but they are not very markedly different. We find the same romantic scenery, with rocky hills and flowering trees, treated, however, in a much more cursory manner; the same groups of neat, compact figures. The rather unusual motives, such as that of a cavalcade half-hidden by a fold in the hill (in the Pursuit scene, Plate XXVI). But in power of co-ordination and arrangement, in the suggestion of spaces and planes, many of the Life scenes in the Stein Collection show an astonishing advance. Between the two, or so we may provisionally suppose, lie the discoveries of Chung-ta the Sogdian, Chan Tzǔ-ch'ien and Yen Li-pēn, together with at least some echo of Wu Tao-tzǔ, Chou Fang, and Chang Nan-pēn.

There are points at which both the landscape treatment and the figure of the *Ingwa Kyō* remind one more of Ku K'ai-chih than of T'ang art. But a detailed analysis of the style would be out of place here, since it is impossible to say how far the Japanese copyist may have deviated from the original.[1]

---

[1] The three surviving scrolls have been reproduced, one in colour, the rest in collotype, by the Fine Art School, Tōkyō. Partial reproductions will be found in *Tōyō*, I, *Shimbi Taikwan*, XVII, and *Kokka*, XI. These reproductions, together with others published by the same school, were sent to me anonymously in 1922. I take this opportunity of thanking the person who sent them.

CHAPTER XI
LANDSCAPE PAINTING

CHAPTER XI
LANDSCAPE PAINTING

LI SSŬ-HSÜN: WANG WEI AND MONOCHROME
PAINTING

Chinese feeling for nature has been, since a time long before the Christian era, of a kind unknown in Europe till the close of the 18th century. The Chinese did not merely love Nature: they were in love with her. So were the European romantics; but whereas their love was a pagan ardour tinged with mysticism and poetry, the Chinese love of Nature grew directly out of a ritual worship.

Like many primitive peoples, the early Chinese adored the divinities of river and mountain-top. By hazardous ascents the early priest-kings renewed their contact with Heaven and fed that mysterious inward power by which they ruled. Sung Yü's *Kao T'ang*[1] was written in order to incite a king to renew his magic weal-bringing power by the ascent of a precipitous crag.

The Chinese call landscape *shan-shui*, "mountains and waters." The rivers and lakes as well as the hills are inhabited by gods, who (apparently as much as any tame gold-fish) depend for their sustenance on human alms. The traveller who crosses a river must feed the god with a libation. One of the best known Chinese plays, the *Rain at Hsiao-hsiang*, describes the shipwreck of a traveller who forgot this rite.

In Sung Yü's poem we see religious fervour already beginning to transform itself into romantic æstheticism. The two attitudes cannot be rigidly divided, for all artists feel that beauty is divine. And indeed in the case of Chinese artists this feeling had always a fuller intensity, for no conception of a personal Divinity competed with it.[2] The mountains were the abode not only of gods, but also of holy men. The word *hsien*, often translated into its Sanskrit equivalent *rishi*, is written with a character which consists of the elements " man " and " mountain." Such hermits certainly existed in China from a very early period, but under the influence of Confucian materialism the Chinese lost all interest in them, and it was not till the revival of Taoist asceticism in the 2nd century A.D. that they again came into prominence. Chinese thought has always tended to be obsessed by the actual problems of social organization. Nor is this strange,

---

[1] 3rd century B.C. Translated in *The Temple and Other Poems*.

[2] I do not think that any divinities, Buddhist or otherwise, ever occupied the same kind of position in the minds of Chinese artists as God did in the mind, say, of Constable.

for China is a continent rather than a single country, and the difficulty of establishing centralized authority over so vast an area has naturally turned the thoughts of its inhabitants constantly towards practical questions of government and control. But even in the days of the loose Chou confederacy the Chinese were obsessed by politics; and the question of exactly what relation ought to exist between the plebs and the nobles, and between the nobles and the sovereign, was continually discussed by Confucius and his school.

Out of this passionate interest in government arose a tendency to over-elaborate its machinery, to weave closer and closer the " web of the world's dust." The function of each individual was registered and docketed; pitilessly the wheels of State caught him up and whirled him into the vortex of administration.

From this jarring workshop of government there were some few who drew back afraid. Dazed by the din and bustle, they stared at the great machine. What was the meaning of it? How could it have happened that they had become part of it?

> *A Mensch hat amal mir gesagt die Bedeutung;*
> *Ich weiss nicht, ich art' nicht—ich werd' a Maschin.*

Civilization, with its irksome restraints and complications, had annexed the plains and valleys. But the mountains remained untenanted. " Why stay? " asked a hundred Chinese poets, who longed to live not as an obscure part of a great machine, but free and fearless in the isolation of the hills. They asked this question, but they knew the answer. The *hsien,* the Mountain Man, must subsist on roots and berries; he must drink from frozen streams, walk barefoot on rocks and snow. He must leave behind him all affections and desires, dwelling in the quiet of his own mind. Such a life is possible; it is led by thousands of hermits in the East to-day. The Mount Everest Expedition found one whose daily nourishment was confined to a few grains of barley; the most accomplished of the Chinese *hsien* lived on dewdrops. The idea that man owes nothing to society and may, if he chooses to face the rigours of isolation, detach himself from it —the ideal of a hermit life and gradual emancipation from the needs of the body—these things were probably very ancient in China; nor is there any evidence that they belong to the south rather than to the north. The *hsien* of the north-east were particularly famous. Still less is there any evidence that the non-social ideal was derived from India. The opposition between this ideal and Confucianism seems to be a fundamental part of the Chinese character, and it was this ideal that inspired the passionate love of mountain scenery which dominates Chinese landscape-painting. Mountains and torrents were adored as symbols of escape, as emblems of a world unsullied by man's scheming and striving. It was not the plastic, the purely visual, side of landscape that inspired these painters, but rather the mood, the spiritual content of the scene.

LI SSŬ-HSŬN

The landscape in the Ku K'ai-chih's "Admonitions" is elementary and hieratic in treatment. He seems, however, to have practised pure landscape-painting. The *Ming Hua Chi*[1] mentions a landscape screen painted by Ku; while his "Owls, wild geese, and an expanse of water," mentioned by P'ei Hsiao-yüan in his *Chēng Kuan Hua Shih* (639), must have come very near to being a pure landscape.

A landscape entitled *The Hills of Kuei-chi*, attributed to Ku K'ai-chih, is in the Metropolitan Museum at New York. We know that Ku admired these hills, but there is no record of his having painted them. The passage which Mr. Ferguson[2] quotes as a description of this picture is in reality Ku's description of his projected painting of the Cloud Terrace Mountain and its fairy inhabitants. The Hills of Kuei-chi are in Chekiang; the Cloud Terrace Mountain far away to the north in Kiang-su, beyond the Yangtze.

The connection of this picture with Ku K'ai-chih is uncertain. The design appears to belong to the 7th century, and the execution may, as Mr. Ferguson suggests,[3] belong to a much later date.

Tai K'uei (died 395 A.D.) painted a picture of "Streams, Hills, and Homesteads of the Land of Wu." His son P'o painted "Famous Mountains of China" and "Wind, Cloud, Water, and Moonlight." But in the whole period from the 4th to the 7th century landscape backgrounds of Buddhist and other paintings were gradually becoming more romantic and varied. Some of the Wei frescoes at Tun-huang[4] have backgrounds of winding fruitful valleys and precipitous wooded hills, which not only show great feeling for nature, but also considerable powers of pictorial arrangement. Unfortunately the artists were unable to bring the figures of their story into any kind of plastic relation with the background. They seem to have painted a romantic piece of country and then to have dumped their figures straight into the middle of it, as one might drop pebbles into a bucket.

[1] V. 8.   [2] *Outlines*, p. 202. See also above. p. 63.
[3] *Catalogue of a Special Exhibition of Chinese Paintings*. Metropolitan Museum, 1914.
[4] E.g. Pelliot, Pl. CXX.

The first great painter in whose work landscape played a prevailing part was Li Ssŭ-hsün. He was a grandson of a nephew of the first Emperor of the T'ang dynasty, and therefore a very great personage. Born in 651, he received an appointment at the capital about 680, got involved in a scandal, and was exiled to Yangchow. Upon the usurpation of the Empress Wu Hou, he resigned his official rank, as a protest against her wholesale execution of members of the Imperial family. In 705 the Emperor Chung Tsung was restored, and Li was invested with a fief and State pension. At the beginning of Ming Huang's reign he was made Senior General of the Winged Forest, a guard regiment composed of young aristocrats. He died between 715 and 719.

Such are the rather uninteresting facts of his life. Although none of his pictures survive, it is possible, since he was a miniaturist working in a well-defined and easily imitable technique, to get a clear idea (from copies and the works of his successors) of what his pictures looked like. He painted in heavy greens and blues, with delicate gold outline. His pictures are said to have reflected the gaiety and glitter of the Court which was his home. He painted " the surface of things, and did not probe the meaning that lies hid beneath."

His technique was derived[1] from the 6th-century painter Chan Tzŭ-ch'ien, two of whose " landscapes in green and blue " still survived in the 16th century.[2] The gold outline seems to have been Li's contribution to this technique. It was developed and perfected by his son Chao-tao, revived by the Sung painters Chao Po-chü and Chao Po-hsü,[3] perpetuated by the 14th-century painter Lēng Ch'ien, and so transmitted to a host of modern imitators. The British Museum possesses an album of " Famous Palaces," which is perhaps a Ming version of a picture by Li Ssŭ-hsün (Plate I); the Freer Collection has a long landscape roll attributed to him.

The Chinese generally refer to Li Ssŭ-hsün as " General Li," and to his son Chao-tao as " The Little General." There has been constant confusion between the two. Thus the picture of " Ming Huang's Flight " (euphemistically known as " Plucking the Melons," from the fact that it shows one of the Court ladies of the retinue so employed) is sometimes attributed to the Old General; but the scene which it represents took place some forty years after General Li's death. Again, Chang Ch'ou attributes to the father the use of a certain method of preparing painting-silk and states that it was derived from Wu Tao-tzŭ. But Li's career was

[1] *Hua Chien*, quoted in *Shu Hua Fang*, IV, 42.
[2] *Shu Hua P'u*, 99. 15.   [3] *circa* 1130–1160 A.D.

almost ended when Wu's was beginning. It is probable that it was the son, Chao-tao, who used this method, which consisted in boiling the silk and then, while it was still hot, basting alum-powder into it and flattening it down till the surface was absolutely smooth, the interstices of the silk being completely filled with white paste. Li Chao-tao's "Sunset" (a subject rare in Chinese art) seems to have survived till the 17th century. The Ch'ien Lung Collection preserved his "Landscape with figures," a large kakemono. He is particularly associated with pictures of architecture placed in a mountainous landscape setting; a rather late copy of such a picture is reproduced in colours as the frontispiece to *Ars Asiatica*.

WANG WEI AND INK PAINTING

Wang Wei was born in 699 at T'ai-yüan in Shansi. In his youth he distinguished himself as a musician. He played the lute and guitar, and composed songs which soon became celebrated. His "Yang-kuan" was for centuries sung at every farewell-gathering:

> *At Wei Castle a morning rain has dabbled the light dust ;*
> *At the Inn side green, green—the new willows' tint.*
> *Stay, stay, and drink again one last bowl of wine ;*
> *For he that issues by the Western Pass[1] will meet few friends.*

He graduated in 721, was appointed assistant in the Grand College of Music, got into a scrape, and was degraded to the post of Secretary to the Granary Intendant of Chi-chou in Shantung. After a while he was promoted to the metropolitan post of Junior Censor. At Ch'ang-an he joined the brilliant group of writers and painters who surrounded the Emperor's brother, Prince Chi. Here are two poems that he wrote at this period :

WITH A CONCOURSE OF ATTENDANTS PRINCE CHI PICNICS AT MASTER YANG'S COTTAGE

> *Where Yang the Scholar talks of Holy Writ*
> *The Prince of Huai came with cup in hand.*
> *Late he drank, till the birds faltered in their song,*
> *And fallen flowers heaped the place where he sat.*
>
> *Homeward he turns, the silver lamps are lit ;*
> *The forest floor is scattered with bells of jade.[2]*
> *The fortress-city sleeps behind solemn gates ;*
> *We pack its entries with a music of pipes and song.*

[1] The Yang Kuan, near Tun-huang. The poem was written at a farewell party given to a friend who was going as envoy to Kucha, in Eastern Turkestan.

[2] Compare p. 98, " fallen . . . jewels littered the road."

CHINESE PAINTING

ATTENDING PRINCE CHI AT A PICNIC IN THE HILLS

The guests are seated, the incense-beasts are full,
The palace wantons have spread their silken screen ;
Flowers from the rivulet dull their painted cheeks,
The mountain moon dims the candle's light.
Black at the window are heaped the ridges of the hill ;
The curtained doors are cold with the fountain's spray.
At last we go—and carry with us in our train
Ballad and dance, lest the way seem dull and long.

Prince Chi died in 726, and his elder brother, Prince Ning, succeeded to his place as leader of society in Ch'ang-an. Ning died in 731 ; the equally hospitable Hsieh, in 734, and his protégés transferred themselves to the Court of Ming Huang, which had hitherto been somewhat eclipsed by the *salons* of his more gifted brothers.

Giles[1] speaks of Wei as retiring, after a short spell of official life, " into seclusion." On the contrary, he lived at Ch'ang-an as a courtier for over thirty years. Like all the grandees of the place he had his country estate, and was fond of making excursions to the neighbouring temples ; but there is no evidence that during all this period he was ever much further from the capital than Croydon is distant from Piccadilly. His villégiature was within an easy day's journey from Ch'ang-an, and he was able to retire thither whenever the Emperor was not actually holding Court at the city. In fact, his life was divided between town and country in just such proportions as any sensible man would choose.

In 755 the An Lu-shan revolution abruptly terminated the most polished epoch that the world had ever seen. Poets, painters, musicians, joined in the wild stampede to the West. Some died by the way, some were captured. Among the latter was Wang Wei ; and, though his medical knowledge enabled him to embark upon a course of ingenious malingering, he was pitilessly incarcerated in the Bodhi-temple at Ch'ang-an.

The rebel An Lu-shan celebrated his victories by a banquet at the Frozen Pearl Lake, to which he summoned the late Emperor's Musicians of the Pear Tree Garden. They stood weeping and could not play ; upon which their chief Lei Hai-ch'ing was done hideously to death in the Riding School. Wang Wei in prison heard of the incident and wrote :

Ten thousand streets (oh piercing to the heart !) smoulder like burning grass ;
The hundred ministers, on what day shall they again assemble round the Throne ?
With fallen leaves of the autumn kuei the Palace paths are blocked ;
At the Frozen Pearl Lake's side—the music of flutes and strings !

[1] *Chinese Literature*, p. 149.

142

Soon afterwards he was compelled to accept a post on the rebel chief's staff.

When the revolution had been crushed, those who had accepted office from Lu-shan were cast into gaol. Wang Wei and two other painters, Chēng Ch'ien (famous for his paintings of fish) and Chang T'ung, both of them, however, better known as statesmen than as artists, were put in the same building. Their gaoler, Ts'ui Yüan, set them to decorate his study walls. Wei was soon released, for it happened that his brother, Wang Chin, who had served gallantly with the Imperial troops, was at this time in high favour with the victorious Prince Regent. He was allowed to ransom Wei, and soon afterwards the Regent, who had now ascended the throne as the Emperor Su Tsung, heard someone recite Wei's *Frozen Pearl Poem*. He was deeply moved, and at once gave the poet a place in the new Crown Prince's household.

His brother, Wang Chin, no longer in favour, had been made Governor of a distant province. Wei memorialized the Throne as follows : " Your servant Wei has five faults to every five virtues of his brother Chin. Yet I am in the Ministry and my brother is banished to a remote district. I wish to give up my appointment in exchange for the recall of Chin." Wang Chin was soon afterwards reinstated at the capital as Counsellor-in-Ordinary (3rd class, 2nd division). In the winter of 759 Wei was taken ill at Ch'ang-an. Chin, who was at Fēng-hsiang, knew he could not reach him in time and sent him a letter of farewell. Wei died soon afterwards. His mother, to whom he was deeply attached, was a devout Buddhist. It is probable that Wei's religious period began after the death of his wife in 730. We are told that he " abstained from meat and fine clothes," and even that he took lessons in Sanskrit. Upon the death of his mother he turned part of his country house into a monastery in her memory and was buried there.[1] After his death the Emperor Tai Tsung said to Wang Chin : " I used to hear the Princes speak very highly of your brother's poetry. Does much of it survive ? " And he sent to Chin's house a messenger who carried back to the Palace many thousand manuscripts, among them four hundred pieces of music.

Wang Wei was the first great poet who was also a great painter.[2] His poems reflect the perfect balance of his nature. Exquisite in their

---

[1] The cremation of laymen was not common in the T'ang dynasty. Wang was probably buried outside the temple enclosure.

[2] The great Han poet Chang Hēng is said to have painted, but his works did not survive and no one thinks of him as a painter.

technique, they are more reflective, more personal, and consequently less completely lyrical than those of Li Po. At the same time, he wholly lacked the political ardour of Tu Fu. His two great contemporaries were impulsive, stupendous, inexplicable; in a word, Gothic. Wei is the most classical of Chinese poets, a master of just such fresh and delicately-ordered art as one finds in the introductions to Plato's Dialogues.

It is not without significance that his second name was Mo-ch'i, an abbreviation of the Sanskrit Vimalakīrti. I have already spoken of this Indian apostle, the patron saint of Chin æstheticism, the " Hermit of Unsullied Fame," whose narrow cell was furnished only by a low white bed. He was, indeed, the favourite saint of all who turned away from gilt and glitter, from the outward show, as Buddhists say, the *rūpa* of the world; and, in particular, of ink-painters. For it is by the word *sĕ*, " colour," that the Chinese translate the Sanskrit term *rūpa*.

One saying about Wang Wei has been so often profaned that I feel impelled to defend his reputation. There is not a book on Chinese paintings, there is hardly even a book on the Far East in general, which does not quote a statement that " Wang Wei's pictures were poems; his poems, pictures." This is, of course, quoted in approbation of his work, for to many people the arts are unpalatable except when jumbled up together; hence the popularity of opera. The dictum is based on a mis-understanding of a passage in which the poet Su Tung-p'o is discussing not Wang Wei's art in general, but a particular picture entitled *Mist-rain at Lan-t'ien* which had inscribed upon it a four-line poem. The point at issue was whether the poem (which does not occur in Wei's collected works) is by him or was added by some subsequent owner of the picture. What Su Tung-p'o says is : " I can taste in the poem something of the picture's flavour; and in the picture I see something of the poem. The poem runs :

From the Blue River white stones jut ;
On its jade waters the red leaves are few.
On the mountain path no rain falls ;
The sky itself wets the traveller's coat.

This is surely by Wang Wei. However, some people think that it was added by an admirer of the painting. . . ."

Later Chinese writers, divorcing Su Tung-p'o's words from their context, have quoted them as though they were a statement about Wei's art in general, not a discussion about the genuineness of a particular poem. Hence the calumny that " Wang Wei's pictures were poems and his poems pictures," spread over Europe. Has it no foundation?

WANG WEI AND MONOCHROME PAINTING

The sting of this slander (as of most) consists in the fact that it is almost true. We have every reason to regard Wang Wei as the ancestor of all subsequent landscape-painters, save those who used the archaistic style in green, blue, and gold. And Chinese landscape-painting as we know it is undeniably poetical. To embody in a picture the emotion caused by reading a poem—such was the ambition of the Sung landscapists who claimed Wang Wei as their ancestor. Their right to regard themselves as his descendants was probably founded not upon the pictures painted during the greater part of his career, but upon those of his mature period.

WANG WEI'S CAREER

When Wang Wei came to Court in the early 'twenties of the 8th century there was only one model that a landscape-painter could follow—the heavily-coloured, decorative, miniature style of Li Ssŭ-hsün which was still being practised at Court by his son Li Chao-tao. There is ample evidence[1] that one of the many styles practised by Wei during his career approximated closely to that of the Lis. It is not credible that this style (when we come to arrange his phases in chronological order) should come in any place but the first. In another phase we find him imitating the landscape style of Wu Tao-tzŭ, under whose influence he fell at the palace of Prince Chi. We are told that it was during his tour to the south-west, somewhere about 725 A.D., that Wu worked out a completely new style of landscape. We cannot be certain what it was, but we may guess that it consisted of an animated, calligraphic outline, discreetly tinted with light colours.

But the style with which Wei is usually associated and, which we may suppose him to have developed in his maturity, was a purely monochrome one, the *p'o-mo* or " broken-ink " style. Before I discuss what this was I must briefly indicate the successive phases of monochrome painting in China.

MONOCHROME PAINTING

It is natural that a painter, if he is embarking upon an elaborate composition, should first of all draw his subject in monochrome. This was certainly the technique of the early Buddhist painters, but there is no reason to suppose that it was not practised in China (for example, in the frescoes on palace walls) long before the introduction of Buddhism. Such preliminary drawings might be in any colour ; but red and black were the

---

[1] E.g. *Shu Hua P'u*, 81, 29.

two colours most generally used. It was natural that a people skilled for many generations in calligraphy (which is, after all, a kind of monochrome painting) should make experiments with these preliminary outline drawings, attempting to give them expressiveness and finality, and should at a later stage sometimes dispense with colour altogether. Such outline-drawings were called *po-hua*, " plain-drawings." Wei Hsieh (4th century), the predecessor of Ku K'ai-chih, did a *po-hua* representing a hunting-scene in the Upper Park at Ch'ang-an.[1] Wu Tao-tzŭ particularly excelled in *po-hua ;* his famous *Tortures of Hell* in the Chao Ching-kung Temple at Ch'ang-an were in this technique. So, indeed, were many of the great T'ang wall-paintings, though colour was frequently added by injudicious decorators. As an example of a red-outline painting Mr. Taki[2] quotes a fragment of fresco brought back by Count Ōtani from Kashgar.[3] The example is not a very good one, for the fragment in question represents a handkerchief with a holy figure stamped upon it in red. The use of red outline is here merely a realistic representation of the figured textile which the fresco portrays.

The next step was the addition of ink washes of varying intensity to indicate contours and folds. This is exemplified by an Avalokiteśvara[4] brought back from Tun-huang by Professor Pelliot. In addition to the light diluted ink there are touches of drier ink and also of light red ; but, substantially, the picture is a *mo-hua*, ink-painting, and, though it belongs to the end of the T'ang dynasty, it is probably the earliest of its kind that survives.

The outline of Wu Tao-tzŭ was, according to all accounts, free and boisterous. His draperies looked as if they were flapping in a gale. The same cannot be said of the picture under discussion, and Mr. Taki concludes that, though the technical method approximates to Wu Tao-tzŭ, the style is rather that of the great 6th-century masters Chang Sēng-yu and Ts'ao Chung-ta.

A third development of the ink-technique, with which Wang Wei's name is associated, was called *p'o-mo*, " break-ink." Here we are on difficult ground, for the term was used in different senses at different times and ultimately became a bone of contention in the curious Tweedle-dum and Tweedle-dee battle between the Northern and Southern Schools.[5] It seems, however, fairly clear that what it originally meant was the breaking

---

[1] *Ming Hua Chi*, V, 3.   [2] *Kokka*, 386.
[3] Reproduced in *Sai-iku Kōko Zufu*, Pl. 6.   [4] Reproduced, *Kokka*, 386.
[5] See below, p. 182.

up or " disarraying " of the ink-outline sketch, so that the result, instead
of being an outline-drawing graduated with washes of ink, looked like a
wash-drawing pure and simple.

Another T'ang artist who used this method was Chang Tsao.[1] He
painted sometimes with a " bald brush " and sometimes with his fingers.
On one occasion, a revolution having broken out, he was obliged to fly for
his life, leaving behind him a half-painted picture ; he had not even
finished " breaking the ink (p'o-mo)."

A fourth method of ink-painting was invented by Wang Hsia, also called
Wang Mo, who lived on into the 9th century. But before describing it
I must return to Wang Wei.

WANG WEI'S PICTURES

I have suggested that Wang Wei's art passed through several phases ;
they correspond to stages of development which we may observe in many
great artists and writers. The decorative period (bright colours and gold
outline) corresponds, say, to Shakespeare's rhyming phase ; the rigid
monochrome period, to Shakespeare's second, blank-verse stage when he
still avoided feminine-endings and other liberties. And, finally, Wei's
p'o-mo corresponds to the untrammelled verse of the later plays. That
one man should have painted in so many styles was a matter of astonishment to Tung Ch'i-ch'ang, the great critic and painter of the 16th century.
It was also awkward for him, because he had spent his life in proclaiming
that his own Southern School alone perpetuated the " true and only "
style of Wang Wei.

At first he was shown paintings in outline. He was sure that these were
not real Wang Weis, because " it is precisely in contour-lines[2] that the
great masters of painting shew their genius " ; therefore outline-paintings
could not be works of genius. Then he came across a Sung copy of the
Wang Ch'uan scroll[3] ; the beloved contour-lines were there, but the
execution was so poor that it could not be made the standard for Wei's
style. Next he met with a Snow Landscape by the 14th-century artist
Chao Mēng-fu, and realized by intuition that it reproduced a picture by
Wang Wei. Strange to say, it was decorated with gold outline and
powdered-white, artisan vulgarities which Tung Ch'i-ch'ang would have
condemned in the works of the Northerners, whom he detested with such

---

[1] Second half of 8th century.
[2] What the Chinese call ts'un, " wrinkles," particularly lines indicating the contours of
hills.   [3] See below, p. 247.

pedagogic acerbity. When he was asked why he thought the style must be Wang Wei's, he answered: " From T'ang till Sung the different methods of ' wrinkle ' are clearly distinguished in the different schools. It is like the five divisions of the Zen sect in Buddhism. A single phrase, often a single word, is enough to tell the listener to which sect a speaker belongs. Now, in the picture the ' wrinkles ' are not like those of Chang Sēng-yu nor of Li Ssŭ-hsün, nor yet of Wang Hsia or Kuan T'ung. Nor do they recall the eclectic styles of Tung Yüan, Chü-jan, Li Ch'ēng, and Fan K'uan. Whose style, then, can it be, if not Wang Wei's ? "

Finally, he saw the *Snow Clearing away on Hills by the River*,[1] which, by its resemblance to the Chao Mēng-fu picture, he at once recognized to be a genuine work by Wang Wei.

Thus Tung Ch'i-ch'ang in the 16th century was able, by an unsatisfactory combination of logic and intuition, to convince himself that he had ascertained Wei's " true and only " style.

But even in the 11th century his pictures were apparently very rare. His one surviving fresco was in the eastern wing of the K'ai-yüan Temple at Fēng-hsiang, some eighty miles west of Ch'ang-an. In the Great Hall of the same temple was Wu Tao-tzŭ's great series of scenes from the Life of Buddha. On the night of the first full moon of the year 1063, Su Tung-p'o arrived at the temple a few hours before dawn and, hurrying to the eastern chapel, examined Wei's fresco by the light of a guttering candle. " Seen in the shifting flickering light the figures of the picture seemed to be moving of their own accord. I stood for a long while gazing in fascinated wonder." Next day he wrote a long poem in which he compares the frescoes of Wu Tao-tzŭ and Wang Wei. Wu he finds " bold and free, violent as an ocean-storm "; the picture[2] shows the Supreme One " speaking quietly of his approaching death, while around him believers wail and weep, and even the unbelieving beat their breasts. The Wild Men with their chiefs, the goblins and their king, press round him, craning their strange tortoise heads." Wang Wei's picture showed Buddha's ascetic disciples in the garden of Jetavana. " In one of his poems he says : *In my old age I wore the sweet thyme at my girdle ; I clad myself in a garment of lilies.* And his fresco has just the exquisiteness and purity of that poem. The disciples of the Garden are gaunt as cranes ;

[1] A version of this subject, in ink and light colours, is reproduced in Strehlneek's catalogue (*Chinese Pictorial Art*), p. 58 *seq.*, 1914.

[2] This Nirvāna of Wu Tao-tzŭ's is described by Shao Po in the *Wēn Chien Hou Lu*, *c.* 1150. See Giles, p. 50.

in them all human longing and passion is dead as the ashes of an extinguished fire. In front of the gate grow two clumps of bamboo, snowy nodules threaded to frost-bound roots. . . . Though Wu be magical and rare, yet he is but a painter; his craft may be dissected and discussed. Wang Wei transcends the mechanical means through which he works; bars cannot confine him; on mystic wings he soars above the cage. Both are stupendous, both divine; but it is before Wei, Wei only, that I bow in silent awe."

The Emperor Hui Tsung, who, as we have seen, was optimistic in his attributions, possessed 126 paintings which he ascribed to Wang Wei. Among them were four " Vimalakīrtis," " Lohan crossing the Sea," and a picture of " Strange Lands." Most of the rest were landscapes.

Kao Shih-ch'i[1] saw at the close of the 17th century Wei's " Snow piled up upon a Thousand Peaks," a long roll presumably painted in colours.

Ch'ien Lung possessed a small album-leaf, " Snow by the Stream," with an inscription by Tung Ch'i-ch'ang, who identifies it with the " Snow by the Ford " which was extant in the 14th century.

FINAL DEVELOPMENT OF INK TECHNIQUE

This is associated with the name of Wang Hsia, also called " Ink Wang " and " Wang the Silent," a wild drunken genius who lived till about 804 A.D. Chang Yen-yüan, the author of the *Ming Hua Chi*, is able to tell us a few facts about him, because Chang's cousin knew the erratic painter.

Wang Hsia was a pupil of the little-known artist Hsiang Jung and of Chēng Ch'ien.[2] When he was drunk he used to dip his head in a pail of ink and flop it on to the painting-silk. Marvellous mountains, lakes, and trees appeared on the silk as though by magic. Having dabbled the picture with a great mass of ink, he would sometimes kick it, rub it, and smudge it, till a sunset or rain-storm appeared, and no trace of the first spilling was left. When the famous poet Ku K'uang (Po Chü-i's first patron) became Inspector of Coastal Defences, Wang Hsia surprised his friends by asking if he might join the Sea Patrol. " Why should you want to do that ? " they asked. " Only because I should like to paint land-

---

[1] It may be as well to mention that Kao Shih-ch'i's book, the *Hsiao Hsia Lu*, is *not* a list of " pictures in the Emperor K'ang Hsi's gallery " (Hirth, *Scraps*, p. 87). On the contrary, the author explains that he has omitted such pictures because it is impossible to tell the truth about objects which belong to royalties. The pictures which he describes belonged to his friends.

[2] Wang Wei's fellow-prisoner; see above, p. 143.

scapes (*shan-shui*) of the sea," he answered. He held the post for a few months, during which time Ku K'uang[1] became his pupil.

Wang Hsia's method came to be known as "ink-flinging." The violence of it has perhaps been exaggerated. It is, at any rate, clear that he dispensed with the preliminary ink-drawing; and it is doubtful[2] whether any of his predecessors had done so. He is thus the inventor of the pure wash-drawing (the *p'o-mo* only looked like one), as opposed to the tinted and gradated outline-drawing.

[1] There has, I think, been some confusion between Ku K'uang and the eccentric Ku Shēng (Master Ku) whom Giles describes on p. 77.

[2] See Mr. Taki, *Kokka*, 387.

CHAPTER XII
ANIMALS, BIRDS AND FLOWERS

CHAPTER XII
ANIMALS, BIRDS AND FLOWERS

ANIMAL PAINTING

In the introduction to *Les Animaux dans l'Art Chinois*, Monsieur Ardenne de Tizac emphasizes the influence of astronomy in giving to animals the important position which they occupy in Chinese art. Many ancient peoples identified certain groups of stars with certain animals. How they came to do so, it is not here my business to enquire. Suffice it to say that the Dragon, the Badger, the Fox, the Tiger, the Bear, the Monkey, and even the Worm all figure in the Chinese firmament. Many early artists painted sets of these astronomical beast-symbols. But clearly the Chinese did not derive their interest in animals from contemplating the stars. I do not think that the preponderance of animal-painting in Chinese art can be attributed to any one cause. It happened for many reasons, most of them not connected either with astronomy or symbolism. It is interesting in this connection to read what is perhaps the only surviving Chinese essay upon " animals in art "—the introduction to the animal paintings in the catalogue of the Emperor Hui Tsung's collection (compiled about 1120 A.D.).

" The horse," says that essay, " is used as a symbol of the sky, its even pace prefiguring the steady motion of the stars ; the bull, mildly sustaining its heavy yoke, is fit symbol of earth's submissive tolerance. But tigers, leopards, deer, wild swine, fawns, and hares—creatures that cannot be inured to the will of man—these the painter chooses for the sake of their skittish gambols and swift, shy evasions, loves them as things that seek the desolation of great plains and wintry moors, as creatures that will not be haltered with a bridle nor tethered by the toe. He would commit to brushwork the gallant splendour of their stride ; this would he do, and no more."

Among the factors which contributed to the development of the animal style are certainly the following :—

Different Conception of Man's Importance. In a small child's conception of the universe animals play quite as important a part as men. In the hierarchy which he constructs it will not necessarily be his parents or the cook or the clergyman who take precedence ; it is just as likely that a rabbit, pig, or goat will have the foremost place. Similarly, primitive people, sharing the streams and jungles with wild beasts (or at a later stage, taming them), do not regard them as less talented, less spiritual, than themselves. On the contrary, owing to the very fact that they cannot communicate with the animals, they tend to idealize them, just as we, intrigued by the silence of shy friends, sometimes attribute to them mythical virtues and capacities.

The Chinese, far more than the western Ancients (to whom everything but Man and his white marble cities was *naturæ horridior pars*), preserved this primitive contact with the beasts. And when in the West Christianity came to set a crown on man's self-conceit by telling him that he alone of creatures was endowed with an immortal soul, Buddhism was teaching the Chinese that the soul[1] of a grasshopper may once have inhabited the body of a king. When at last the " lower orders of Creation " came into their own in Western painting it was as actors in a droll parody of human situations (" Dignity and Impudence "), or in maudlinly sentimental melodrama (" The Friend of Man ").

This sentimental attitude towards animals is, I think, unknown in Chinese art. It is to be sought for, if it exists at all outside 19th-century Europe, in certain examples of late Greek and Græco-Roman sculpture.

Magic Animals. Of the dragon, part winged-horse, part serpent, and part octopus, I have already spoken. The T'ang dynasty was more interested in seeing than in imagining, and the dragon does not on the whole play a very important part in T'ang art. But he had been of immense importance during the first centuries of Chinese painting ; whereas his spiritual counterpart, the tiger, symbol of strength and nobility, occurs very rarely in the early period, almost equally seldom in T'ang times, and does not become part of the stock-in-trade of Chinese painting till the 10th century.

During the T'ang dynasty a stream of exotic animals (some of them hard to identify) poured into the Chinese Court from India, Central Asia, and Annam. As soon as the presents arrived, Court artists were ordered to make pictures of them—a wise precaution, for the unfortunate creatures frequently succumbed after a short time to the unfamiliar rigours of the Chinese climate. Of these visitors the lion was, of course, the most distinguished ; he was depicted by a steady succession of artists from the 6th century onwards. In decorative art he rapidly degenerated into a species of hieratic puppy.

As a symbol he represents not courage or kingship, as he does with us, but the Buddhist Church Triumphant.

---

[1] Buddhists dislike the *word* ; but they are not averse to theories which imply the existence of the *thing*.

Domestic Animals.   The Chinese, particularly the northern Chinese, had enough of the Tartar in them to make horses and horsemanship of immense importance in their lives.   The horse dominates secular Chinese sculpture and to such an extent pervades European collections of Chinese paintings that one might well be led by them to suppose that all Chinese pictures represent horses, and that there was in all history but one painter ; his name, Chao Mēng-fu.   This plethora of horse-paintings is due to the fact that Chinese dealers, quickly perceiving that their Western clients were more interested in subject than in treatment, in the " what ? " than in the " how ? " have unloaded upon them every representation of an animal which they rightly supposed to play an important part in the life of every rich Occidental.   In recent years, however, the supply of " antique " horse-pictures has declined.   We have become more interested in petrol-engines than in horseflesh—a taste which the manufacturer of Chinese antiquities is powerless to gratify.

Tao-lin, a priest of the 4th century, was rebuked for spending so much of his time in the stables.   " The company of horses," he answered, " is not incongruous with my sacred calling; there is divinity in their fleetness."   Prince Ning, the patron of Wu Tao-tzŭ, was a great horse-fancier ; one of Tu Fu's most celebrated poems is a verse-treatise on horse-painting.

The Bull.   The bull, in its secular aspect, is the symbol of idyllic rural life ; on its back sits the happy herd-boy with his two-foot switch, himself the symbol of the triumph of art over force.   I do not think that the bull under its mystic aspect, the bull of the Zen parable, occurs till Sung times, but it will be convenient to treat of it here.   A T'ang priest, K'uo-an, invented the parable, which is the story of Man's quest for transcendental truth.   The seeker is represented as a man who is looking for a stray bull. He finds its tracks, he sights it, he catches it, pastures it, and rides it home in triumph, only to discover—that the shed is empty.   He has captured the bull and brought it home, but there is no bull.   There was no question, therefore there can be no answer.   A mystical conclusion follows, which would require a lengthy exposition.   The parable was told in ten stanzas, which are often illustrated in a series of ten paintings.[1]

Another animal of religious significance was the monkey.   One day the Zen-master Hsüeh-fēng[2] was walking with a disciple in the mountains. Some baby-monkeys were playing on the rocks near by.   Hsüeh-fēng said, " Even those tiny creatures carry their little Buddha-mirrors at their hearts."   The meaning of this remark will be made clearer in my chapter

[1] For another story in which the bull figures, see p. 206.   [2] 822–908 A.D.

on Zen. Pet dogs, too, were much in favour during the T'ang dynasty, but they were not commonly painted till Sung.

THE ANIMAL PAINTERS

Ts'ao Pa and *Han Kan*. Ts'ao Pa was a descendant of the fourth Emperor[1] of the Wei dynasty. About the year 720 he had already made his name as a horse-painter. About 750 he was commissioned to paint the Emperor's horses and Ministers. (They are mentioned in this order.)

He is chiefly known as the teacher of Han Kan. The poet Tu Fu in his " Song of Painting," which is an eulogy of Ts'ao Pa, compares him favourably with his pupil. " Han Kan," he says, " only paints the flesh. Ts'ao paints the bones."

Han Kan was probably born about 715 A.D. During Ming Huang's reign the tributary nations of Central Asia were continually seeking the Emperor's favour by sending to him presents of fine horses. It became Han Kan's business to make pictures of them when they arrived. And as he was also horse-painter in chief to the Princes Ning, Chi, and Hsieh (among whom we know that Prince Ning, at any rate, was a polo-player), he had unique opportunities of study. A great mass of legend has gathered round his name; many of these stories are told by Giles in his *Chinese Pictorial Art*, and I will not repeat them here. He seems sometimes to have painted in ink, for the Ch'ien Lung Collection contained an ink-roll, " The Inner Natures of Horses," which was confidently attributed to him. In the same collection there was a " Monkey and Horse," a hanging-picture, in colours. Han Huang, a considerable figure in public life, was born in 723 and died in 787. He spent his leisure (his duties as Special Commissioner of the Fleet were perhaps not more arduous than Pepys's business at the Admiralty) in painting idyllic scenes of rural life, counterparts to the pastoral poems of Ch'u Kuang-hsi. Since we cannot look at Han Huang's pictures, let us read one of Ch'u's poems :

THE HERDBOY

What cares he if the path goes on and on ?
What does it matter if the dyke stretch far away ?
All he asks is a bull that minds the prong
And by no prank disturbs the chain of his thoughts.
A round-brimmed hat droops over the herdboy's head ;
A cloak of straw trails over the herdboy's breast,—

---

[1] Born 241 ; died 260. The Wei dynasty in question is of course the early native dynasty of that name, not the later Tartar one.

156

Shelter enough to baffle sun or shower,
Wrap enough to frighten cold or snow. . . .
The big bull is hidden by a fold of the hill,
The little bull has nosed into the near wood—
With others of his trade the herdboy dances and claps ;
All that happens he fits to verse and song ;
Takes his pleasure while pleasure comes his way,
And does not care if his rhymes be false or true.

We are told of Han Huang that his painting was extremely realistic, that " he pushed outward resemblance to the furthest point." Ch'ien Lung possessed two coloured rolls by him, the " Abundant Harvest " and " Scenes from Rural Life," in nine sections, each showing a different agricultural operation. Mr. Eumorphopoulos has an ink-painting of bulls which is attributed to Han Huang.

Tai Sung, another famous painter of cattle, was employed by Huang as a clerk when he was Governor of part of Chekiang. He took lessons from his chief. Many existing paintings are attributed to him, probably for no better reason than that they represent bulls.

FLOWER-PAINTING

Flower-painting as a separate art does not seem to have existed in China till the middle of the T'ang dynasty. It has its origin in the floral accessories of Buddhist painting. It was the custom to surround religious paintings and bas-reliefs with margins of floral pattern, the motifs of which (as may clearly be seen in the Life of Buddha reliefs at Yün-kang) were derived from Sassanian art. Such floral margins are to be found on some of the Stein banners. The 6th-century painter Chang Sēng-yu was, as we have seen, famous for his flowers, " painted so as to look as if they stood out in relief." These were probably done as " frames " for large religious frescoes. Flower-painting did not reach its zenith till the 10th century ; but one T'ang dynasty painter must be mentioned, Pien Luan, who flourished at the beginning of the 9th century. At the Tzŭ-shēng Temple he painted a Bhaishajya-rāja ; " the Tibetan-mallows in the Bodhisattva's head-dress were particularly fine." Here we see flower-painting as an accessory to Buddhist art.

COURT SCENES

The painting of Court scenes was the speciality of a succession of painters. The first of these was Chang Hsüan, who belongs to the first half of the

8th century. Of his technique we know nothing except the insignificant fact that he touched the lobe of the ear with a dot of red. His follower Chou Fang was also known as a Buddhist painter. About the year 800 he was employed (owing to the influence of his brother, who had distinguished himself in a campaign against the Tibetans) in the painting of the Chang-ching Temple, which the Emperor Tē Tsung restored. He immediately altered any part of the frescoes which was adversely criticized. Months passed before he could at last make up his mind to leave a figure as it stood. Similar stories are told (with approbation) of the Greek painter Apelles. He is said to have originated the conception of " Avalokiteśvara (Kuan-yin) sitting by the water in moonlight." It was perhaps at about this time that a definitely female type of Kuan-yin began to be represented. (I know of no evidence that any of Wu Tao-tzŭ's Kuan-yins were female.) Another creation of Chou Fang's was the erotic picture. In this branch of painting he had many successors ; but their works remain unexplored.

Two versions of his " Listening to Music," probably neither of them originals, are known to exist : one in China[1] and one in the Freer Collection. It is one of the most interesting early secular compositions which survive. Already we see strongly developed the Chinese tendency to express not so much a plastic as a spiritual situation. The figures, strangely scattered over the ample space of the picture, are emblems of highly concentrated, critical attention. Yet there is an extraordinary intensity in the composition ; and one feels that the painter has expressed something which could not have been expressed through the medium of any other art (Plate XXVII).

Li Chēn, a contemporary follower of Chou Fang, is of considerable interest to us because five of his works actually survive. He decorated various temple walls in a style closely modelled upon that of Chou Fang during the period c. 780–805 A.D. A poem written about the middle of the 9th century says that it is hard to decide whether Chou Fang or Li Chēn were the better painter. He occupies, in fact, an obscure but safe niche in native art-records.

In 804 the Japanese priest Kōbō Daishi arrived in China, learnt the doctrines of the Magic Sect from the sixth patriarch,[2] Hui-kuo, and returned to Japan three years later, bringing with him a number of paintings, including portraits of the third, fourth, fifth, sixth, and seventh patriarchs

---

[1] Reproduced, *Shēn Chou*, VI, 15, and *Burlington Magazine*, XXX (1917), 211. I am told that Lo Chēn-yü has published an article in which four versions of the picture are discussed.

[2] Or seventh ; there are several different enumerations.

of the Magic Sect. These are now preserved in the Tōji at Kyōto and are attributed to Li Chēn.

The third patriarch, Vajrabodhi, a Southern Indian, reached China in 719 and died there in 732. The picture of him, the first of the series, is hopelessly defaced. It cannot, of course (for Li Chēn was certainly not at work much earlier than 780), have been made from life. Nor can that of the fourth patriarch, Šubhākara, son of a Central Indian prince, who arrived in China in 716 and died there, aged ninety-nine, in 735.

The fifth patriarch, Amogha-vajra, a Northern Indian, who had enjoyed great prestige under the reign of Ming Huang, died in 774. The picture of him (as also those of his two predecessors) may well have been done from life. Fortunately it is in better condition than the rest. It is reproduced in *Kokka*, 198, in Curt Glaser's *Die Kunst Ostasiens*, and in many other books.

The portrait of Hui-kuo, Kōbō Daishi's teacher, is reproduced in *Kokka*, 344. The main figure is badly damaged, but that of the attendant, very delicately drawn, is almost intact. Hui-kuo died during Kōbō Daishi's visit, and was succeeded by I-hsing. His portrait, reproduced in *Kokka*, 345, is in exceedingly bad condition.

The importance of the above paintings is that they are the only certain works by a known T'ang master which survive. They confirm the impression that Chou Fang and his school had the good sense to realize the folly of apeing the arbitrary calligraphic outline of Wu Tao-tzŭ, a style too personal for imitation. They also have great interest as early specimens of Chinese portraiture.

Portraiture. We have seen that in early times portraiture occupied a preponderating place in Chinese painting. To the Chinese a portrait is not merely a picture which happens to take as its plastic basis the forms of a particular human being. The discovery that a human figure may be treated as impartially as a sack of potatoes, that Pontius Pilate and a coffee-pot are both "upright cylindrical masses," was—fortunately, I am sure most of my readers will say—never made by the Chinese. They never disentangled the forms they depicted from the human associations with which these forms were enveloped. They accepted portraiture as a composite art, an amalgam of picture-making and biography. But from the first they realized that it entailed something more than a mere transcription of the sitter's features. Thus Ku K'ai-chih speaks of *chuan-shēn*, "transmitting the (sitter's) soul," and to obtain this result literal representation must often be sacrificed. His theory assumes that a man's features and pose do not fully reveal his character; for if they did so, an accurate representation of the body would at the same time depict the inner qualities of the mind. *Chuan-shēn* therefore requires an act of psychological clairvoyance on the part of the painter; he must read the sitter's soul.

Portraiture of this kind has existed in Europe, often quite dissociated from plastic merit. Anders Zorn's etching of Renan, unimportant as a work of art, is a perfect example of *chuan-shēn*, an astounding caricature. So little survives from the great period of Chinese portrait-painting that we are unable to guess how far they pushed this art of *chuan-shen*, of pictorial psychometry. By the end of the 10th century landscape had gained complete supremacy and portraiture gradually fell into more and more mechanical hands. It was revived in the 16th and 17th centuries by the great literary painters, who loved to paint one another in landscape-settings or upon a background of rustic cottages, fruit-gardens, or the like. The minute figure of the " sitter " was cursory in treatment; the *chuan-shēn* went rather into the surroundings and accessories, which were made to typify the character of their owner, for the subject was generally a gentleman enjoying the amenities of his country estate.

The bourgeoisie imitated this *genre*. It became customary for a son to secure *hsiao-ching*, " small views," in which were commemorated the habits of his deceased parents. They were shown busy in the pursuit of their everyday occupations, the wife directing her household, the husband reading, writing, or drinking his cup of tea.

Funeral Portraits. Those who can afford to do so procure full-length, highly coloured portraits of their deceased parents. In some cases these portraits are made from life; but more often the painter is called in to draw the head after death. He then makes notes as to the proper costume in which to show the deceased, and finishes the picture at his workshop. The pose is always full-face, stiffly seated. An official is shown in his State robes and cap; a private person, in the ceremonial attire worn by the father when acting as high-priest of the family.

The portrait is carried in the funeral procession and afterwards hung up in the hall or in the ancestral temple of the dead man's clan, if such a temple exists. The object of these portraits is to afford a lodging-place for the soul of the deceased. Hence, that the soul may not realize that it is being tricked, an absolutely convincing likeness is necessary. " The painter is in many instances compelled to do the face over and over again, until he succeeds. . . ."[1] The funeral portrait has, in fact, a purely ritual

[1] De Groot, *Religious Systems of China*, I, 113.

aim. In a few cases it may chance to be a work of art, but the odds are heavily against it. The task which confronts the artist (if the funeral-painter happens, as is seldom the case, to be more than a mere artisan) is to weld into a plastic whole the realistically rendered features, the elaborate ceremonial costume and insignia, the highly ornamental arm-chair. A few of the earlier[1] portraits go some way towards achieving this; but the far more richly patterned and decorated costume of the Manchu dynasty made the problem definitely insoluble.

Large numbers of 18th and early 19th-century funeral portraits have found their way to Europe. They are, artistically speaking, some of the most repulsive paintings in existence.

ART CRITICISM IN THE T'ANG DYNASTY

The canons of the early writers were framed with reference to figure-painting, and their successors were reluctant to apply those standards to landscape. The author of the treatise on landscape-painting which is attributed to Wang Wei[2] enunciates few general principles, contenting himself with observations proper rather to a naturalist than to an æsthetician: " Wind without rain only affects the tree's branches, but rain without wind causes the tree-tops to nod. . . . When the rain clears the clouds pack away, the sky is pearly grey, a thin mist floats across the scene, the mountain is tinged with a deeper blue. . . . In summer, ancient trees cover the sky, waters run green and waveless, waterfalls seem to pierce the clouds. . . ."

Occasionally, however, he commits himself to a more general observation: " In landscape, the idea must come first: the carrying out of the idea follows." Or, again: " Ink-painting is the foremost branch of the whole art. It perfects nature and completes the Creator's work." In this last sentence, thrown off casually and not again referred to, we meet with a conception which has formed the basis of many European theories of art. Why he ranks ink-painting above other branches, Wang does not explain. " Profound truths," he says at the end of one essay, " cannot be explained in words," showing thereby his adherence to the teaching of Zen Buddhism.

Chang Yen-yüan, who lived in the middle of the 9th century, was an art-historian rather than a philosopher. His theory of art becomes apparent

---

[1] None earlier than Ming are, I think, at present known.
[2] The *Catalogue of the Four Libraries* regards it as a Sung forgery.

only incidentally in his writings. "Painting," he says, "perfects education, aids morality, explains to us the operations of the Spirit, helps us to penetrate the mysteries of Nature. It shares the merit of the Six Scripts and the potency of the Four Seasons. It proceeds not from effort, but from Nature."

One of the principal objects of painting is to record the actions of the virtuous. "Those who had distinguished themselves by loyalty or filial piety were portrayed in the Cloud Terrace Museum; those whose heroism had been conspicuous found their way to the galleries of the Unicorn Tower. The sight of good is in itself a warning against evil; the sight of evil arouses thoughts of virtue. . . . Ts'ao Chih says: 'There is no one who in front of a picture of the Three Kings and Five Emperors (the mythical paragons of Confucianism) would not raise his head in thankfulness; nor any that before a painting of the depraved monarchs of the Decadence would not heave a sigh. There is none who, contemplating the picture of a good and honest man, would not forget his meals; . . . nor any that coming upon the image of a licentious husband or abandoned wife would not hastily avert his gaze.'"

Chang, then, considered the aim of painting to be chiefly a moral one; but he lets slip certain reservations. It is something which "proceeds not from effort, but from Nature," and to this touch of mysticism he adds the doctrine of Hsieh Ho's first Canon. "Be the resemblance never so great," he says, "yet if the operation of the Spirit (*Ch'i-yün*) be lacking, it will be of no avail."

Chang Yen-yüan's (almost unconscious) art-philosophy refers solely to figure-painting; in his essay on "Landscape, trees, and rocks," he confines himself to retrospect and anecdote. He begins by complaining of the lack of realism in landscape-painting previous to Wu Tao-tzŭ: "The peaks of their mountains were like the teeth of a comb; their water does not look as if anything would float on it; the men are larger than the mountains!" "The revolution in landscape painting began with Wu and was completed by Li Ssŭ-hsün and his son." But in what this revolution consisted Chang does not tell us.

CHAPTER XIII
THE FIVE DYNASTIES

CHAPTER XIII

THE FIVE DYNASTIES

FIRST HALF OF THE 10TH CENTURY

At the beginning of the 10th century China dissolved into a number of minor kingdoms, some of which survived for a considerable time after the establishment of the Sung dynasty. These local courts were great centres of artistic activity. Civilization was for a while decentralized, as it had been under the feudal princes at the beginning of the Han dynasty. It was at this time that a new kind of poetry, the *t'ien-tz'ŭ*, which had already been played with experimentally by a few T'ang poets, became an accredited literary form. The man who raised it to this position was Li Hou-chu,[1] last Emperor of the Southern T'ang dynasty, deposed by the Sungs three years before his early death in 978. Many of his *tz'ŭ* were written after his deposition, when he was wandering forlornly through his former Empire, " High Heaven fallen among mortal men." I will quote one which I have translated elsewhere :

> *Immeasurable pain !*
> *My dreaming soul last night was king again.*
> *As in past days*
> *I wandered through the Palace of Delight,*
> *And in my dream*
> *Down grassy garden-ways*
> *Glided my chariot smoother than a summer stream ;*
> *There was moonlight,*
> *The trees were blossoming,*
> *And a faint wind softened the air of night,*
> *For it was Spring.*

It is said to have been at his Court that women first bound their feet, thus imparting to their gait a swaying motion which was found attractive by the æsthetes of the day. All the accessories of Li Hou-chu's life, his clothes, his fans, his food were of the most exquisite quality. Even the paper that he wrote on, manufactured by a firm called the Hall of Untroubled Thought, was of such surpassing texture that the writers and painters of the 11th century vied with one another in obtaining small strips of it.

The somewhat decadent splendours of his Court at Nanking were portrayed by Chou Wēn-chü, to whom is attributed the very much repainted *Court Ladies on a Terrace* in the British Museum.

[1] Giles, *Biographical Dictionary*, No. 1236. For an account of the *tz'ŭ* see *The Temple and Other Poems*.

165

It was often on the marvellous paper which I have mentioned that Hsü Hsi, another Court artist, painted his flower-pieces; or again he would use a wide-ribbed silk, " coarse as cotton-cloth." Two paintings at the Chionin, Kyōto (" Lotus in the Wind " and " Lotus and White Heron ") are doubtfully attributed to him.[1] So is a " Bird on Apple-tree Bough," reproduced in *Kokka*, No. 88. His works became very rare at an early date. The Ch'ien Lung Collection contained one specimen entitled " Riches and Honour in the Jade Hall." This would seem to have been a figure-subject.

Of his style we know little except that it was always contrasted with the highly realistic manner of his contemporary Huang Ch'üan, who worked at the Court of the Latter Shu emperors in Western China. Both painters are said sometimes to have dispensed with ink-outlines. Hsü Hsi sketched directly from nature in light washes of colour; Huang Ch'üan painted (without preliminary groundwork) in minutely applied opaque colours.

Another painter who worked in Western China was the priest Kuan-hsiu. Born in 832, he became a novice at the age of seven. During the early part of his life it was as a poet that he chiefly distinguished himself. I have read his poetical works.[2] They seem to me to be highly conventional and colourless, which has indeed been the general verdict of posterity. About the year 895 he was summoned to the Court of Ch'ien Liu, who was ruling at Hangchow. Soon afterwards he moved to Ch'ēng-tu, the capital of the Latter Shu State, and it was here, when he was already well over sixty, that he did his most important work. His biography[3] tells us nothing else about him that is to the point, save that he was short and fat.

There are in Japan several sets of Lohan which are attributed to Kuan-hsiu.[4] The most famous is that which belongs to the Kōdaiji, Kyōto. This was brought from China in the 12th century.[5] There is a similar series at the Shōmyōji (Kanazawa), and another (which has not, so far as I know, been published) at the Tōkaian. At the Bukkokuji in Fushimi there is a set of thirty-two Kwannons, illustrating the aspects of the Merciful One, which are described in the *Saddharmapundarīka Sūtra;* these, too, are ascribed to Kuan-hsiu.

But the series which Japanese connoisseurs consider to be his most

---

[1] *Tōyō*, VIII.

[2] The *Hsi Yo Chi*, recently republished in the series *Ssū Pu Ts'ung K'an*, Shanghai.

[3] Translated by Chavannes, *Journal Asiatique*, 1916 (Sept.–Oct.), p. 298.

[4] The Japanese usually call him Zengetsu Daishi.

[5] See *Tōyō*, VIII, or *Shimbi Taikwan*, VI, 9. *Kokka*, 253.

authentic work is in a completely different style from those mentioned above. This is the set of Lohan which belongs to Baron Takahashi (Plates XXXI and XXXII). It was published in a separate volume by the *Shimbi Shoin* in 1909. I am told that the originals have been extensively repainted. Finally, Ch'ien Lung possessed a large kakemono in black and white, representing the Eighteen Lohan. The paintings attributed to Kuan-hsiu in Japan are, I think, all in colour.

The problem of Kuan-hsiu remains to be solved. It is possible that the Takahashi Lohan, if allowance be made for repainting, are, after all, by the same hand as the other sets. Kuan-hsiu was over sixty when he painted his great series of Lohan at Ch'ēng-tu. May not the Takahashi set (which stands nearer to T'ang than to Sung art) be an *œuvre de jeunesse*? Students of European art have realized that if the connecting links were missing it would often be difficult to detect that the earliest and latest works of a master were by the same hand.

The *I-chou Ming-hua Lu*, or " History of Painting at Ch'ēng-tu," gives a description of Kuan-hsiu's style which presumably applies to the work he did at Ch'ēng-tu, that is to say, in his old age. It concords exactly with the Kōdaiji series, but not at all with the Takahashi set : " He painted the Sixteen Lohan in a style modelled upon that of Yen Li-pēn, some with *bushy eyebrows* and huge eyes, some with pendulous cheeks and *high-hooked noses*, some leaning against pine-sheltered rocks, some sitting amid hills and streams. Every outlandish type was there, whether of Indian or Persian mien and countenance. To those that asked him where he had seen such men, he answered, ' I saw them in a dream.' His ' Ten Disciples of Shākyamuni ' was in the same style, and all who saw it were amazed."

Kuan-hsiu does not occupy an important place in native works on Chinese painting, nor have European writers paid much attention to him. Yet he (or, if you will, the artist of the Takahashi Lohan) is the first great individual painter whose work still exists, or at least the first whose works are of purely plastic rather than of historical importance. Indeed, to many European students of Chinese art his Lohan will, I think, in the future seem to be the most important of all Chinese pictures which have survived.

THE LIANG KINGDOM (907–923 A.D.)

This local dynasty was founded by a rather disreputable adventurer named Chu Wēn.[1] His capital was first at Pien-chou (the modern K'ai-fēng Fu) and afterwards at Lo-yang. Unlike the local monarchs of Ch'ēng-tu and

[1] Giles, *Biographical Dictionary*, No. 475.

Nanking he was not a patron of art, but it happened that the two great landscape-painters of the period were his subjects.

Ching Hao. Ching Hao fled from the disorders which marked the close of the T'ang dynasty to a secluded valley of the T'ai-hang range, and there took to painting as a distraction in his solitude. He also composed a treatise on landscape-painting, from which I shall presently quote a few passages. He used to say : " Wu Tao-tzŭ in painting landscape had brush (i.e. outline) but not ink (i.e. tone). Hsiang Jung had ink, but not brush. What I want to do is to combine the two styles." He was not only a landscape-painter ; at the Shrine of the Twin Forests in Lo-yang he painted a fresco of " Avalokitēśvara upon Mount Potalaka."[1]

Kuan T'ung. Kuan T'ung set himself to imitate with passionate assiduity the works of Ching Hao, " eschewing both sleep and food." Of his landscapes an 11th-century critic[2] writes : " The jagged summits of the crest, the uttermost caverns of the abyss, giant precipices gashing the mountainside—all such strange cloven or tapering forms he could depict with a single sweep of the brush, swiftly these rose under his hand as a spring that darts from the earth. Blue mists lying on lofty rocks, stones and soil of wood and dene ; far-spreading distances, interminable causeways disappearing at last among remote hills, bridges and stiles, hamlets and dykes half-wrapped in cloudy dimness—all these he could portray. . . ."

" Most of all," says the Hui Tsung catalogue,[3] " it delighted him to paint autumn hills and wintry forests, with groups of cottages, river-crossings, hermits, recluses, fishermen selling their catch, mountain-hostelries. Look well at his picture and you will find yourself suddenly transported to the scenes which it portrays. You are standing, perhaps, ' on Pa Bridge[4] amid the wind and snow,' or travelling up the Three Gorges[5] ' where gibbons scream from either shore.' You who but a moment ago were a common courtier or grubber in the dusty markets of the world are suddenly transformed.

" Kuan T'ung's style," the writer of the catalogue continues, " is indeed negligent and swift ; yet the more cursory his strokes, the stronger grows the soul[6] of the picture ; the smaller his scene, the deeper his conception."

[1] Concerning this cult, see Eliot, *Hinduism and Buddhism*, II, 15.
[2] Quoted, *Shu Hua P'u*, 49, 2.
[3] *Circa* 1120, quoted, *Shu Hua P'u*, 49, 3.
[4] In Shensi. I think the lines of poetry are quoted from Wang Wei.
[5] On the Yangtze.
[6] *Ch'i*, " spirit."

Kuan T'ung was, in fact, the inventor of the typical Chinese " landscape with figures," the remote ancestor of thousands of pictures, thousands of fans ; indeed, of a whole pictorial world stretching down from the 10th century to the days of the Willow Pattern. The Ch'ien Lung Collection contained two pictures attributed to him ; the one, a long roll in ink, entitled " Autumn Hills and Distance " ; the other, a coloured kakemono, " Causeways in the Mountains of Ssechuan."

CHING HAO'S ESSAY

By a pleasant literary artifice Ching Hao puts his precepts into the mouth of an old man whom he met whilst sketching pine-trees on the Hill of the Sacred Gong, in the T'ai-hang Range.

" Painting," the old man said, " is delineation[1] ; to measure the shapes of things, yet with grasp of Truth ; to express outward form as outward form, and inner reality as inner reality. Outward forms must not be taken as inner realities. If this is not understood, resemblance may indeed be achieved, but not pictorial Truth. A ' resemblance ' reproduces form, but neglects spirit ; but Truth shows spirit and substance in like perfection. . . . In landscape painting there are six essentials—*Spirit, Harmony, Thought, Atmosphere, Brush,* and *Ink. Spirit* makes the heart travel with the brush and seize unerringly the shapes of things. *Harmony,* without visible contours, suggests form ; omits nothing, yet escapes vulgarity. *Thought* segregates the essential and concentrates the mind on the shapes of things.

" The master of *Atmosphere,*[2] while yet observing the laws of the seasons, can search out the Mysterious and establish Inner Truth. The master of thr *Brush,* though he follow the laws and ordinance of painting, can yet move among them unimpeded ; all is flight and motion, nothing solid or fixed. The master of *Ink* can heighten or lower his tone at will, to express the depth or shallowness of things ; creating what seems like a natural brilliancy, not derived from the line-work of the brush. Again, there are four categories : *The Divine, The Mysterious, The Marvellous,* and *The Skilful.* The *Divine Painter* makes no effort of his own ; his hand spontaneously reproduces natural forms. The *Mysterious Painter* first experiences in imagination the instincts and passions of all things that exist in heaven or earth ; then, in a style appropriate to the subject, natural forms flow spontaneously from his hand. The *Marvellous Painter* is profuse in ill-considered forms. Often while achieving resemblance in

---

[1] Or delimitation. There is here a play on two senses of the Chinese word *hua.* I may mentioned that I have used the text of the *Hua Hsüeh Hsin Yin,* checked by that of the *Shu Hua P'u.*   [2] Lit. " seasonal aspect."

detail, he misses the universal principles of the view before him. This is the result of mechanical dexterity without intelligence. The *Skilful Painter* scrapes together little prettinesses and welds them into the pretence of a masterpiece. But the more he loads his design with decoration, the further it recedes from the true spirit of the scene which he depicts. This is called excess of outward forms with poverty of inner meaning. . . . There are two kinds of faults. Those that depend upon representation, and those that do not. When flowers or trees are out of season, when a man is larger than a house, or a tree taller than a mountain, when a bridge does not rest on its banks, these are demonstrable faults of form. . . . But when the operation of the spirit is weak, all the forms are defective ; and though the brush be active, its productions are like dead things—then we speak of ' faults unconnected with representation.' "

Then follow notes on the " growth " of different trees, on the technical terminology of landscape painting, and on the painters of antiquity. The essay closes with an ode in praise of pine-woods. Unlike Chang Yen-yüan, Ching Hao does not demand that art should be " improving." He takes Hsieh Ho's philosophy of figure-painting and adapts it to landscape. It did not occur to him to take into account anything outside his own branch of painting, still less to construct a general philosophy even of the plastic arts. But he shows a vivid perception of the fact that art consists of something more than mere representation, and by leaving certain vital questions unanswered, at any rate avoids falling into the absurdities which entrapped his successor, Kuo Hsi.

CHAPTER XIV
NORTHERN SUNG
HUI TSUNG AND THE ACADEMY
KUO CHUNG-SHU AND BOUNDARY-PAINTING

NORTHERN SUNG

HUI TSUNG AND THE ACADEMY
KUO CHUNG-SHU AND BOUNDARY-PAINTING

In the latter part of the T'ang dynasty society had been lacerated by the contentions of the rival parties which supported Confucianism and Buddhism. The Sung Emperors were determined not to take sides in this dispute, and from the first they gave equal support to both parties. During the Five Dynasties Buddhism had been gradually recovering from the blow dealt to it in 845. The Zen sect, which dispensed with the worship of superhuman cult-figures, was becoming predominant; such divinities as survived tended to shed their remote celestial splendours and to appear in friendly humanized forms.

Avalokiteśvara was more popular than ever, particularly as The White-robed One and The Dweller amid the Rocks. The Lohan and Vimala-kīrti, who were patriarchs rather than divinities, were also in favour; so was Vaiśravana crossing the Ocean. Portraits of famous priests tend to replace cult-images of Bodhisattvas. But Shākyamuni, Bhaishajya (The Medicine Buddha), and Vairochana (The Sun Buddha) still occasionally appear; and, among the familiar Bodhisattvas, Kshitigarbha and Mahās-thāmaprāpta. Only Amitābha (Amida), the central figure of the Trinity, who was already dwindling in the T'ang dynasty, has now completely vanished.

A great deal of fresco-painting was done in the temples at Pien-ching, the familiar T'ang subjects still being preferred. Thus we read of walls being decorated with Hell Scenes, the Miracles of Maitreya, Devarājas and dragons.

Sung Philosophy. Europeans, having heard of Confucius as philosopher, have often been surprised on referring to his works to discover that there is not in them a particle of what we in Europe have generally associated with the term philosophy. They are astonished to find in his sayings no enquiry into the nature of knowledge, or truth, or of good, but only dogmatic assertions about the right sort of bonnet to wear or the most genteel way to lie in bed. Yet we are told that since the Middle Ages Confucianism has served the Chinese not only as a philosophy, but even as a substitute for religion. The reputation of Confucius has naturally led the Europeans to suppose that he founded a school of thought as (say) Hegel did, and that his followers merely continued to develop his speculation in this direction or that. Such a belief ignores the peculiar conditions under which the mediæval philosophies developed.[1] Every philosopher was the servant of some Church; his task consisted in pushing freedom of thought to the farthest point consistent with the articles of his faith. In India schools of philosophy grew up which, while making formal allegiance to the Buddhist Church and pledged to its cardinal doctrines, pushed their independence as far as the " rules of the game " would permit. Such, again, was the philosophy of the Arabs and the scholasticism of our own schoolmen. What we call Confucianism, the system erected fifteen hundred years after the Sage's death by the Sung philosophers, was not a system of thought founded by Confucius, any more than Mahomedan philosophy was founded by Mahomet; it was a school of speculation which deliberately circumscribed itself by the dogmatic teachings of Confucius. The intellectual sport of these Sung schoolmen consisted in concocting ingenious links between their own cosmic speculations and the practical dogmatism of the Master.

Between the period of Confucius and the foundation of the Sung school, Confucianism showed very little sign of transforming itself into anything like a philosophy. In the Han and T'ang dynasties it consisted chiefly in textual criticism. With the rise of Buddhist philosophy the monasteries became the principal seats of intellectual life. The Confucians, who cut a ludicrous figure whenever they attempted to compete with intelligences such as that of the great Buddhist teacher Hsüan Tsang, retrieved their discomfiture by a marvellous outburst of poetry. Only the stolid Han Yü (died 824 A.D.) raised any noteworthy protest against the spread of Buddhist thought; but it is as a Conservative politician, not as a philosopher, that he argues in his famous anti-Buddhist tract. Some thirty years later the Conservatives triumphed; Buddhism was proscribed; and only one sect, that of Dhyāna or Zen, ever again influenced Chinese thought. Against the subtleties of Indian metaphysic the Confucians had had no chance of making any kind of fight; against the somewhat decadent and largely de-Indianized mysticism of the Zen sect they found themselves at last in the 11th century able, with the aid of much Imperial encouragement, to hold up their heads. Most of the Sung philosophers had studied Buddhism, all were deeply indebted to it and correspondingly virulent in their denunciation of it. Chu Hsi[2] (whose teaching, though he lived under the Southern Sung dynasty, was to a large extent a commentary upon the works of his Northern Sung predecessors) began as a Buddhist. Subse-

[1] See above, p. 91.   [2] See J. P. Bruce, *Philosophy of Human Nature*, p. 199.

quently he had great difficulties with his pupils, who, impregnated with Buddhism, insisted on interpreting his scientific observations in a mystic sense. Thus after listening to the tolling of a temple bell he makes a remark which his pupil understands as meaning that the sound of the bell has caused in him one of those sudden intuitive apprehensions of Truth at which some of the Zen sects arrived.[1] " That is not at all what I meant," protests Chu Hsi. " I was only remarking upon the rapidity of thought, and pointing out how before one stroke of the bell has ceased to sound the mind has passed through an infinity of transitions."

The early Chinese cosmogoners believed that the universe had once been an undifferentiated Chaos. This Chaos ultimately divided itself into two principles, Positive and Negative, which in combination produced the huge brood of phenomenal existence. The Han philosophers made various very unsuccessful attempts to account for the splitting up of Chaos into two elements. The Sung philosophers much more reasonably postulated an aboriginal, eternal duality of Positive and Negative, Active and Passive, Matter and Spirit. Between these two poles all things perpetually alternate. What lives is slipping towards death ; what is dead is creeping towards life. (Freud, in the new view which he sets forth in " Jenseits des Lustprinzips," comes very close to the Sung school.) The great problem of Confucianism was the problem of evil. To the deist this problem consists mainly in the question : Why does God, who is supposed to be good, appear to behave so wickedly ? To the Chinese materialist it consisted in the question : Why does man, whose very name (*jēn*) implies generosity and love, generally behave as ruthlessly as a tiger ? To this question Mencius replied that man's nature is good. He sins only in ignorance ; if he has apprehended good, he will pursue it. Hsün Tzǔ (3rd century B.C.) held that man's nature is evil ; Yang Tzǔ (1st century B.C.), that it is a mixture of good and ill. Han Yü, to whom we have already referred, would accept none of these theories. It was evident to him that the natures of Conservatives like himself were good ; but it was equally evident that the nature of a Liberal (such as Po Chü-i) must be bad. So he divided natures into classes ranging from good to bad. Finally, Chu Hsi sensibly declared that it is not true to say of any man that his nature is good or bad. Its actual state at any minute depends upon the balance of the two elements, Active and Passive, of which our nature is composed.

[1] For Zen, see next chapter

175

CHINESE PAINTING

THE NEW SOCIAL CONFLICT

The conflict between Buddhism and Confucianism continued during the 11th century, but in a more definitely political form. In 1069 Wang An-shih, the leader of the Radicals, introduced his great programme of economic and administrative reform. In order to secure the support of some at least of his adversaries he represented each of his proposals as being founded upon some injunction of the Confucian Canon. This involved a new critical interpretation of the Confucian texts. There is, I think, no doubt that Wang An-shih's vastly ingenious glosses (reminding one of Verrall at his most reckless moments) were parodies of the current methods of interpretation.

His opponents (they had been his friends and admirers a few years before) were no mere coterie of obstructionists or die-hards. Foremost among them was Ou-yang Hsiu, poet, archæologist, and historian; he had been Wang An-shih's earliest patron. Although a theoretical opponent of Buddhism, he maintained friendly relations with priests; his gentle, easy-going nature made him a very different Conservative Leader from Han Yü.

To a slightly younger generation belonged Ssŭ-ma Kuang, to whom we owe the *Mirror of History*,[1] upon which the current European histories of China are based. The idea of turning history into a Confucian text-book had already occurred to Han Yü, to whom edification seemed a nobler object than mere truth.

The most remarkable man of this generation was Su Tung-p'o. He thought the proposals of Wang An-shih impracticable and resisted them with all his power; but in the cast of his mind there was no Confucian rigidity. His hero was Po Chü-i, between whose life and his own he loved to find or imagine analogies. The very name " Tung-p'o," by which he is best known to posterity, was adopted by him in allusion to Po Chü-i's garden on the Eastern Embankment (Tung-p'o) at Chung-chou, where Po consoled the days of his remotest exile among

Red flowers that hang like evening's clouds,
White flowers that gleam like a fall of snow.

Su Tung-p'o's own poetry is very varied. Sometimes he imitates T'ao Ch'ien, sometimes Po Chü-i, or again writes in a somewhat fantastic whimsical vein of his own. In one poem he sympathizes with the pre-

---

[1] Completed in 1084, carried down to Ming times by subsequent writers. Upon it are based Wieger's *Textes Historiques* and (indirectly) Cordier's *Histoire Générale de la Chine.*

dicament of God assailed by so many conflicting prayers. The boatmen going down the river pray for a west wind ; the returning boatmen for the reverse. Those who are sowing, for rain ; those who are hoeing, for fine weather. This train of thought was suggested to the poet by the fact that his boatmen, when the ship was becalmed, insisted upon his disembarking to pray for wind at a neighbouring shrine.

He was a great botanist and observer of nature. His curiosity was unbounded. He not only discovered that plants had sex, but discoursed as learnedly as Mr. Julian Huxley upon hermaphroditism in the poultry-yard. Here is one of his poems :

MOUNT LU

From that side it seems a peak ;
From this side, a range.
View it from on high, view it from below,—
It is never twice the same.
How comes it that we cannot know
This mountain's real form ?
It is, oh friend, it is that we
Are dwellers on the Mount of Lu.

In this poem Mount Lu represents the " World of Happening and Being-so " (*Der Sinn der Welt muss ausserhalb ihrer liegen*).[1]

THE ACADEMY

The foundation of the Painting Academy is usually ascribed to Li Hou-chu, ruler of the fragmentary Southern T'ang Empire. When, in the middle of the 10th century, China was reunited, painters from the various local Courts thronged to the new capital and placed themselves at the Sung Emperor's disposal. The Academy was as yet merely a department of the Literary College. The Emperor Hui Tsung (1100–1127) being himself a painter did not suffer the Academy to remain an appanage of the Literary College, but organized it into a State Department of equal importance. Ministers were chosen not only because of their proficiency in the Classics and in defunct forms of literary composition, but also frequently because of their skill in painting. Painting examinations were instituted, modelled as closely as possible upon the literary examinations. The themes set by the examiners were discussed by the candidates pictorially instead of in writing. Painting became, in fact, a new branch of literature.

[1] Wittgenstein, *Tractatus Logico-philosophicus*, p. 182.

Professor Giles[1] has given several examples of the puerile ingenuity with which the candidates acquitted themselves of their task. Thus when the line,

The hoof of the steed comes back laden with the scent of trampled flowers,

was set as the subject, the winning candidate solved this difficult problem of illustration by painting a cluster of butterflies following at a horse's heels, thus showing that the hoofs were scent-laden.

HUI TSUNG

He came to the throne at the age of nineteen in 1100–1. The associates of his youth had been Wang Shēn (who had married his sister) and Chao Ta-nien. Both were literary men and painters, cultivated members of the ultra-Conservative *haute-noblesse*. The first was known for his romantic pictures of Fairyland painted in green, blue, and gold ; hardly distinguishable, we are told, from the landscapes of the T'ang painter Li Ssŭ-hsün. The second (also a member of the Imperial family and a cousin of Hui Tsung's) imitated the poetic landscapes of Wang Wei. Possibly such pictures as the " Autumn " and " Winter " reproduced in the second volume of *Shimbi Taikwan* belong to the period when the young prince was still under the influence of his brother-in-law Wang Shēn and his cousin Chao Ta-nien. In 1101, accident set this cultured aristocrat upon the throne ; for Minister it gave him Ts'ai Ching, Wang An-shih's successor, a Reformer and Realist of commanding personality. The Minister was fifty-five and had long experience of office ; the sovereign was in his 'teens, knew much of art and books, but nothing of politics. It was natural that he should fall completely under Ts'ai's sway. The political aspects of this influence do not here concern us ; but Ts'ai was also interested (from a political point of view) in art and learning. In the first year of Hui Tsung's reign the following regulations were issued in regard to the study of painting at the Academy : " Painters are not to imitate their predecessors, but to depict objects as they exist, true to colour and form. Simplicity and nobility of line is to be their aim."

That these recommendations proceeded rather from Ts'ai Ching, with his fierce hatred of obsolete conventions, than from the young Emperor who had been trained to a romantic veneration for ancient art and learning, is assumed by Wieger,[2] and can hardly be questioned. But gradually the new Emperor found his feet. The influence of Ts'ai Ching waned, and

[1] *Chinese Pictorial Art*, p. 137.   [2] Wieger, *Textes historiques*, III, p. 1873.

178

Hui Tsung reverted to the respectable theories of his boyhood. In 1106 he dismissed the Radical leader and six years of reaction followed. In 1112 Ts'ai was recalled, to be finally ejected eleven years later when the Sung empire was already tottering.

As a painter Hui Tsung was chiefly famous for his realistic pictures of birds and flowers. " In painting birds he gave them eyes of lacquer the size of a bean, which stood out in relief," says Tēng Ch'un, writing about 1180 A.D. The *Hua Shih Hui Yao* tells us that he " excelled in mono-chrome paintings of rocks and flowers. His method in ink-paintings of bamboos was very tight and minute. He used one tone of dry ink without gradations (without *nōtan*, as the Japanese would say), getting the effect of density, where required, by letting less of the white ground show." His glorification of extreme realism was evidently only a phase. However, of the sixteen paintings by him which the Emperor Ch'ien Lung possessed only two were landscapes. Almost all the rest were realistic bird-and-flower paintings.

Hui Tsung was a great collector. I have frequently referred to the catalogue of his paintings. He also accumulated in his palaces enormous quantities of books, bronzes, and *objets de vertu*, which were also described in catalogues which still survive. The greater part of all these treasures was destroyed when the Tartars captured K'ai-fēng in 1127. Hui Tsung himself died in captivity in 1135 at the age of fifty-two.[1]

OTHER BIRD-AND-FLOWER PAINTERS

The Northern Sung dynasty produced a vast number of bird-and-flower painters. Their works passed into the huge collection of Hui Tsung and for the most part perished during the sack of Pien-ching.

The name of Chao Ch'ang is of special interest to European students of Chinese painting, because it is inscribed upon the well-known picture of Two Geese which is now at the British Museum.

Chao Ch'ang. He was a native of Ch'ēng-tu, the capital of Sse-chuan. He lived in the early years of the 11th century and was the most celebrated flower-painter of his time.

" His paintings of plucked flowers all give the impression of life and growth ; his methods of colouring were particularly subtle. Every

---

[1] He died at Wu-kuo Ch'ēng (" Castle of the Five Lands "), which according to one account lay in the modern Manchurian province of Kirin, close to its Korean frontier. But a " tomb of Hui Tsung " is shown at Hwe-yöng in the Korean province of Hyam-gyong.

morning, just as the dew was falling, he wandered round the flower-beds with his brush and colours in his hand, painting as he walked. He gave himself the nickname 'Paint-from-Life.' He painted in successive washes of water-colour, never using solid or opaque pigments. The surface of his pictures was absolutely even, and it was by this peculiarity that his genuine works were recognized by connoisseurs, who would pass a finger across the silk, and if there was the least ' relievo,' pronounce the work to be a forgery.[1]

" He was not so good at painting birds and rocks. In his later years he bought up many of his own paintings, so that genuine specimens became more difficult than ever to procure."

So rare was his work that the Emperor Ch'ien Lung possessed only one painting by him—a roll of " insects and butterflies."

Another source[2] tells us that he was a man of haughty pride, one that would bow neither to violence nor authority. His life was spent in wandering through the lands of Pa and Shu, Tzǔ and Sui.[3]

He took his first lessons in painting from the 10th-century painter T'ēng Ch'ang-yu, but soon surpassed him. Magistrates and Governors vied with one another in acquiring his paintings; but Ch'ang was very loath to part with them. In the early years of the 11th century one Ting Chu-ai sent him a present of five hundred pieces of silver. Ch'ang felt touched, and went to thank him in person. Chu-ai pressed him into the Hall of Reception and begged him to paint from life a few leaves of lettuce, a ripe melon, and some other fruit. Ch'ang painted what was set before him and then went away without a word.

THE TWO GEESE

It is convenient to discuss this picture here. The fact that Chao Ch'ang's name is written upon it is not, however, of much significance.

The outlines of the design (which are very harsh and contrast strangely with the extreme sensitivity with which the heads, tail-feathers, etc., are rendered) seem to have been determined by strokes made from outwards, towards the outline of the birds. It therefore seems likely that the picture originally had a background. This background became hopelessly damaged by damp or the like, and was deleted by some restorer with acid. The bleached silk of the background was then darkened to the tone of old silk. If my surmise is right, what we possess is only a fragment of the

---

[1] I disagree with Giles's translation of this passage, *Chinese Pictorial Art*, p. 111.
[2] See *Shu Hua P'u*, L, 28.   [3] i.e. the province of Sse-chuan.

original design. It is by no means certain that it dates from the Sung period.

THE BAMBOO

Petrucci, in his *Encyclopédie de la Peinture Chinoise*, has spoken of the bamboo as the symbol " de la sagesse et de la fermeté." It seems to me that the Chinese have regarded the bamboo rather as the symbol of culture, of refinement, of " gentility " in the mediæval sense of the word. There is the story of Wang Hui-chih, son of the famous calligraphist Wang Hsi-chih, who " if he stayed for a while in lodgings or even in an empty house, would always plant a clump of bamboo outside his window." " Is gardening worth while when you are making so short a stay ? " some one once asked him. Wang Hui-chih, pointing to the bamboo which he had planted, answered with a sigh, " I cannot live a day without the company of these dear gentlemen."

The word which I have translated " gentlemen " means " prince," " lord," " aristocratic," and there is emphasis upon it. The bamboo, then, is the symbol of high-breeding, fastidious taste, of what the Chinese call *fēng-liu* (which is the opposite of vulgarity). It can bring distinction and grace even into the squalor of casual surroundings. An account of the history of bamboo-painting in China is given by Li K'an[1] in a famous essay, which begins with an account of his own career. His first masters were Wang T'ing-yün and Wang Man-ch'ing, two northern painters who had lived under the Tartar occupation.[2] Both of them founded their style upon that of Wēn T'ung, the close friend of Su Tung-p'o, who died suddenly at the age of forty-odd in 1079.

Both Su Tung-p'o and Huang T'ing-chien, of whose literary eminence Li K'an stood in awe, had declared that Wēn T'ung's was the " true style " of bamboo-painting. It is evident from what we know of Wēn T'ung that he was a man of extremely attractive personality. The admiration of his contemporaries for his painting may have been in part a tribute to the charm of his character. But for Li K'an the commendation of such men as Su and Huang was a sufficient guarantee. He set out upon one of those curious quests, so common in the art-history of China, a country where archælogical curiosity has always been so intense and the means of gratifying it so exiguous. It is as though a modern artist, convinced by the testimony of Macaulay that Sir Thomas Lawrence alone possessed the art of portraiture, should be forced to spend a dozen years in discovering

---

[1] *Shu Hua P'u*, 53, 4. He lived *c.* 1240–1310.   [2] See below, p. 203.

a genuine Lawrence and the rest of his life in extracting from the true masterpiece those secrets which in this latter age the Gods no longer bestow.

At last, in 1285, he was shown at Nanking what he believed to be a genuine Wēn T'ung. He traced it with oiled paper and went away happy. Soon afterwards this picture and three others by Wēn T'ung passed into his possession. Armed with these documents he rejected all that he had learnt from his early teacher, and began the study of bamboo-painting anew.

He was now assailed by a fresh curiosity concerning the origin of his *métier*. He chanced to come across a stone incision after a bamboo-painting by Wang Wei. He realized that such a crude method of reproduction would give him no idea of the original, but it proved that the *genre* existed as early as the 8th century. Soon afterwards he found a coloured bamboo-painting by Po Chü-i's friend, Hsiao Yüeh. It was in bad condition, but opened up new vistas, for the models which he had hitherto studied had been monochromes. Finally, he became the possessor of a fine coloured painting of bamboos by the 10th-century master Li P'o. Upon this material he built a new and more authentically archaic style. The origin of monochrome bamboo-painting is, in fact, uncertain. It is traditionally associated with the name of Wu Tao-tzŭ.

LANDSCAPE

The Southern School. The successors of Ching Hao and Kuan T'ung were Chü-jan (a priest), Li Ch'ēng, Tung Yüan, and Fan K'uan,[1] all of whom lived at the beginning of the Sung dynasty. This line of painters (together with their successors) was afterwards known as the Southern School. The distinction is not a geographical one. About 684 the Zen sect of Buddhism split into two schools. The legitimate sixth patriarch, Hui-nēng, continued to reside in Anhui; his unsuccessful rival, Shēn-hsiu, in answer to the summons of the Empress Wu-hou, established himself at Ch'ang-an. " Instead of commanding his presence at Court, the Empress came in a litter to his lodgings and actually knelt down before him. The friendship of this capable but murderous woman procured for him temporal dignities which in the eyes of the world completely outshone the rustic piety of the Sixth Patriarch, Shēn-hsiu, at the capital became as it were the Temporal Father of Zen, while Hui-nēng at his country monastery remained its spiritual Pope. The successors of Hui-nēng became known

[1] Thus enumerated by Tung Ch'i-ch'ang. His contemporary Mo Shih-lung makes Li Ch'ēng the founder of the Northern School!

as the Fathers of the Southern School; while the courtly and social Zen of Shēn-hsiu is called Zen of the North."[1]

Such, at any rate, is the popular view of the two Zen Schools. It probably does not do justice to the philosophic side of Northern Zen. It was on the analogy of Zen history that the writers of the 16th century invented an "apostolic" succession of landscape painters, beginning with Wang Wei and continuing with the painters whom I have named at the beginning of this section. The distinction emanated from partisans of the Southern style; they lumped together as Northern all painters who did not seem to them to belong to the true apostolic line. Furthest beyond the pale were the followers of Li Ssŭ-hsün, who painted only "the world's outer show," the miniaturists with their heavy blues, greens, and gold outline. Less wholly reprobate were those Sung "Northerners" who, using as their basis the style of contour-line typical of Li Ssŭ-hsün, developed styles of bold monochrome and impressionistic tinted sketch.

Such was the theory; but it was not developed till a comparatively late time. Sixteenth and seventeenth century writers talk glibly about the minutiæ of Wang Wei's style, but upon what is their patter based? We know that Tung Ch'i-ch'ang, who was in a better position than any one else in China to see ancient paintings, spent his whole life searching for a genuine Wang Wei.

The Patriarchs were not nearly so orthodox as their successors. We are told, for example, that Li Ch'ēng often used Li Ssŭ-hsün's method; so did Tung Yüan. Chinese information about the painters of the Southern School is singularly monotonous. The biographical information given by Professor Giles in his *Pictorial Art* is quite adequate, and I must leave the discussion of their work to those who in the future are fortunate enough to discover it. But before I close this chapter I want to give an account of certain painters who stand somewhat apart.

KUO CHUNG-SHU

Born about 920 A.D., he entered the service of the Latter Chou dynasty (one of the local kingdoms which preceded the Sung dynasty) somewhere about 951. One day, excited by drink, he came to blows with the Imperial Censor in the Government Hall. The Censor impeached him, but Chung-shu stole the indictment from the official who should have carried it to the Throne, and destroyed it. He was then sent as Military Secretary

---

[1] See below, p. 222.

to Kienchau in Hunan. Here again in a fit of drunkenness he struck a fellow-official and, without permission, quitted his place of exile. Henceforward he wandered aimlessly about the country, drinking as much wine as he could get and greeting with ribaldry all whom he encountered, " whether peasant or prince." If the scenery of a district pleased him, he would linger for a week or two. " He could go without food for a month ; in the summer he could expose himself all day to the sun and take no harm ; in winter when the rivers were frozen he would hack away the ice and bathe in the hole that he had made.

" He was a skilful painter, particularly of intricate groups of buildings. He would often go to the house of some prince or great gentleman in the hope of getting wine. His host, you may be sure, would spread painting-silk upon the wall, and, if the humour seized him, Chung-shu would paint a picture in quittance of his entertainment. The Emperor T'ai Tsung[1] summoned him to Court, gave him a large allowance, and lodged him in the Imperial Collection, where he was set to work upon a history of Chinese epigraphy. But he proved to be incapable of working methodically or according to a set plan. The Emperor recognized his genius and treated his eccentricities with great forbearance." When, however, he took to spreading slanders about members of the Cabinet and selling government property for his own benefit, the Emperor lost patience with this Autolycus and banished him to Shantung (977 A.D.).

When he had reached the outskirts of Ch'i-chou he turned suddenly to his companions and cried, " I am going to die." He then scooped in the ground a hole large enough to admit his head, peered into it, and died. The friends who not long afterwards came to remove the body found it " light as a cicada's shell."

CHIEH-HUA (" Boundary Paintings ")

The Ch'ien Lung Collection contained three paintings by Chung-shu. Two were copies of Wang Wei ; the third, of Ku K'ai-chih. But he is best known for his elaborate architectural painting. " He painted pagodas and palaces set among the hills with an accuracy and minuteness that contrasted strangely with the wild lawlessness of his life."[2] He is credited with the invention of *Chieh-hua*, " boundary painting," a style upon which the 14th-century writer T'ang Hou makes the following remarks :—

" It is commonly said that there are thirteen branches of painting, of which the first is landscape and the last ' boundary-painting.' This has

[1] 976–998 A.D.   [2] *Shu Hua P'u*, LXXXII, 19.

led to the assumption that 'boundary-painting' is an easy matter. Squares, circles, angles, lines, relations of height and distance, recession and projection involve difficulties which even the most skilful carpenters and architects cannot wholly master. How much the less is the manipulation of such matters a simple task for the painter who seeks with brush, ink, ink-stone, and foot-rule to commit his conception to silk or paper, who must accommodate his design to the plumb-string! Every other branch of painting has its typical representative in ancient times. Only boundary painting has no representative even in T'ang times. It is with Kuo Chung-shu at the end of the Five Dynasties that the history of this method begins. . . . Recently Chao Mĕng-fu, in teaching his son Chao Yung how to make 'boundary-paintings,' said to him, 'All other sorts of painting may be fudged. But in boundary painting the fitting of things into their places necessarily demands a certain degree of skill.'"

In its technical sense, then, "boundary-painting" means painting in which the straight lines are drawn with a plumb-string or ruler ; and since straight lines do not occur to any considerable extent in nature, the term is in this technical sense applied only to pictures of buildings. Thus the *Tz'ŭ Yüan*, a dictionary recently published by the Shanghai Commercial Press, defines " boundary-paintings " as " pictures of buildings in which the straight lines are drawn with the help of a *chieh-ch'ih* (" boundary foot-rule "). In fact, *chieh* in the term *chieh-hua* is short for *chieh-ch'ih* (" boundary foot-rule ").

This is certainly by far the most common use of the term. But there is another to which Professor Giles has called attention in the second edition of his *Pictorial Art* (p. 201). A Ming (?) writer[1] says of a painting by Wang Mĕng : " This picture contains only three or four trees. It is surrounded by a border (*chieh-hua*). Beyond the border are inscribed several poems, the first of which says . . ." Such " bordered paintings," oval, square, or fan-shaped, are fairly common.

The same writer says that the *chieh-hua* attributed to Ma Yüan and Hsia Kuei (see below, p. 209) were really painted by Ting Yeh-fu, an Uighur who worked in China during the 14th century. In this passage the context is not sufficient to show in which sense the term *chieh-hua* is to be understood.[2]

---

[1] Quoted by the great *T'u Shu* Encyclopedia (XVII, 796, 2, 41), apparently from the *T'ai-p'ing Ch'ing Hua* (16th century ?).

[2] Giles (p. 145) misunderstood this passage. The sentence which he translated : " They (i.e. Ma and Hsia) were both descendants of wild men, by which is meant inhabitants of the Western countries," should run, " . . . proceed from Yeh-fu. Yeh-fu was an inhabitant

CHINESE PAINTING

CHAO TA-NIEN

Chao Ling-jan, better known as Chao Ta-nien, has been mentioned above as the mentor of the young Emperor Hui Tsung, whose kinsman he was. During the greater part of his life he was, in consequence of his exalted rank, tied to the monotonous routine of Court duties. He said of himself jestingly that he, a landscape-painter, knew no more of Chinese scenery than what was to be seen on the road from the Palace to the Imperial Tombs.

He loved above all to paint winter-scenes and trees standing amid pools. The painting by him reproduced in *Shimbi Taikwan*, Vol. XIX, and again in *Kokka*, 41, " Lake Shore in Autumn," is then his most typical surviving work.[1] It should not be judged by the black-and-white reproduction in *Tōyō Bijutsu Taikwan*, which makes it appear to be a much more blurred and impressionistic work than it is.

Chao Ta-nien had studied the T'ang masterpieces in the collections of the aristocrats whose houses he frequented in his youth, and it is said that his style had in it something of T'ang formality.

of the Western Lands." This Uighur, Ting Yeh-fu, is known as an imitator of Ma Yüan and Hsia Kuei. The quotation is not (as Giles states) from the *Yen Ch'i Yu Shih*, but apparently from the *T'ai-p'ing Ch'ing Hua*. For Yeh-fu, see *Shu Hua P'u*, 54, 11.

[1] Assuming the correctness of the attribution.

CHAPTER XV
KUO HSI AND HIS WRITINGS
MI FEI: LI LUNG-MIEN

CHAPTER XV
KUO HSI AND HIS WRITINGS
MI FEI: LI LUNG-MIEN

Kuo Hsi was born c. 1020. He specialized in the painting of vast landscapes on the walls of princely palaces. Consequently few if any of his works have survived. The *Kokka* Company has reproduced (as a separate publication) a roll attributed to him and formerly possessed by Tuan Fang. But Mr. Taki, editor of the *Kokka*, has himself doubted its authenticity. The catalogue of the Emperor Ch'ien Lung's paintings mentions seven pictures attributed to Kuo Hsi; but in so curt a way as to suggest that the compilers could not accept them as genuine. Fortunately he was a writer as well as a painter. His essay on " The Sublime in Landscape Painting," edited by his son, Kuo Ssǔ, may still be read and has been noticed by several European writers. Fenollosa (*Epochs of Chinese and Japanese Art*, Vol. II, pp. 12–19) gives considerable extracts from it, using a translation made for him by Japanese friends. As is sometimes the case with English renderings of Chinese texts made by Japanese, this translation is inaccurate and in places nonsensical. Petrucci (*Ostasiatische Zeitschrift*, I, 395) has translated and annotated two passages. The essay is devoted entirely to landscape-painting; the sentence (Fenollosa, p. 15) where Kuo Hsi seems to be discussing flower-painting, has been mutilated by Mrs. Fenollosa, who made extracts from the complete Japanese version. The reference to flowers, etc., is a comparison: " Just as in flower-painting . . . so in landscape . . ."

Kuo Ssǔ's introduction opens with the usual quotation from Confucius and etymological speculations. The actual essay of Kuo Hsi begins as follows :—

" Wherein lies the reason that good men so much love landscape ? It is because amid orchards and hills a man has ever room to cultivate his natural bent; because streams and rocks never fail to charm the rambler who goes whistling on his way.[1] It is because fishing and wood-gathering are the natural vocations of the hermit or recluse, hard by where the flying birds and chattering apes have made their home.

" Noise and dust, bridles and chains—these are what man's nature is ever weary of. Haze and mists, saints and fairies—for these man's nature pines eternally, and pines in vain."

In times of tyranny and misrule, Kuo Hsi continues, it is natural that wise men should betake themselves to the hills and forests. But in times

---

[1] From a poem by T'ao Ch'ien.

of peace we are held to the city by filial and feudal ties. Woods and streams, nature-spirits and fairies, are seen by us only in our dreams.

" Now comes a painter, and by his skill all these things are suddenly brought to us.[1] Still in our home, stretched on the divan, we hear the cries of gibbons by many streams, the song of birds down many valleys ; while our eyes are flooded by the gleam of hills,the hues of falling streams. Does not this illustrate the saying, ' Charmed by another's purpose, I attain my own desire ' ?

" It is for these reasons that the world honours the painting of landscape. If it be approached under the dominance of any other spirit, carelessly or light-heartedly, it is as though one should defile the sanctuary of a God, or cast impurities into the clear wind of heaven. . . . Landscapes have been classified as those fit to walk through, those fit to gaze on, those fit to idle in, those fit to live in. A painting of any of these may reach the standard called ' miao,' pre-excellent. But those fit to idle in and those fit to live in make better subjects than the others. Why is this ? Look at the landscape paintings of to-day. In a panorama of several hundred leagues not more than three or four parts in ten will be such as might be dwelt in or idled in. Yet the painter will certainly regard the scenery as of the ' residential ' or ' pleasure ' class. Now it is just for the sake of these beautiful spots (suitable for residence or pleasure) that wise men thirst and pine for the country. The painter and the critic must both bear this in mind. To do so is what is called ' not losing sight of the essential.' "

The above account of the purpose of landscape-painting seems to us very absurd ; but it corresponds exactly to the view of most people in Europe to-day. The average man admires a landscape-painting because it reminds him of some place where he has pleasantly " idled or dwelt." The painter who ignores this has, in several senses, " lost sight of the essential." Kuo Hsi speaks, and speaks charmingly, for the great majority—those for whom art has only an associational value. A few lines later Kuo continues :

" In painting any view, whether it be large or small, whether it contain many details or few, the artist must concentrate his powers in order to

---

[1] The view that the object of possessing landscape-paintings is to save one the trouble of going out-of-doors is also expressed by Tsung Ping (375–443) in an essay which the *Ming Hua Chi* reproduces. This essay is omitted by the *Shu Hua P'u*, which was compiled with minute care by a large committee of scholars. I cannot believe that the omission was an oversight. I therefore conclude that the essay in question was not considered to be genuine. It is possible that it is a late addition to the *Ming Hua Chi*. See *Kokka*, 297 and 298. The Imperial Catalogue, in discussing valuable early works which the *Ming Hua Chi* has preserved, also omits all reference to Tsung Ping's essay.

unify the work. Otherwise it will not bear the peculiar imprint of his soul.

" His whole soul must attend the completion of the task. Otherwise his energies will be dulled. He must have deep seriousness wherewith to dignify his work; else it will lack depth of conception. He must use reverent toil to perfect it; else it will be incomplete.

" If a painter forces himself to work when he feels lazy his productions will be weak and spiritless, without decision. This is because he cannot concentrate. If, when he is feeling distracted and bothered, he decides to muddle[1] through, his forms will be evasive and incomplete. This defect comes from lack of seriousness. If it is hurried on feverishly, the composition will be rough and arbitrary; it will lack consistency. This defect comes from lack of reverent toil.

" Now indecision leads to loss of lucidity; lack of freshness destroys charm; incompleteness mars composition; lack of consistency leads to sudden transitions.[2]

" These are the main defects of painters. But they can only be discussed with those who understand the subject."

The above passage calls for no comment. It expresses admirably the conditions under which a work of art is produced, and shows Kuo Hsi speaking no longer as a member of the undistinguished public, but as that rare and individual thing, an artist. It should be mentioned that the term " immobilité d'esprit," which Petrucci finds so felicitous, occurs only in his translation and not at all in the Chinese text.

The editor of the essay, Kuo Ssŭ, annotates this passage as follows:

" I, Ssŭ, remember that when my father was at work on several pictures, he would often suddenly put them aside and not return to them for ten or twenty days. . . . This was because he felt disinclined. And disinclination, what is it but the ' laziness ' of which he speaks above ? If, however, he was in a good humour and his work was going well, everything else was forgotten. But if the least thing happened to distract or disturb him, he would at once stop painting. This is what he means by saying that one must not attempt to paint if one is feeling ' distracted and bothered.'

" On days when he was going to paint, he would seat himself at a clean table, by a bright window, burning incense to right and left. He would choose the finest brushes, the most exquisite ink; wash his hands, and clean the ink-stone, as though he were expecting a visitor of rank. He waited till his mind was calm and undisturbed, and then began. Is not

[1] A literal translation.
[2] Lit. " To the quick-slow method." I do not see how Petrucci gets his " méthode de la composition " out of this. He seems to have borrowed it from the clause before.

this what he meant by saying that one should not dash off one's work light-heartedly?

" What he had completed, he would sift again. What he had enlarged, he would amplify. When once might have seemed enough, he would not even be content with twice, but would improve upon it! He would re-commence each picture many times, as though at war with a pitiless adversary—till at last he was content. Is not this what he meant when he said that a work of art must not be hurried-on?

" The men of the world think that my pictures are produced by a mere wave of the brush; they have no idea that painting is a difficult matter. The philosopher Chuang Tzŭ says: ' The painter must take off his coat and sit cross-legged '; he knew what painting means. The artist must have a heart full of generous and lively emotions; a mind teeming with gay and pleasing thoughts. ' His disposition must be simple and sincere; he must be indulgent, affable, and kind.'[1]

" Upon the heart of such a one every human emotion, every attitude whether of joy or sorrow, the particular shapes and planes of every in-animate thing will be spontaneously recorded; and will flow unconsciously from his brush.

" Ku K'ai-chih of the Chin dynasty, wherever he was living, always built himself a studio at the top of a high tower. He was indeed a true sage of antiquity! For if a man's thoughts are constrained, confused, clouded, or clogged, or his purposes all twisted to one bend, how can we hope to portray the shapes of things or express the thoughts of men?

" It is as when a workman is to make a lute. He has found ' a lonely eloeococca of Mount I-yang '[2]; his skill of hand and genius of invention lie mysteriously buried within him, and while the tree still stands in the earth, long before its leaves and branches are lopped, he sees clearly as though it stood before him a finished lute carved by the hand of the master Lei.

" But if his thoughts are troubled and disordered, if he be doltish, ignorant, melancholy, or morose, he will gaze at his chisels and knives, not knowing where to begin. Could such a one have caused ' Burnt Tail's '[3] five notes to well their sounds down the clear breeze and over the flowing stream? In fact, as one of my predecessors has said, ' A poem is a formless picture;

[1] Out of these adjectives Fenollosa's Japanese collaborator concocted a queer proper-name " Ichokushi," which he apparently took to be that of a Chinese philosopher. But the passage in inverted commas is quoted verbatim from the *Book of Rites*; see Couvreur's version, Vol. II, p. 297.

[2] Quotation from the *Book of History*.

[3] T'sai Yung (born 133 A.D.) came across some peasants cooking their dinner on a fire of eloeococca-wood. By the peculiar crackle that it made he knew it to be wood of marvellous quality. He asked them to give him a log, and out of it he fashioned the celebrated lute " Burnt Tail," charred at one end, yet producing notes of surpassing beauty. (*Annals of the Han Dynasty*.)

a picture is a form-poem ' ! Wise men have often discussed these words, and we have made them our law. On leisure days I have looked through poems, ancient and modern, of the Chin dynasty and of T'ang, and many times found a verse which expressed with perfection some striving of man's heart, or brought vividly before the mental eye some aspect of nature.

" But if I was not seated at leisure in a quiet room, at a bright window, with a clean table before me, with a stick of incense lighted to dissipate the gloom of care—then, even though a fine verse or noble thought were before me, it would not take shape ; even though a subtle feeling or rare mood presented itself, it would not fructify. How then can it be said that the final conception of a painting is easy to reach ? When environment is already ripe, when hand and heart correspond, just when one is beginning ' here and there to find a crossing, now and again to meet with a source,' some man of the world arrives, distracts one's thoughts, buffets one's feelings—and all is confusion.

" For that reason I, Ssŭ, have recorded some of the fine pieces and choice passages of the ancients which my father was in the habit of reciting. There will not be lacking among them some which might inspire such high thoughts as stir a painter's mind. Moreover, I myself have sought far and wide for such lines, and here insert those of which my father approved."

The reader may reasonably expect that, having carried him to this point, I should proceed to translate some of the verses in which Kuo Hsi delighted. I do so reluctantly, fearing that in translation these fragments will lose all their beauty. It should be remembered that they are stanzas and couplets, not complete poems.

(1) *On Lady's Table Mountain-top spring snows melt ;*
By the roadside apricot-flowers bud on tender twigs.
My heart is ready ; I long to go. Yet when shall the day be ?
Sadly I watch the homeward coach roll over the field-bridge.

By YANG Ē-SHIH (c. 800, written when detained in the city).

(2) *Alone I seek the mountain-hut, now resting, now travelling.*
A thatched roof's slant joins behind the pine-tree leaves !
I hear the voices of men within ; the door is still closed.
By the wild lettuce of the hedge there flutters . . . a yellow butterfly.

By CH'ANG-SUN TSO-FU (T'ang).

(3) *O southward-wandering brothers mine, will you ever come back again ?*
Far off, between the Three Rivers and the Five Hills you roam.
Alone I stand by the farm-door and the autumn waters wide ;
A shivering crow starts away ; the sun drowns in the hills.

By TOU KUNG (9th century).

193

(4) *My fishing is over ; my lonely boat I moor to the bullrush bough ;*
Of wine I open a new cask ; of " cha "[1] a new box ;
For twice ten years I have fished the waters of the Kiang and Che ;
Yet never once in salutation have my two hands been joined.

ANON.

(5) *South of my home, north of my home—all is spring flood ;*
Nought I see but a host of gulls coming day by day.
Water-fording, the lame ass straightens both its ears ;
Wind-cringing, the lean groom humps one shoulder.

By " LU OF THE SNOW POEM " (i.e. LU LUN, *fl. c.* 750–780).

(6) *I walk till I reach the place where the waters end ;*
Sit, till I see the last cloud arise.

By WANG WEI (the famous painter and poet of the 8th century).

(7) *In the sixth month, with my holly staff, I come to the rocky road ;*
In a noon-shadows-many place I listen to the murmuring stream.

By WANG AN-SHIH (the famous reformer).

(8) *A distant water joined to heaven clear ;*
A lonely rampart shadowed in cloud-wrack deep.

By TU FU (famous poet of the 8th century).

(9) *From the thick bamboos the last rain-drops drip ;*
On the high hill-top lingers the evening light.

By HSIA-HOU SHĒN (8th century, 2nd half),

(10) *Sky distant : approaching geese small ;*
River wide : departing sail lovely.

By YAO HO (9th century).

(11) *Snowy purpose unfulfilling—clouds to the earth cling ;*
Autumn-cried never ceasing—geese to the sky cleave.

By CH'IEN WEI-YEN (C. 1000 A.D.).

(12) *The spring river is girt with rain ; swiftly the night comes ;*
None stands by the ferry in the fields ; the boat drifts aslant.

By WEI YING-WU (8th century, 2nd half).

MI FEI'S CLOUDY MOUNTAINS

Another artist whose name is associated with a peculiar technique is Mi Fei,[2] of whose eccentricities an account has been given by Professor Giles

---

[1] A preparation made of rice, dried fish, etc.
[2] 1051–1107. " Mi Fu " is certainly the correct pronunciation, but " Fei " has managed to oust it.

in his *Chinese Pictorial Art*. Fastidious to the verge of madness, he would not take food out of a bowl from which others had helped themselves, nor drink from his friend's cup. Overborne by a continual sense of pollution, he was for ever washing himself and changing his clothes. He was a great connoisseur of antiquities, a passionate collector of painting and calligraphy. Among his paintings were an Apsara or Buddhist Angel, by Ku K'ai-chih; six snow-views by Wang Wei; "Training Horses," by Han Kan; landscapes by Ching Hao, Kuan T'ung, Tung Yüan, and Li Ch'ēng; four flower-pieces by Hsü Hsi; "Birds among the Rushes," by I Yüan-chi.[1] He was continually copying and recopying these masterpieces. At night they were propped on a table by his bedside and followed him into his dreams. So strong was his passion for the past that he dressed in the costume of the T'ang dynasty.

It is strange that out of all this archæological romanticism arose a new and very distinctive style of landscape-painting. He began to paint wood-clad, cloud-enveloped mountains entirely in brush-blobs of ink, without preliminary drawing, or contour-lines to mark the folds of the hills. The style was developed by his son Mi Yu-jēn, and practised in a modified form by the 13th-century painter Kao K'o-kung. Since then the "Mi style" has been used as an occasional resource by many landscape-painters. But it is doubtful if any actual work by Mi or his son survives.

It is probable that he painted comparatively few pictures in the style which is popularly associated with his name. He died at fifty-seven, and the style is one which seems to belong to a mature age. The Ch'ien Lung Collection contained four paintings by him. Two were in colour, two in ink. The same collection possessed two pictures by Mi Yu-jēn, both makimonos in ink.

Though Mi Fei's pictures are lost, his book, the *Hua Shih* (" Records of Painting "), still survives. It is a work of about 100 pages, consisting of anecdotes about painting and connoisseurship and records of paintings which he had seen. He was, as we have seen in the case of Wu Tao-tzŭ,[2] extremely sceptical about " Old Masters." I do not think that the following anecdote has been translated : There was at Soochow an ignorant grandee who collected pictures. He decided the date of them by reading what was written at the back and looking out the names in Chang Yen-yüan's *Ming Hua Chi*. Thus he possessed a painting of the " Seven Astral Phases " which bore on its label the name of no less a personage than the Emperor Wu of the Liang dynasty (6th century). Encouraged by this

[1] 11th century, famous for his paintings of monkeys.   [2] See above, p. 114.

acquisition, he plunged ever deeper into the past and bought a picture of Fu Hsi's Eight Trigrams which was ascribed on the label to Shih Huang, minister to the mythical Yellow Emperor (3rd millennium B.C.!). When asked how he had come by it, the grandee answered, " I got it from his grandson " ; but whether he meant the Yellow Emperor's grandson or Shih Huang's grandson was not clear. . . . All his pictures were of that kind.

On one occasion he was shown the Vimalakīrti by Ku K'ai-chih which belonged to Mi Fei's family. Without examining the brushwork he at once exclaimed, " Modern pictures of this sort are quite easy to obtain," and turning to his attendant, " Tell Hu Ch'ang to-morrow to take a look round and buy me two of this subject."

A few days afterwards two very low-class pictures arrived, one labelled " Vimalakīrti by Ku K'ai-chih," the other " Vimalakīrti by Lu T'an-wei."

The Ku K'ai-chih was a single figure of Vimalakīrti without Manjuśrī, and was evidently by some one who had seen the famous painting at the Tile Coffin Temple.[1] The other included Manjuśrī and the dozing lion, and was by some one who had seen the lion in Lu T'an-wei's picture at the Kan-lu Temple.[2]

LI LUNG-MIEN

Li Kung-lin, better known as Li Lung-mien, was born about 1040 A.D. A distinguished archæologist, calligrapher, and poet, he held high office at Court, where he enjoyed the friendship of Su Tung-p'o, Ou-yang Hsiu, and Huang T'ing-chien. Another of his friends was Ts'ao P'u, the Master of the Stables, through whose influence Lung-mien was able to study the marvellous horses which had recently been presented to the Emperor by the rulers of Khotan and other Western countries. It seems that after a few years he suddenly abandoned horse-painting and devoted himself to copying the religious painters of the T'ang dynasty. This change is probably to be attributed not to any sudden conversion to Buddhism, but to the fact that in 1087 his friend in the Imperial stables was removed to a post in the distant province of Fuhkien.

Except when trying to produce an actual simile of older paintings, it was his practice to translate the coloured pictures of his predecessors (for even his horse-paintings, though studied from life, were based upon the tradition of Ts'ao Pa and Han Kan) into outline-drawing, using a thin, wiry ink-line.

[1] See p. 45.　　　[2] See p. 71.

This technique was a revival of the *po-hua* or uncoloured outline-paintings of early T'ang and pre-T'ang times; it became known (perhaps not till some centuries after Li Lung-mien's death) as *po-miao*, "plain limning." He did not (except when making an actual replica of an old painting) use silk, but drew upon the exquisite paper made by the Hall of Untroubled Thought at Nanking for the 10th-century poet-ruler Li Hou-chu.

His copy of Ku K'ai-chih's "Admonitions" has already been mentioned. In his work the narrative element played a large part. His rolls were picture-books, agreeable guides to the manners of ancient times and distant countries, pleasantly informative panoramas and charts. His inspiration lay not so much in nature as in the great works of man—the poetry of Ch'ü Yüan (which "hangs with the sun and moon"), the paintings of Ku K'ai-chih, Yen Li-pēn, and Wu Tao-tzŭ.

In the last years of his activity he witnessed the triumph of the realistic movement. It was, indeed, at the moment when Hui Tsung ordered the painters of the Academy to draw from life and from life only that Lung-mien's rheumatism suddenly obliged him to quit the Court. Already in 1076 he had bought a plot of land on the Sleeping Dragon Mountain (Lung-mien Shan). In 1100 he retired permanently to this retreat, where he died six years later.

The disasters which not long after his death began to threaten the Sung dynasty culminated in the loss of Northern China.[1] Huddled south of the river in shame and insecurity, the men of Southern Sung turned their thoughts inward. Painting became dreamy and subjective, three parts poetry, expressive of a mood rather than of outward realities.

Li Lung-mien was China's last great prose-painter.

We need not doubt the genuineness of all the 107 pictures in the Hui Tsung Collection which were attributed to him. To discuss them here would be too long a task. A series of his pictures which this collection apparently did not include was "Confucius and his 72 Disciples," which was engraved upon stone at Hangchow by order of Kao Tsung, first Emperor of the Southern Sung dynasty.[2]

Turning to the seventeenth catalogue of Kao Shih-ch'i,[3] we find fourteen pictures listed; all but two or three of them are traditional Buddhist subjects—"Lohan," "The Hunt for the Bowl" (of which so many modern copies are extant), Vimalakīrti, illustrations to the Lo Shēn Fu

---

[1] In 1126-7.   [2] See *Chin Shih Ts'ui Pien*, 149, 1.
[3] No. 8 of my native sources.

(probably founded upon Ku K'ai-chih's picture) and to Su Tung-p'o's famous *Red Wall*.

The Ch'ien Lung Collection possessed about twenty of his pictures. Of these more than half were in outline, two or three in ink, and two in full colour. All except three are illustrations to stories or poems. There is one picture of " Two Horses," and there are two famous landscape rolls, the " Hsiao-Hsiang Rivers " and the " Upper Yangtze." The latter (reproduced in *Kokka*, 273) is dryly topographical, severely objective—the antithesis of that poetical mystic interpretation of nature which prevailed in the succeeding centuries.

No. 380 of the *Kokka* reproduces the " Five Horses," a roll which entered the Ch'ien Lung Collection too late to be included in the catalogue, but is still in the possession of the Manchu Imperial family. It was (assuming its genuineness) painted in the summer of 1087, and a few months before Li Lung-mien severed his connection with the Imperial stables. The section which I reproduce[1] represents a Khotanese horse, with its native groom, and has therefore, I presume, considerable zoological and anthropological interest. As an example of the slightly-tinted outline style it far transcends in sensitivity and expressiveness of line the general run of *po-miao* paintings which survive. It is a piece of delicate and subdued realism that is merely commemorative and makes no attempt at being a picture.

The Clerical Orgy. At the beginning of the 6th century Chang Sēng-yu[2] painted a picture with the above title. We are reminded of the unpleasant discovery[3] made by the Wei Emperor in 446, not long before Chang's birth, when, visiting a temple in the north, he found a secret distillery in the cloisters and a harem in the crypt. At the beginning of the 6th century most of the monks in China were still foreigners, so that Chang's picture probably represented an orgy of Westerners—Indians or Central Asians. It was resented by the Buddhists, who in the 7th century persuaded Yen Li-pēn to paint a picture of a Taoist orgy. Both paintings were copied[4] by Li Lung-mien. The latter contained twenty Taoist priests, with seventeen attendants. The former (which was in Hui Tsung's collection) is very briefly referred to by Tung Ch'i-ch'ang, who, writing at the beginning of the 17th century, says that it was made to illustrate a poem called " The Drunken Priests," by Su Hsün (1009–1066). I venture tentatively to suggest that a fine early painting of this subject which is now in the

[1] See Plate XXXIII. [2] See above, p. 84. [3] See above, p. 79.

[4] He seems in general to have reproduced his models closely, but it is not certain that in these cases he got anything more than his conception from his predecessors.

collection of Monsieur A. Stoclet, at Brussels, may possibly be Li Lung-mien's original. More than any other Chinese painting which I have seen this gives me the impression of coming from the hand of a great master. What above all distinguishes it from later paintings of similar subjects is that it is definitely composed in receding space. Later artists, such as Ch'iu Ying in the Ming dynasty, convey to us in a perfectly lucid way the relative positions of figures and objects; but these relations are apprehended by us intellectually—we do not " feel " recession and space. But in Monsieur Stoclet's picture we are able to " walk to and fro," which is just the characteristic of Li Lung-mien's painting which Tung Ch'i-ch'ang notices when commenting upon the " Drunken Priests." Other striking features of the picture are the ambitious foreshortening of the recumbent figure in the right-hand corner and the hunched shoulder of the priest who is holding the arm of the central figure; this last effect (which gives the priest the air of being a humpback) is, I am sure, an effort to render exactly some effect seen in life. For Li Lung-mien was a great realist; " his figures," says Tung Ch'i-ch'ang, " have the exactitude of lantern-projections." A great part of the beauty of this picture is due to its exquisite colour; the tree on the left with its contrast of green against white is particularly fine.

A small point of contact with Li Lung-mien is the face of the man with a drum, which strikingly resembles that of the Khotanese groom in the " Five Horses." The central figure reminds me of another painting which, like the Horses, was accepted in the 18th century as Lung-mien's work.[1]

The Calligrapher Huai-su. This picture passed through the hands of the New York dealer Mr. Lu, who in 1916 presented a photograph of it to the British Museum. It belonged, like the " Admonitions," to Hsiang Mo-lin and An I-chou, finally passing into Ch'ien Lung's collection about 1747 A.D., too late to be included in the main catalogue. It also bears the seal of Ch'ien Lung's successor.

Its former possessor, An I-chou, identified it as the " Drunken Priests " picture, and this title has stuck to it. The misunderstanding arose in this way: it is really (I am convinced) a picture of the bibulous priest-calligrapher Huai-su[2] and illustrates his poem:

> *Everybody brings me wine, so that I never have to buy it ;*
> *All day I sit in the woods with my flask tied to a tree.*
> *I am just turning into a calligraphic genius when suddenly the madness comes—*
> *Alas! I deserve that my portrait should be inserted in the Drunken Priests picture!*

[1] See Plates XXXIV, XXXV and XXXVI.

[2] 7th century. A pupil of Hsüan Tsang; author of a commentary upon the *Abhidharma Kośa Śāstra.*

On the left a boy holds up a scroll upon which Huai-su writes, his flask is (as in the poem) tied to a tree. On the right serving-boys are arriving with fresh presents of wine. The quality of the painting is not nearly so fine as that of Monsieur Stoclet's picture or even as that of the " Five Horses." It presents in its present form a curious example of the recklessness with which the Chinese deface works of art, its surface being almost completely covered with seals and inscriptions. But as most of the seals and all of the inscriptions are those of the Emperor Ch'ien Lung, they must be considered, according to Chinese standards, as enhancing the beauty and value of the picture.

CHAPTER XVI
THE ROMANTICS

SOUTHERN SUNG

THE ROMANTICS

The Tartars captured Pien-ching[1] in the spring of 1127. The Emperor Hui Tsung was, as we have seen, carried away to the " Castle of the Five Lands," a northern fortress somewhere in the direction of the modern Vladivostock,[2] where he died twelve years later at the age of fifty-two.

One of his sons who had been sent to Nanking to levy troops was now proclaimed Emperor and established his Court at Lin-an, the modern Hangchow. The troubles of the Chinese were not over. Having spent a year in systematically reducing the north of China, the Tartars crossed the Yang-tze and at the end of 1129 overran most of Chekiang, including the great towns of Nanking, Hangchow, and Ningpo. But they were suffering from difficulties of transport, internal dissent, and perhaps already from Mongol pressure upon their distant northern frontier. Having burnt Hangchow and other towns, the Tartars withdrew to the north.

A new cleavage now divided Chinese political life. There was a " die-hard " party which insisted that the Tartars could and must be driven out of the lost provinces, and a party of reconciliation led by Ch'in Kuei, who having been a prisoner in the hands of the Tartars had formed the conclusion that they were irresistible. Ch'in Kuei's own story was that he had escaped from captivity by killing his gaoler. There is, however, a strong suspicion that he was released on the understanding that he would persuade the Chinese to make peace.

The " die-hards " corresponded, of course, roughly to the old Conservative party. Ch'in Kuei found arrayed against him the whole eloquence of the Confucian Schools. But at last, in 1142, he triumphed. The Chinese resigned their claim to the provinces north of the Yang-tze ; but their diplomats were able to point to one small triumph : the body of the late Emperor Hui Tsung was returned to his son at Hangchow.

The Tartars gave trouble from time to time, but they made no further serious effort to extend their conquests, and were soon afterwards immersed in difficulties of their own.

Gradually the fugitives from Pien-ching began to recover from their fright. They looked about them and saw that Fate had wedged them into a singularly beautiful corner of the world. They did not know how long it would be theirs to enjoy, for at any moment the vast Hyperborean steppe

---

[1] Modern K'ai-fēng Fu.   [2] See above, p. 179.

might pour upon them its irresistible hordes. So they enjoyed the gardens of Hangchow, the waters of the Western Lake, with a tender, half-hypnotized delight, their thoughts deliberately averted from every aspect of life but its beauty—sunk in the sensuous lethargy which won them Marco Polo's scorn.[1] The reunion of China became, even with the Confucian party, a day-dream rather than a policy. Lu Yu, the greatest poet of the period, longed passionately all his life to see the Chinese armies marching northward, and in a famous death-bed poem begged his son to send news to the underworld when the great day of victory at last should come:

> *When I am dead, I shall understand, I know,*
> *That the world was not real.*
> *Yet I grieve that I have not seen*
> *The Nine Lands made one.*
> *When at last the Imperial armies march*
> *To conquer the Central Plain ;*
> *At your Household Rites do not forget*
> *To whisper it to your father's ghost.*

He died in 1209. In that year Genghiz Khan was already advancing upon Kansuh. China was soon to be reunited, but not in a way which can have given any satisfaction to the poet's ghost.

The Mongols captured Hangchow in 1276. The spirit of Southern Sung æstheticism winged slowly northward to Japan. The Ashikaga period (1393–1573 A.D.) reproduces with astonishing completeness the characteristics of Southern Sung. Meanwhile in China a tremendous reaction had set in. The marvellous organizing capacity of the Mongols had set everyone to work. Dreams, introspections, mysticism, were forgotten, or if anyone relapsed into them there was a wild Tibetan or Uighur at his elbow to jog him back into utilitarian action. No one in the succeeding centuries took any interest in the mystical Zen painting of Hangchow, and few cared for the brooding, romantic art of the 13th-century Academy. Consequently the Japanese were able to remove to their own country practically the whole output of the Zen monasteries and a large part of the work of such romantic Court landscape-painters as Ma Yüan and Hsia Kuei. Many of these paintings have been published in Japanese journals, but the work of critically sifting them is only just beginning. I shall therefore not attempt to do more than discuss them in a general way. Before doing so, I

---

[1] " Sachez qu'ils n'étoient mie une gent d'armes. Car tous leur délices n'étoient que des femmes, et proprement le roi sur tous ; si qu'il n'avoit d'autre chose cure, hors de femmes et de bien faire aux pauvres gens."

must mention a few of the realist Academy painters who, after the transfer of the capital to Hangchow, continued to paint in a " concrete," objective style.

Academy Realists. Chao Po-chü and *Liu Sung-nien.*

First of all there were the painters in the " blue, green, and gold-outline " style of Li Ssŭ-hsün.   The best-known of these were the brothers Chao Po-chü and Chao Po-hsü, who are always cited by " Southern School " writers as a warning against the tiresomeness of minute realism.   Yet Tung Ch'i-ch'ang concedes to Po-chü a certain " liberality of spirit " which his successors lacked.   Early in the 18th century his " Idling away the Summer at the Lotus Arbour "[1] still survived, and the Ch'ien Lung Collection contained one genuine picture by him, a roll entitled " In a Lotus Boat under the New Moon."

Liu Sung-nien flourished about 1170–1230.   He took lessons in painting from the aged Chang Tun-li, a son-in-law of the Emperor Chē Tsung.[2]   During the period 1174–1189 he held the rank of " scholar " in the Academy ; about 1191 he was raised to the rank of Painter-in-ordinary (*tai-chao*).   The Emperor Ning Tsung[3] bestowed upon him the Order of the Golden Girdle, in reward for a set of pictures illustrating " agriculture and weaving," says the *Hua Shih Hui Yao.*[4]   He was nicknamed " Liu of the Dark Gate."   This has hitherto been taken as an indication that he belonged to some mystic sect.   But the wording of the *Hua Shih Hui Yao* seems rather to suggest that " Dark Gate " was an alternative name of the Blue Wave Gate (Ch'ing Po Mēn) at Sung-nien's native place, Ch'ien-t'ang.   His house was just outside this gate.   We are told that he loved to paint " pine-tree covered with snow.   He would first draw the outline in faint ink ; then he would indicate the pine-needles with rough brushwork, afterwards tinting them with a stippling of grass-green.   The branches he tinted with light ochre, leaving the upper half blank to give the appearance of snow."   Most of his pictures illustrated famous moments in history (such as the treaty of Pien Bridge being signed by the Chinese Emperor and the Turkish Khan in 626 A.D.), or popular legends such as that of the " Four Greybeards " (after a picture by Yen Li-pēn) and the " Gathering of Wits in the Western Garden " (after Li Lung-mien).

Ch'ien Lung possessed three originals : " Po Chü-i and his Eight Friends at Hsiang-shan," " Silkworms and Weaving," and a hanging-picture called " Bamboos on the Eastern Hills."   I have reproduced here two parts of

---

[1] *Hsiao Hsia Lu*, I, 18.   [2] Reigned 1086–1100.   [3] 1195–1225.
[4] Published in 1631.   Professor Pelliot has shown (*Mem. concernant l'Aise Orientale*, I, 96) that it was probably not Liu Sung-nien who painted this series.

a roll entitled " The Three Incarnations of Yüan-tsē,"[1] which is now in Mr. Eumorphopoulos's collection. It, too, seems to have belonged to Ch'ien Lung, though it does not appear in the published catalogue of his collection. The story which the roll illustrates is as follows : A priest, Yüan-Tsē, and his friend, Li Yüan, are travelling by boat. One day they see upon the shore a woman who is carrying a pitcher. It is obvious that she is pregnant. Yüan-tsē says : " That woman has been with child for three years. She cannot be delivered till some living person gives up his soul to enter into the body of her child. I will die for her. Go to her house in three days, and I will greet you through the lips of the new-born child." The priest died that night, and his soul entered the body of the unborn child. The woman was delivered, and when Li Yüan visited her, the infant greeted him with a smile which was recognizably that of the deceased Yüan-tsē. Thirteen years afterwards Li Yüan met a boy, evidently about thirteen years old, riding on the back of a bull. He was singing to himself a song about the rebirth of Yüan-tsē, but heedlessly as though the words had no meaning. Li Yüan knew instantly that he was face to face with the reincarnation of his old friend. But the boy rode on, and was never seen again.

This, obviously, is the story of only two incarnations. It is probable that the first incarnation explains in some way the intimacy of Yüan-tsē and Li Yüan, telling, for example, how in a previous existence they had been brothers.[2] The earliest painting of the subject seems to have been that of Li T'ang.[3] Wang Shih-mou, writing in the second half of the 16th century, describes it as follows[4] : " It shows a herdboy riding on a bull's back ; Li Yüan stretches forward to greet him ; a second roll shows the boatman face to face with the pregnant woman, who is drawing water in a vessel that has a brocaded pad at the bottom. It is a companion piece to the other roll." Again, Chang Ch'ou, writing *circa* 1620, says : " Li T'ang's picture of the second of the Three Incarnations has an inscription by Yü Chi."[5] It is rather odd that the two parts of the picture are mentioned in the wrong order.

Somewhat later another version of the subject was produced by the two artists in collaboration. Chao Po-chü painted the meeting with the

---

[1] See Plates XXXVII and XXXVIII.

[2] That this was so is indicated in the text which is appended to the roll.

[3] See below, p. 208.

[4] Quoted by *Nan Sung Yüan Hua Lu*, II, 6.

[5] 1266–1342 A.D.

pregnant woman ; Liu Sung-nien painted the herdboy scene. The same Chang Ch'ou says[1] : " The roll of the Three Incarnations of Yüan-tsē was jointly produced by Chao Po-chü, who painted the former incarnation ; while Liu Sung-nien painted the recognition scene. . . . It is a pity that the figures are too large in proportion to the scenery, which consequently does not produce a proper effect. The first part of the roll is in the collection of my fellow-townsman, Vice-President Han Shih-nēng ; the second belongs to Mo Yün-Ch'ing[2] of Sung-chiang. Both have inscriptions by Wang Shih-mou. What a pity the two parts of the roll should be separated ! " There is a notice of Liu Sung-nien's section of the picture in the works of Wu K'uan[3] : " The picture of the Three Incarnations was attributed to Liu Sung-nien by Chao Mēng-fu ; at the end of the roll are twenty inscriptions by well-known priests—a tribute to the popularity of Yüan-tsē."

The twenty poetical inscriptions by priests are to be found at the end of Mr. Eumorphopoulos's roll ; it is wrapped in a cloth which bears the label " Catalogued by Chang Chao in 1744," and there is no reason to doubt that it belonged to Ch'ien Lung, for it was purchased by Messrs. Yamanaka from Prince Shun, the father of the Emperor Hsüan T'ung. But whether it is the Sung original which Chao Mēng-fu attributed to Liu Sung-nien is much more doubtful. For some reason Liu Sung-nien is a favourite of the Chinese antique-dealers. They have put his name upon innumerable 17th- and 18th-century rolls, many of which have not the remotest connection with him.

Hsiao Chao. Of numerous other Southern Sung artists who worked in the solid, highly-coloured style I have not space to speak. An intermediate place between the realists and idealists is held by Hsiao Chao,[4] a picturesque character who has been neglected by European writers. A native of Huo-tsē in Honan, in 1126 he fled before the invading Tartars to the T'ai-hang mountains, where he maintained himself by highway robbery. A traveller whom he one day apprehended turned out to have nothing in his bag but a colour-box and brushes. It was the famous painter Li T'ang, fleeing southward to the new capital. The highwayman, who had often heard Li T'ang's name, made friends with his victim and

---

[1] *Nan Sung Yüan Hua Lu*, IV, 7.

[2] i.e. Mo Shih-lung, a well-known painter and writer on art, c. 1600. Author of the *Hua Shuo.* Han Shih-nēng (c. 1570) is better known as Han Ts'un-liang.

[3] Born 1432 ; died 1472. An important calligrapher.

[4] See *Nan Sung Yüan Hua Lu*, III, 16.

accompanied him to Hangchow. Here he was assisted by Li T'ang to a government appointment, became his pupil in painting, and ultimately his son-in-law. He ended his career as a Painter-in-Ordinary at Court.

He was a rapid worker. It was once discovered that the walls of a pavilion which the Emperor was about to visit next day were undecorated. The courtiers were in consternation. Hsiao Chao was hurried to the spot. He began to work at dusk, asking only that four flagons of wine should be placed in the room. At each watch, punctually as the watchmen beat their drums, he finished a wall and drank a flagon. By four in the morning the whole room was frescoed and Hsiao Chao completely intoxicated. Shortly afterwards (the habit of early rising is a perversity not confined to Western monarchs) the Emperor arrived with his suite and was delighted with the decoration of the pavilion walls. Hearing that they were the work of Hsiao Chao, he bestowed upon him a bounty of gold and silk.[1]

Hsiao Chao's most famous work was a series of twelve paintings illustrating the " auspicious omens " with which the reign of Kao Tsung began. Each painting was accompanied by a long descriptive text. At the beginning of the 18th century the series was in the possession of the Wu family of Kuang-ling in Kiangsu. Of his importance as a painter very different opinions were held. The *Hua Chuan*[2] says that his style resembled that of the great 10th-century landscapist Tung Yüan, but was more vigorous and lively; while the 13th-century writer Yeh Shao-wēng says that his pictures " have no other merit save that by their extreme verisimilitude they positively brace the beholder, as though he were actually standing on some great mountain-top or by some splendid stream."

Other Court artists were Mao Sung and his son Mao I, who were wise enough to specialize in miniatures of kittens and puppies. Li An-chung, who is better known in Japan than in China, was a bird and flower painter of very individual style. His work exercised a great influence upon Japanese artists such as Tosa Mitsu-oki.

Several Buddhist painters of this period (for example, Chou Chi-ch'ang, master of the Daitokuji Arhats, and Lu Hsin-chung, whose " Kings of Hell " are preserved in the Chionin and Shōkokuji, Kyōto) seem to have found a market in Japan for their coloured wares at a time when Zen monochrome ruled supreme in China.

The Romantics. Li T'ang, whom I have already mentioned, must have been born about 1090 A.D. or a little later. He became one of Hui Tsung's Court painters and worked in the old-fashioned Li Ssŭ-hsün style. He

---

[1] The story is in the main a variation upon an old theme.   [2] 16th century?

left Pien Ching before the final catastrophe. Settling at Hangchow, the new capital, he kept alive by selling an occasional picture. Having deserted the late Emperor, he dared not ask to be employed by Kao Tsung, his son. But after a time Kao Tsung heard of his presence at Hangchow and summoned him to Court, where he became head of the Academy. At first he continued to paint in the " blue, green, and gold " style, but after a while emancipated himself from the miniature tradition of the Academy and painted large pictures in bold, jagged brushwork, abandoning (for example) the convention by which water must be represented by a series of little wriggly lines.[1]

The fact that Li T'ang is credited with having effected by these means a complete revolution in landscape-painting seems at first sight to indicate that his predecessors were much more archaic, stiff, and formal than the accounts of them would have led us to suppose.

As regards coloured paintings, that is probably true. But until absolutely certain specimens of 10th-century and Northern Sung painting are known to us (which is not at present the case) we shall not clearly understand the nature of the change brought about by Li T'ang. In the case of ink-painting we can hardly doubt that a cursive freedom of brushwork had already existed for centuries, the transition from cursive calligraphy to cursive ink-painting being an inevitable one.

The name of Li T'ang is always coupled with that of his pupils Ma Yüan and Hsia Kuei, both of them Academy painters. Ma Yüan is generally thought of in Japan and Europe as a landscape-painter. But such titles as " The Three Religions," " The Demon-Queller," " The Four Grey-beards," " Portrait of Sung-ch'üan," " Illustrations to Book XV of the Odes," show that he was also a subject-painter.[2] He is thought of as working chiefly in ink, with light touches of colour; but out of the eleven pictures by him in the Ch'ien Lung Collection six were in full colours, four in ink alone, and one only in " light colours."

Hsia Kuei's paintings were from Ming times onwards excessively rare. The Ch'ien Lung Collection contained only two specimens, one a roll in ink (" Autumn River in Wind and Rain "), dated *Jēn-yin*, i.e. 1182; the other a roll in full colours (" Views of River and Hill "), dated *chia-tzŭ*, i.e. 1204.

---

[1] See *Shu Hua Fang*, 10, 31.
[2] In 1176 Ma Yüan (in conjunction with Li T'ang, Li Sung-nien and Hsia Kuei) stooped to the comparatively humble task of drawing the illustrations for the *Ku Yü T'u P'u*, a catalogue of jade objects in the Imperial Collection.

The critics of the 16th century abused the art of Ma Yüan and Hsia Kuei, relegating it to the " Northern School," that promiscuous repository of all their *bêtes noires*. It is quite clear why they disliked it. They regarded " northern " landscape as turgidly romantic. To them Ma Yüan seemed a sort of Lhermontoff. They were irritated by the preciosity of the figures who in Northern School painting sit thinking deep and poetic thoughts upon the edge of a precipice by moonlight.

What the adherents of the Southern School valued was elegance, charm, good taste ; theirs (at least, as we know it from the Ming painter Shēn Chou onwards) was essentially a happy art. They regarded any display of deep feeling as somewhat ill-bred ; to them art was an escape from the turbulence of human emotion into a world of refinement and grace. And if they make occasional excursions into Romanticism, it is in the style of Diderot rather than of Lhermontoff. Previous European writers have attributed the disfavour into which Ma Yüan and Hsia Kuei so rapidly fell, to the revival of orthodox Confucianism ; and it is true that Confucianism provided the natural background to an anti-mystical " 18th-century " state of mind. But it is worth noting that Tung Ch'i-ch'ang, the most bigoted opponent of the Northern School, was by no means an orthodox Confucian ; indeed, he dabbled more than a little in the very Zen doctrines which inspired 13th-century painting. He even gave sympathetic consideration to the tenets of Christianity.

The technique, but not, I think, the spirit, of the Ma-Hsia school, was inherited by Tai Chin as a reaction against the formalism of the Ming Academy. That there were already at this time persons who were profoundly irritated by the work of Ma Yüan and Hsia Kuei is illustrated by the story that when someone spoke to the 15th-century painter Kuo Shun of Ma and Hsia's pictures, the infuriated painter burst in with " What have I to do with their tail-ends of mountains and truncated streams, productions of ignoble refugees ? "[1] referring to the truncated state of China at the time when Ma Yüan lived. It would be painful to think that many Chinese judged works of art by such standards as these.

A less wholly insane point of view is expressed by Tu Mu, writing about 1500 A.D. :[2]

" Most of the Old Masters set great store by detail and high finish, and this lasted through T'ang down to the end of the Northern Sung dynasty. It was Ma Yüan and Hsia Kuei who painted with a free style in diluted ink, disguising their outlines and using rough contour-marks. This made

---

[1] Mistranslated by Giles, p. 144. [2] *Shu Hua P'u*, 84, 19.

the imitation of the Old Masters impossible, and the art of painting fell into decay. Connoisseurship is to-day at a low ebb, and consequently great importance is attached to the works of Ma and Hsia. But one has only to show their admirers a number of ancient paintings and they soon revise their judgment."

Several points here are of interest. The name of Li T'ang is omitted: we see that the popularity of Ma and Hsia had not wholly abated at the beginning of the 16th century: we find attributed to the two painters a great divorce from tradition, an absolute break with the past.

CHAPTER XVII
ZEN BUDDHISM
THE DRAGON

CHAPTER XVII
ZEN BUDDHISM
AND ITS RELATION TO ART

THE ZEN PAINTERS. THE DRAGON

Books on the Far East often mention a sect of Buddhism called Zen. They say it was a " school of abstract meditation " and that it exercised a profound influence upon art and literature ; but they tell us very little about what Zen actually was, about its relation to ordinary Buddhism, its history, or the exact nature of its influence upon the arts. The reason of this is that very little of the native literature which deals with Zen has yet been translated, perhaps because it is written in early Chinese colloquial, a language the study of which has been almost wholly neglected.

In the year 520 A.D. there arrived at Canton a missionary from Southern India. His name was Bodhidharma, and he appears to have been the younger son of an Indian prince. The reigning Emperor of China was a munificent patron of Buddhism. He had built monasteries, given alms, distributed scriptures, defended the faith. Hearing that a Buddhist prince had arrived from India, he summoned him at once to his capital. The following conversation took place in the Palace at Nanking :—

Emperor : You will be interested to hear that I have built many monasteries, distributed scriptures, given alms, and upheld the Faith. Have I not indeed acquired merit ?

Bodhidharma : None at all.

Emperor : In what then does true merit consist ?

Bodhidharma : In the obliteration of Matter through Absolute Knowledge, not by external acts.

Emperor : Which is the Divine and Primal Aspect of Reality ?

Bodhidharma : Reality has no aspect that is divine.

Emperor : What are you, who have come before my Throne ?

Bodhidharma : I do not know.

The Emperor could make nothing of him. Monasticism, a huge vested interest, decried him, and after a short stay in Nanking he started northward, towards the capital of the Wei Tartars, who, as we have seen, then ruled over a large part of China. The Wei Emperor, like his Chinese confrère, was also a great patron of Buddhism, and he, too, desired an interview with the Indian priest. But Bodhidharma had done with the Emperors, and settled in a small country temple, where he lived till his

215

death nine years later. Some say that he tried to visit the capital of the Weis, but was prevented by the intrigues of the monks there.

He left behind him a few short tractates, the substance of which is as follows:

There is no such person as Buddha. Buddha is simply a Sanskrit word meaning "initiate." The Absolute is immanent in every man's heart. This "treasure of the heart" is the only Buddha that exists. It is no use seeking Buddha outside your own nature. Prayer, scripture-reading, fasting, the observance of monastic rules—all are useless. Those who seek Buddha do not find him. You may know by heart all the Sūtras of the twelve divisions, and yet be unable to escape from the Wheel of Life and Death. One thing alone avails—to discover the unreality of the World by contemplating the Absolute which is at the root of one's own nature.

Some one asked him: "Why may we not worship the Buddhas and Bodhisattvas?" He answered:

"Ogres and hobgoblins can at will assume the outward form of Bodhisattvas: such are heretical and not of the true Buddha. There is no Buddha but your own thoughts. Buddha is the Way. The Way is Zen. This word Zen cannot be understood even of the wise. Zen means ' for a man to behold his own fundamental nature.'[1]

"The highest truths cannot be written down or taught by speech. A man who cannot write a word, can yet contemplate his own heart and become wise. Knowledge of 1000 Sūtras and 10,000 Śāstras cannot help him to realize the Absolute within him."

He was asked: "Can a layman with wife and children, one given over to the lusts of the flesh, achieve Buddhahood?" He answered:

"Provided he contemplates his own inner nature, he will achieve Buddhahood. It does not matter about his lusts. Even a butcher can achieve Buddhahood, if he searches in his own heart."

"What!" cried his listeners, "a butcher, who lives by taking life, and *he* achieve Buddhahood?" The master replied:

"It is not a question of the man's trade. If he has learnt to know his own nature he will be saved.

"I have come from India only to teach you that Buddha is Thought. I care nothing for monastic rules or ascetic practices. As for walking on water or through fire, climbing sword-wheels, fasting, sitting upright for hours without rest—all such practices are heretical; they belong to the World of Being.

[1] Zen (*Sanskrit : dhyāna*) means literally "contemplation."

216

" Thought, Thought, Thought ! It is hard to seek. Expanding, it covers the whole world ; shrinking, it is too small to lodge a pin.

" I seek the heart ; I do not seek Buddha. For I have learnt to know that the outer world is empty and untenanted."

Such was the teaching of Bodhidharma. It was Vedantic[1] rather than Buddhist. The terms " thought," " Buddha," etc., used by Bodhidharma, correspond exactly to the *brahman* of the Upanishads. Mystic contemplation or *yoga* had been used by the Brahmins and was not unknown to the early Buddhists. But Bodhidharma was the first to insist upon it as the sole means of salvation.

Yet though his whole teaching turned on this " meditation " or " Zen," he left behind him no exact directions for the practice of it. Having shown the end, he left it to each individual to find his own means. Rules, dogmas, and definitions were precisely what he set out to destroy. Less than a hundred years after his death another Indian, Buddhapriya, came to China and there defined with exactitude and blunt materiality the various forms of meditation. The transition from the spirituality of Bodhidharma to the grossness of his follower is, however, typical of religious history. The poetry of Christ turns into the theology of Paul; the hovel of Saint Francis into the mansion of Brother Elias.

BUDDHAPRIYA

He first describes the different attitudes in which Zen may be practised, with an exact account of the correct position of hands, feet, head, etc. The normal attitude of meditation, cross-legged, with upright back and hands locked over the knees, is familiar to every one.

Zen could also be practised while walking and, in cases of sickness, while lying down. Buddhapriya's instructions are in the form of question and answer.

Question : How does the Zen practised by heretics and by the other schools of Buddhism differ from our Zen ?

Answer : The Zen of the heretics is not impersonal. The Zen of the Lesser Vehicle is material. The Zen of the Greater Vehicle only abstracts man and phenomena.

Question : How ought one to set about practising Zen ?

Answer : First put far away from you all anger and malice, and fill your heart with kindness and compassion.

[1] Dr. McGovern tells me that Zen would seem to be more immediately derived from the Nihilistic School of Nāgārjuna (1st century A.D.), but Sir Charles Eliot (*Hinduism and Buddhism*, III, 305) emphasizes its connection with the Vedānta.

Question : Can the beginner at once proceed to the contemplation of non-Being?

Answer : By no means ! He must by stratagems gradually enter in. I have never yet seen one who straightway achieved the vision of non-Reality. If, for example, he were meditating in this room he must first banish from his mind every part of the world except the city of Ch'ang-an. Next, every building in the city except this monastery. Next, every room in the monastery except this cell, every object but himself, every part of himself except the end of his nose. Finally, the end of his nose hangs in space like a drop of dew, and on this nose-end he concentrates his mind.

This is only a preliminary exercise. There are others of the same kind. For example, persuade yourself that your navel is a minute rivulet running through the sands. When this conception is firmly achieved, you will see a bright light, and ultimately, the body growing transparent, you will behold the working of your bowels.

Or, again, regard your head as the top of a hollow pipe which runs straight down through your body into the earth. Meditate upon the top of your head, that is to say, upon the mouth of the drain-pipe, and then gradually ascend in your thoughts to a height of four inches above the head, and concentrate firmly on this conception. You will thus easily pass into the contemplation of non-Being, having performed the transition from elementary to complete Zen as comfortably as a workman climbs the rungs of a ladder.

Question : Are there any signs whereby I may know that I have attained to Samādhi?[1]

Answer : To be sure there are. Sometimes you will feel a sensation as of bugs or ants creeping over your skin ; or, again, it will appear to you that a cloud or mass of white cotton-wool is rising immediately behind your back. In neither case must you be discomposed or put out your hand. Sometimes it will seem as though oil were dripping down from your head and face ; sometimes a light will shine from out of the ground you are sitting upon.

These are all preliminary signs.

Sometimes, when you have been sitting for a long while and your back is aching, you will suddenly hear a sound of rapping with the fingers or a noise as of someone bumping against the door. Do not be disquieted. These are the Good Spirits of Heaven, come to warn you against sleep.

[1] " Concentration."

Again, it may happen that you have an agreeable sense of lightness and floating; this is a good sign. Beware, however, of a *painful* sense of lightness; for this may merely indicate flatulence.

Patches of heat on the body are a sign of Fiery Samādhi. A light filling the whole room is a premonitory sign of Zen; to smell strange fragrances not known on earth is a sign of whole and utter Abstraction.

Such and many more are the signs of Zen. The practicant must not heed them; for if by them he be encouraged or dismayed, all his work will be undone.

Question : Can Zen be practised in a Buddha Shrine ?

Answer : No, indeed ! Zen should be practised in a quiet room or under a tree or among tombs or sitting on the dewy earth.

Question : Can Zen be practised by many sitting together ?

Answer : To be sure it may; but each must face his neighbour's back. They must not sit face to face. When there are many sitting together at night, a lamp or candle may be lit; but when there are few together, it ought not to be used.

Question : Need I wear monastic vestments at my meditations ?

Answer : Vestments ? Why, you need wear no clothes at all, if so be you are alone.

LATER DEVELOPMENT OF ZEN

Zen was at first a purely personal discipline, non-monastic, non-ethical, not demanding the acceptance of any Scripture or any tradition. In modern Japan it has to some extent regained this character. In China the habit of quoting written authority was too strong to be easily discarded. The Zen masters soon began to answer difficult questions by quoting from the Buddhist Scriptures. Convenience dictated that practicants of Zen should live in communities, and monasticism was soon established in their sect, as in every other sect of Buddhism. Questions of conduct arose, and Zen was squared with the contemporary ethical outlook; though in mediæval Japanese literature wicked and cynical persons are generally depicted as adepts of Zen.

Bodhidharma denied the existence of Good and Evil; but it was pointed out by later apologists that the Zen adept, having viewed the Absolute, is convinced of the unreality and futility of those pleasures and possessions which are the incentive to sin. The Zen practicant, though he makes no moral effort, nevertheless is certain not to sin, because he is certain not to be tempted.

Finally, Zen forged itself a tradition. Probably during the 11th century a Scripture[1] was fabricated which recounts how once, when Buddha was preaching, he plucked a flower and smiled. Only the disciple Kāśyapa understood the significance of this act. Between him and Buddha there passed a wordless communication of Absolute Truths. This communication was silently passed on by Kāśyapa to his disciple, and so ultimately to Bodhidharma, who brought it to China.

The method of teaching by symbolic acts (such as the plucking of a flower) was extensively used by the Zen masters. For example, when a disciple asked Yen-kuan a question about the nature of Buddha, he answered: " Bring me a clean bowl." When the priest brought the bowl, the master said, " Now put it back where you found it." He signified that the priest's questionings must return to their proper place, the questioner's heart, from which alone spiritual knowledge can be obtained.

The object of the Zen teachers, as of some eccentric schoolmasters whom I have known, seems at first sight to have been merely to puzzle and surprise their pupils to the highest possible degree. A peculiar " brusquerie " was developed in Zen monasteries. The literature of the sect consists chiefly in an endless series of anecdotes recording the minutest happenings in the lives of famous Zen monks and their (apparently) most trivial sayings. But behind these trifling acts and sayings a deep meaning lay hid. The interpretation of such teaching depends on a complete knowledge of the symbolism used. I am not inclined to agree with those students of Zen who assert that its written teaching is wholly devoid of intellectual content or so completely esoteric as not to admit of explanation in words. Like other Buddhist philosophers, the Zen masters were chiefly concerned with the attempt to define the relation between the One and the Many, between the subjective and objective aspects of life.

The idealism of Zen does not mean that the phenomenal world has no importance. To those who have not reached complete self-realization the urgencies of that world remain paramount and are the only stepping-stones upon which they can climb higher.

On the day of his arrival at the monastery a novice presented himself before the abbot, begging to be allowed to begin his spiritual exercises without further delay. " Have you had supper ? " asked the abbot. " Yes." " Then go and wash your plate."

[1] *Ta Fan-t'ien-wang wēn-Fo chuĕh-i Ching.*

ZEN BUDDHISM: THE DRAGON

THE ZEN MASTERS

Let us begin with Hui-nēng, a master of the 7th century. He lost his parents when he was young and earned his living by gathering firewood. One day when he was in the market-place he heard someone reading the *Diamond Sūtra*.[1] He asked where such books were to be had, and was told " From Master Hung-jēn on the Yellow Plum-blossom Hill." Accordingly he went to Hung-jēn's monastery in Anhui and presented himself before the master. " Where do you come from ? " " From the South." " Bah ! In the South they have not Buddha in their souls." " North and South," replied Hui-nēng, " are human distinctions that Buddha knows nothing of."

Hung-jēn accepted him as a lay-brother and put him to pound rice in the bakery.

Hung-jēn was growing old and wished to choose his successor. He therefore instituted a poetical competition in which each monk was to epitomize in a quatrain the essence of Zen. The favourite candidate was the warden Shēn-hsiu, who sent in the following verses :

> *The body is the trunk of the Bodhi-tree,*
> *The mind is the bright mirror's stand.*
> *Scrub your mirror continually,*
> *Lest the dust eclipse its brightness.*

Hui-nēng, as a lay-brother, was not qualified to compete. Someone told him of Shēn-hsiu's quatrain. " Mine would be very different," he exclaimed, and persuaded one of the boys employed in the bakery to go stealthily by night and inscribe the following poem on the monastery wall :

> *Knowledge is not a tree,*
> *The Mirror has no stand;*
> *Since nothing exists,*
> *How could dust rise and cover it ?*

The authorship of the poem was discovered, and the abbot Hung-jēn visited Hui-nēng in the bakery. " Is your rice white or no ? " he asked. " White ? " answered Hui-nēng ; " it has not yet been sifted." Thereupon the abbot struck three times on the rice-mortar with his staff and departed. Hui-nēng understood his meaning. That night at the third watch he came to Hung-jēn's cell and was invested with the abbot's mantle, thereby

[1] Translated by W. Gemmell, 1912. Its use by Hung-jēn shows that Zen did not long eschew the scriptures.

221

becoming the Sixth Patriarch of the Zen Church. He died in 712 A.D., without having learned how to read or write.

FASHIONABLE ZEN

The warden Shēn-hsiu had lost the Patriarchate and with it the spiritual headship of Zen. But as a compensation Fate had in store for him worldly triumphs of the most dazzling kind. Leaving the rural monastery of Hung-jēn, he entered the Temple of the Jade Fountain in the great city of Kingchau. His fame soon spread over Central China. He was a man of " huge stature, bushy eyebrows and shapely ears." The Empress Wu-hou, who had usurped the throne of China, notoriously cultivated the society of handsome priests. About 684 A.D. she summoned him to the capital. Instead of commanding his presence at Court she came in a litter to his lodgings and actually knelt down before him. The friendship of this woman procured for him temporal dignities which in the eyes of the world completely outshone the rustic piety of the Sixth Patriarch. Shēn-hsiu at the capital became as it were the Temporal Father of Zen, while Hui-nēng at his country monastery remained its spiritual pope. The successors of Hui-nēng became known as the Fathers of the Southern School, while the courtly and social Zen of Shēn-hsiu is called Zen of the North.[1]

Was it in sincere goodwill or with the desire to discredit his rival that Shēn-hsiu invited Hui-nēng to join him at the capital? In any case, Hui-nēng had the good sense to refuse. " I am a man of low stature and humble appearance," he replied ; " I fear that the men of the North would despise me and my doctrines "—thus hinting (with just that touch of malice which so often spices the unworldly) that Shēn-hsiu's pre-eminence in the North was due to outward rather than to spiritual graces.

Shēn-hsiu died in 706, outliving his august patroness by a year. To perpetuate his name a palace was turned into a memorial monastery; the Emperor's brother wrote his epitaph, his obsequies were celebrated with stupendous pomp.

His successor, P'u-chi, at first remained at the Kingchau monastery, where he had been Shēn-hsiu's pupil. But in 724 the irresolute Emperor Ming-huang, who had proscribed Buddhism ten years before, summoned P'u-chi to the Imperial City. Here princes and grandees vied with one another in doing him honour. " The secret of his success," says the historian,[2] " was that he seldom spoke and generally looked cross. Hence his rare

---

[1] See above, p. 182–3.   [2] *Old T'ang History*, 191.

words and occasional smiles acquired in the eyes of his admirers an unmerited value." He died at the age of eighty-nine. On the day of his interment the great streets of Ch'ang-an were empty. The whole city had joined in the funeral procession. The Governor of Honan (one of the greatest functionaries in the State), together with his wife and children, all of them clad in monastic vestments, followed the bier, mingling with the promiscuous crowd of his admirers and disciples.

Religion was at that time fashionable in the high society of Ch'ang-an, as it is to-day in the great Catholic capitals of Munich, Vienna, or Seville. When I read of P'u-chi's burial another scene at once sprang to my mind— the funeral procession of a great Bavarian dignitary, in which I saw the noblemen of Munich walk hooded and barefoot through the streets.

I shall not refer again to the Northern School of Zen. One wonders whether the founders of religions are forced by fate to watch the posthumous development of their creeds. If so, theirs must be the very blackest pit of Hell.

Let us return to the Southern School, always regarded as the true repository of Zen tradition.

HUANG PO[1]

Huang Po lived at the beginning of the 9th century, and was thus a contemporary of the poet Po Chü-i. He enjoyed the patronage of a distinguished statesman, the Chancellor P'ei Hsiu, of whom the Emperor said, " This is indeed a true Confucian." It is to the Chancellor that we owe the record of Huang Po's conversations, which he wrote down day by day. I will make a few extracts from this diary :—

P'ei Hsiu. Hui-nēng could not read or write. How came it that he succeeded to the Patriarchate of Hung-jēn? The warden Shēn-hsiu was in control of 500 monks, gave lectures, and could discourse upon thirty-two different Sūtras and Śāstras. It was certainly very strange that he was not made Patriarch.

Huang Po (replying): Shēn-hsiu's conception of Thought was too material. His proofs and practices were too positive.

" The master told me that when he was studying with Yen-kuan, the Emperor Tai Chung came dressed as a monk. The master happened to be in the chapel prostrating himself before an image of Buddha. The Emperor, who thought he had learnt the lesson of Zen idealism, said to him : ' There is nothing to be got from Buddha, nothing from the Church,

---

[1] So named from the Huang Po Mountain in Fuhkien, where he taught.

nothing from Man ; for nothing exists. What do you mean by praying at your age ? '

" Huang Po answered him : ' I seek nothing of Buddha, the Church, or Man ; I am in the habit of praying.' The Emperor said : ' What do you do it for ? ' Huang Po lost patience and struck him with his fist. ' You rude fellow,' cried the Emperor. ' Since nothing exists, what difference does it make to you whether I am rude or polite ? ' and Huang Po struck him again. The Emperor retreated hastily."

In his old age Huang Po visited his native village and stayed a year in his mother's house without revealing his identity. After he had set out again for his monastery, his mother suddenly realized that he was her son and went in pursuit of him. She reached the shore of a certain river, only to see him disembarking upon the other side. Thereupon she lost her reason and flung herself into the water.

Huang Po threw a lighted torch after her and recited the following verses :

> *May the wide river dry at its source, to its very bed*
> *If here the crime of matricide has been done ;*
> *When one son becomes a priest, the whole family is born again in Heaven ;*
> *If that is a lie, all that Buddha promised is a lie.*

Henceforward the throwing of a lighted torch into the bier became part of the Zen funeral ceremony ; it was accompanied by the reciting of the above verses. Probably formula, ritual, and story alike belong to a period much more ancient than Buddhism.

In the 17th century a Chinese priest named Yin-yüan[1] carried the teaching of Huang Po to Japan, where it now possesses nearly 700 temples.[2]

MA TSU

Ma Tsu was a master of the 9th century. One day he was sitting with his feet across the garden-path. A monk came along with a wheelbarrow. " Tuck in your feet," said the monk. " What has been extended cannot be retracted," answered Ma Tsu. " What has been started cannot be stopped," cried the monk, and pushed the barrow over Ma Tsu's feet. The master hobbled to the monastery, and, seizing an axe, called out : " Have any of you seen the rascal who hurt my feet ? " The monk who had pushed the barrow then came out and stood " with craned head." The master laid down his axe.

[1] 1592–1673 A.D.   [2] Huang Po is in Japanese pronounced Ōbaku.

To understand this story we must realize that the wheelbarrow is here a symbol of the Wheel of Life and Death, which, though every spoke of it is illusion, cannot be disregarded till we have destroyed the last seed of phenomenal perception in us.

LIN-CHI[1]

Huang Po, as we have seen, taught wisdom with his fists. When the novice, Lin-chi, came to him and asked him what was the fundamental idea of Buddhism, Huang Po hit him three times with his stick. Lin-chi fled and presently met the monk Ta-yu.

Ta-yu : Where do you come from?

Lin-chi : From Huang Po.

Ta-yu : And what stanza did he lecture upon?

Lin-chi : I asked him thrice what was the fundamental doctrine of Buddhism, and each time he hit me with his stick. Please tell me if I did something I ought not to have done?

Ta-yu : You go to Huang Po and torture him by your questions, and then ask if you have done wrong.

At that moment Lin-chi had a Great Enlightenment.

Lin-chi substituted howling for Huang Po's manual violence. He shouted meaningless syllables at his disciples ; roared like a lion or bellowed like a bull. This " howling " became a regular part of Zen practice, and may be compared to the yelling of the American Shakers. Upon his death-bed Lin-chi summoned his disciples round him and asked which of them felt capable of carrying on his work. San-shēng volunteered to do so. " How will you tell people what was Lin-chi's teaching? " asked Lin-chi. San-shēng threw out his chest and roared in a manner which he thought would gratify the master. But Lin-chi groaned and cried out, " To think that such a blind donkey should undertake to hand on my teaching ! "

It was in the 12th and 13th centuries that Zen most completely permeated Chinese thought. Upon the invasion of the Mongols[2] many Zen monks from Western China took refuge in Japan ; the same thing happened during the Manchu invasion in the 17th century. But by that time Zen had a serious philosophic rival.

In the 15th century the philosopher Wang Yang-ming began to propagate a doctrine which, in all but names, strongly resembled the philosophic side

[1] Lin-chi (" coming to the ford ") is, like Huang-po, a place-name. It is not (as Eliot conjectures it might be) a translation of the Pali term *sotāpanno.*

[2] On the attitude of the Mongol rulers to Zen, see an article by Prof. Kunishita, *Tōyō Gakuhō,* xi, 4, 87.

of Zen. He taught that in each one of us is a " higher nature," something which, borrowing a phrase from Mencius, he called " Good Knowledge." Of this inner nature he speaks in exactly the same terms as the Zen teachers spoke of their " Buddha immanent in man's heart." He even uses the same kind of doggerel verse as a medium of teaching.

Rigid Confucianists, who would not have listened to any doctrine of professedly Buddhist origin, were able through Wang Yang-ming's tact to accept the philosophy of Zen without feeling that they were betraying the Confucian tradition. The followers of Yang-ming are to-day very numerous both in China and Japan. They cultivate introspection, but not the complete self-hypnosis of Zen.

In China, where Zen is almost forgotten, the followers of this later doctrine are not even aware of its derivation.

ZEN AND ART

I said at the beginning of this chapter that Zen is often mentioned by writers on Far Eastern art. The connection between Zen and art is important, not only because of the inspiration which Zen gave to the artist, but also because through Zen was obtained a better understanding of the psychological conditions under which art is produced than has prevailed in any other civilization.

Art was regarded as a kind of Zen, as a delving down into the Buddha that each of us unknowingly carries within him, as Benjamin carried Joseph's cup in his sack. Through Zen we annihilate Time and see the Universe not split up into myriad fragments, but in its primal unity. Unless, says the Zen æsthetician, the artist's work is imbued with this vision of the subjective, non-phenomenal aspect of life, his productions will be mere toys.

I do not mean that in Zen Chinese artists found a short cut to the production of beauty. Zen aims at the annihilation of consciousness, whereas art is produced by an interaction of conscious and unconscious faculties. How far such an interaction can be promoted by the psychic discipline of Zen no layman can judge ; moreover, the whole question of the artist's psychology is controversial and obscure.

Perhaps it is not even very important that the artist himself should have a sound æsthetic ; but it is of the utmost importance to the artist that the public should have some notion of the conditions under which art can be produced—should have some key to the vagaries of a section of humanity which will in any case always be found troublesome and irritating.

226

Such a key Zen supplied, and it is in the language of Zen that, after the 12th century, art is usually discussed in China and Japan.

Zen paintings are of two kinds. (1) Representations of animals, birds, and flowers, in which the artist attempted to identify himself with the object depicted, to externize its inner Buddha. These were achieved not by study from the life, as the early Sung nature-pieces had been, but by intense and concentrated visualization of the subject to be painted. This mental picture was rapidly transferred to paper before the spell of concentration (*samādhi*) was broken. (2) Illustrations of episodes in the lives of the great Zen teachers. This branch of Zen art was essentially dramatic. It sought to express the characters of the persons involved, subtly to reveal the grandeur of soul which lay hidden behind apparent uncouthness or stupidity. Typical of this kind of paintings are the pictures of " Tan-hsia Burning the Image."[1]

One night Tan-hsia, a Zen priest, stayed as a guest at an ordinary Buddhist monastery. There was no firewood in his cell. As the night was cold he went into the chapel, seized a wooden statue of Shākyamuni, and, chopping it up, made himself a comfortable fire. To him the idol of Buddha was a mere block of wood ; his indignant hosts took a different view. The controversy is the same as that which occupies the central place in the Nō play *Sotoba Komachi*.

Other common subjects are Bodhidharma with tightly closed lips, as he appeared before the Emperor of China ; Bodhidharma crossing the Yangtze on a reed ; Hui-k'o, the Second Patriarch, cutting off his own arm in order to persuade Bodhidharma that he was in earnest ; Hui-k'o waiting waist-deep in the snow till Bodhidharma deigned to admit him ; Tē-shan tearing up his commentary on the *Diamond Sūtra*.

THE ZEN PAINTERS

Shih K'o. Before considering the Southern Sung Zen painters I must deal with their rather mysterious forerunner, Shih K'o. His master is said to have been the late T'ang Buddhist painter, Chang Nan-pēn, of whom I have already spoken. Chang flourished[2] c. 874–889 ; but we do not know his exact dates. He may well have been alive at the beginning of the 10th century. Shih K'o was a native of Ch'ēng-tu, at which town Chang Nan-pēn had worked between 881 and 885. He was sharp-tongued and of a satirical turn of mind. If he was out of humour with his customers,

[1] See Kümmel, *Die Kunst Ostasiens*, Pl. 118.   [2] See *Shu Hua P'u*, 48, 8.

however rich and influential they might be, he would make game of them in the pictures which they had ordered. The 16th-century writer Tu Mu[1] tells us that in his comic pictures Shih K'o " drew " only the faces, arms, and feet of his figures; the draperies were indicated by " rough strokes."

The Hui Tsung Collection possessed (in the first quarter of the 12th century) twenty-one pieces attributed to him—Taoist subjects, star-divinities, Madame Chung K'uei, and one Lohan. From the pen of Su Tung-p'o's friend Li Ch'ien we have a description of an elaborate mytho-logical picture by Shih K'o, " The Jade Emperor Holding His Court "[2]: " Celestial fairies and magical officers, Golden Boys and Jewel Maidens, the Three Marshals, the Great Unity, the Seven Aboriginals, the Four Holy Ones, Rain, Thunder, and Lightning, the presiding spirits of every hill and stream, all powers and dominations whether above the earth or below it—these and no less are seen assembled in the Emperor's Presence. The Jade Emperor himself, great Lord of Heaven, sits with his face to the south, robed in stately apparel. . . .

" It was from Shih K'o's wild mockery of the world in which he lived that his painting derived its masterly freedom; he can break all the rules of his art and yet delight and surprise us. If the types he depicts are sometimes uncouth, odd, or repulsive, this is only that he may display the variety of Nature. In this picture, for example, he has, in order to make game of us, bedecked the persons of some of the water divinities with fish or crabs.

" I have seen a painting by Shih K'o of an old man and woman drinking vinegar, their wrinkled noses and wry mouths vividly expressing its sour-ness. I also remember his ' Demons' Hundred Gambols.' Chung K'uei and his wife are seated at a table with wine and victuals in front of them. They and their attendants are all marvellously portrayed. In the fore-ground are groups of big and little demons who are amusing the bridal pair by doing tricks to the accompaniment of music. . . .

" In this picture of the Jade Emperor he did not dare to carry his jesting too far; but he could not resist decking the water-gods with crab-pendants, that he might get at least one smile from posterity."

Upon Shih K'o's picture of the " Three Laughers "[3] Su Tung-p'o wrote the following inscription : " The three of them are laughing in chorus ;

---

[1] See *Shu Hua P'u*, 12, 10.

[2] *Ibid.*, 82, 20. The Jade Emperor is the paramount Taoist divinity.

[3] See above, p. 41.

228

even their clothes, hats, shoes all have an amused air. The acolyte behind them is beside himself with laughter."

The 14th-century writer Chu Tē-jun[1] praises the " beautiful and delicate colouring " of Shih K'o's " Madame Chung K'uei and her Little Sisters " and finds in it an interesting survival of T'ang style. This is presumably the same picture that was in the Hui Tsung Collection. The story of Chung K'uei was as follows : One night the Emperor Ming Huang of the T'ang dynasty dreamt that he saw an imp stealing Yang Kuei-fei's jade flute. Presently a huge figure in a broken Court hat and top-boots came striding in, seized the imp between his finger and thumb, gouged its eyes out, and ate it whole. When the Emperor asked who he was, he answered that he was the spirit of a certain student named Chung K'uei, who in the 7th century, having failed to pass his examinations, dashed out his brains against the steps of the Examination Hall. The Emperor of the day, taking pity on him, ordered him to be given a Court burial. In gratitude for this he had vowed to devote his spirit-life to protecting the Emperors of China from all elves, goblins, and evil influences. Next day Ming Huang described his dream to Wu Tao-tzŭ, who thereupon painted the famous picture of Chung K'uei beating a small imp with his stick.[2]

The picture probably suggested the story. It is said that the name Chung K'uei means " stick " in Shantung dialect, and that Chung K'uei is simply The Man with the Stick. It existed as a personal name from early times, and was apparently used by both men and women.[3]

There arose (probably towards the end of T'ang) the legend of a female Chung K'uei, sometimes treated of as the demon-queller's wife. It seems to be thus that she figures in the picture of the " Demons' Hundred Gambols " mentioned above. In the picture praised by Chu Tē-jun were represented " a young bride with four female imps in attendance upon her." These were presumably her sisters, but the legend of Madame Chung K'uei is hard to disentangle. In any case, both the Chung K'ueis are commonly shown with a retinue of attendant imps. Favourite subjects are " Chung K'uei's Wedding," " Chung K'uei Playing the Lute by Moonlight " (by Ma Yüan, for example), and " Chung K'uei Moving House." These subjects gave scope for a great deal of *grotesquerie* similar to that of the Arhat pictures by Lu Lēng-ch'ieh.

[1] *Shu Hua P'u*, 82, 20.   [2] A copy of it is reproduced in *Kokka*, 30.
[3] It was borne by Yao Hsüan of the N. Wei dynasty (5th century) in conjunction with the name Pi-hsieh, " Exorcist," and by an aunt of the 5th century general Tsung Ch'io, famous for his campaigns in Indo-China.

Shih K'o's pictures in Japan. The Shōhōji, near Kyōto, possesses a pair of paintings[1] inscribed with an inscription to the effect that they were painted in the first year of the period Ch'ien Tēn (965 or possibly 919) by Shih K'o of Ssechuan. They were given to this temple by a Court lady in the 17th century; their previous history is quite unknown. The one which represents a man leaning on a tiger is inscribed: *Ērh tsu tiao hsin*, which may mean either "The Second Patriarch Attuning his Heart," or "Two Patriarchs Attuning their Hearts." The difficulty of accepting the first explanation is that the Second Patriarch of the Zen sect is not particularly associated with the tiger. If we accept the alternative and consider the pictures to represent two unnamed Patriarchs, we are still left in doubt as to which of the Zen Patriarchs can possibly be meant, for clearly the Patriarchs of the Magic Sect cannot come into consideration.

Kokka, 95, identifies the figures with the two Lohan Bhadra and Jivaka. This seems very improbable; and are Lohan ever referred to as Patriarchs (*tsu*)? Were it not for the inscription the figure leaning on the tiger would probably have been taken for Fēng-kan, the frequent companion (particularly in Japanese paintings) of Han-shan and Shih-tē.[2]

It is also true that were it not for the inscription which attributes the pictures to Shih K'o they would certainly have passed as the work of a Southern Sung artist. And it is this fact which gives them their archæological importance. They seem to prove that we must regard the ink-technique of the 13th-century Zen painters as a revival rather than a discovery.

THE LIU-T'UNG-SSŬ SCHOOL

One institution, about which till recently very little was known, seems to have been an important factor in the propagation of Zen art and ideas. About 1215 A.D. a Zen priest came from the far south-west of China to Hangchow, the capital, and there refounded a ruined monastery, the Liu T'ung-ssŭ, which stood on the shores of the famous Western Lake. His name was Mu-ch'i. He seems to have been the first to practise in connection with Zen the swift, erratic type of monochrome invented more than two hundred years earlier by Shih K'o. In hurried swirls of ink he sought to record before they faded visions and exaltations produced whether by the frenzy of wine, the stupor of tea, or the vacancy of absorption.

[1] *Kokka*, 95; *Shimbi Taikwan*, III; *Tōyō*, VIII.
[2] The pictures are accompanied by an inscription by the 14th century calligraphist Yü Chi. The publication of it might throw light on the subjects of the paintings.

Sometimes his design is tangled and chaotic; sometimes, as in his famous " Persimmons," passion has congealed into a stupendous calm.[1] Of his fellow-workers the best known is Lo-ch'uang, a painter of birds and flowers. Liang K'ai,[2] once a fashionable painter, left the Court and with his pupil Li Ch'üeh worked in the manner of Mu-ch'i. Examples of Liang K'ai's work before and after his conversion are still preserved in Japan.

Finally, about the middle of the 14th century, a Japanese priest, Mokuan, came to China and, under circumstances which I have elsewhere[3] described, confusingly became Mu-ch'i II. It may be that it was he who sent back to his own country some of the numerous pictures signed Mu-ch'i which are now in Japan. Which of them are by Mu-ch'i and which by Mokuan is a problem which remains to be solved.

Very little is known of the lives of these 13th-century Zen artists. Numerous works in Japan have been assigned to them. Many of them have been published in Japanese art-journals; others have never been shown except as accessories to the tea-ceremony. The work of critically examining and sifting this material has only just begun. For this reason I have treated them with a brevity which does not at all do justice to their importance.

P'u-ming. In the 14th century Zen did not flourish, giving place in many instances to the Lamaistic Buddhism which was the religion of the Mongols. But some of the earlier Mongol rulers patronized Zen, and " south of the River," particularly at Soochow, Zen priests carried on the thought and art of their Southern Sung predecessors.

At the Ch'ēng-t'ien-ssŭ in Soochow the priest P'u-ming, called Hsüeh-ch'uang (" Snowy Window "), painted ink-orchids. One of his pieces is in the collection of Mr. Masao Gejō.[4] Neither of the two other Mongol dynasty priests of whom I am about to speak was a member of the Zen sect, and one of them ought not perhaps to be classified as a Buddhist at all. But their art was very closely allied to that of their Zen confrères.

P'u-kuang. Of this artist Professor Pelliot writes : " Il fut au début du XIVe siècle le chef d'une secte religieuse reconnue comme une véritable religion par les souverains mongols, la secte des *dhūta*."[5] Upon the recommendation of Chao Mēng-fu[6] he was made professor in the Chao-wēn College. In 1312 he wrote a preface to the *Sūtra of the 42 Articles.*

In mediæval Japan the *dhūta* (called *zuta kotsujiki*) were mendicant

---

[1] See Plate XLIV. [2] See Plate XLV.

[3] See my *Zen Buddhism*, Luzac, 1922. [4] See *Bijutsu Shūyei*, Vol. 3.

[5] *T'oung-pao*, 1922, p. 351. See also *Bulletin de l'école française d'Extrême-Orient*, III. 315–16 ; IV, 438. [6] See below, p. 237.

Buddhist friars; they certainly did not constitute a separate religion. The part they played in China will no doubt be clearer when Professor Pelliot has published his notes on the subject. It is as an artist that P'u-kuang here concerns us. His best-authenticated work is an album of nineteen leaves representing Bodhidharma, P'u-tai, and seventeen Lohan[1]—rapid sketches of astounding dexterity and economy of line. It is not surprising to learn that P'u-kuang was famous chiefly for his calligraphy; his painting, indeed, seems to be a side-product of that art. Here we have the Lohan in their last stage of secularization. Starting as cult-figures, they became in Kuan-hsiu's hands impressive Indian magicians; and in Li Lung-mien's, Chinese sages. P'u-kuang treats them with as little reference to their sacred charatcer as would a Japanese artist in a *surimono*.

He is, in fact, the precursor of *Wēn-jēn-hua* (" Literary Man's Painting "). His dexterous wayward urbanity belongs to the milieu of the Ming eclectics rather than to the over-gilded setting of the Mongol Court which honoured him.

Po-tzŭ-t'ing. Po-tzŭ-t'ing came from Chia-ting in Ssechuan. At one time he expounded the doctrines of the T'ien-tai Sect at Ch'ih-Ch'ēng in Chekiang. " But by nature he loved the track of waves and journeying of clouds. He begged his way from village to village, saying little to those he met, but mixing that little with strange jests. He loved to paint rocks and irises, and would cover his pictures with poetical inscriptions."

Zen art was revived at the beginning of the Manchu dynasty by a small group of which the most important was the priest Tao-Chi (born about 1630, died about 1717). This new Zen art was, like that of the 14th century, allied to the Literary Style (*Wēn-jēn-hua*), of which the greatest contemporary exponent was Chu Ta,[2] who himself became a priest in 1644. Both men were members of aristocratic Ming families; both sought to drown with painting and religion the shame of the Manchu conquest. " In their pictures," wrote Chēng Hsieh,[3] rather over-rhetorically, " the tear-stains outnumber the brush-marks."

Rather junior to them was K'un-ts'an, a priest in the Bull's Head Temple at Nanking; it was said that, whereas Tao-chi achieved complete " realization " in his art but not in his religious life, K'un-ts'an " failed to convey in his painting the full measure of his spiritual illumination."

[1] Reproductions in *Kokka*, 333. The album belongs to Baron Koyata Iwazaki.
[2] Called Pa-ta Shan-jēn, " the Eight-Great Hermit," in allusion to his devotion to the *Sūtra on the Eight Great Awakings of Man* (Nanjio's Catalogue, No. 512).
[3] Called " Plank-bridge," a famous 18th-century poet.

In art Tao-chi preached a doctrine of individualism. " One may imitate the old masters' methods of brushwork, but still one has not painted ' their landscape.' By all these categories and rules one becomes a slave to the old masters and is reduced to feeding upon scraps from their table. But the whiskers of the Ancients can never sprout upon my cheeks. . . . Once my motto was *My own way*. But now I realize that, after all, there is only one way, and that which I discovered for myself and called my own way was really the way of the Ancients."[1] The Yu-chēng Shu-chü at Shanghai has published a collection of his landscapes, under the title *Shih-T'ao Shang-jēn Shan-shui ts'ē*.

THE DRAGON

Allied rather to Taoist than to Zen mysticism is the art of dragon-painting, which reached its zenith in the 13th century. The British Museum possesses a dragon-painting in ink with washes of light red. The monster descends across the picture from right to left, hollow-eyed, noseless, with three huge teeth protruding from its lower jaw ; the prongs of its beard hang like pink icicles under its chin. From each side of its forehead coiling antennæ sprout. Its scaly trunk is wreathed in a swirl of mist and darkness. White clouds of billowy shape hem it in below and above ; on the lower cloud is the cursive signature " So-wēng." The creator of this dim monster presents that extraordinary combination of Bohemianism and administrative efficiency which so often startles us in reading Chinese biographies. He was Lord Cromer, with a touch of Aubrey Beardsley.

Ch'ēn Jung. Ch'ēn Jung, called So-wēng, was born at Ch'ang-lo in Fuhkien about 1200. He passed his examinations in 1235 and became clerk to the Imperial Academy. Later he was made Governor of P'u-t'ien in Fuhkien, and rose to a high rank at Court. " In his early days he was a magistrate in Shansi. Here he built roads and aqueducts, instituted schemes of poor relief, and repaired temples and schools. He showed great forbearance in the discharge of his office ; and in his private life, the utmost simplicity. He would often gather round him the scholars of the neighbourhood and discuss with them the obscurities of the Classics. On his holidays he would talk of literature with men of refinement or compose poems in their company. Chia Ssǔ-tao[2] once invited him to serve under his banner ; but Jung was drunk when the invitation came and answered flippantly. Ssǔ-tao, who had a great respect for his character, did not take

---

[1] His essay on painting was published in 1728 under the title *K'u Kua Ho-shang Hua Yü Lu*. It was reprinted in 1908.   [2] Died 1276.

it ill. " The vigour of his prose and verse won him a great reputation in the era Pao Yu.[1]

" He would make clouds by splashing ink and mists by spitting water. When excited by wine, he would give a great shout, and seizing his cap, use it as a painting-brush, roughly smearing his design. Afterwards he finished the picture with a proper brush. Sometimes it would be a complete dragon ; sometimes only an arm or the head was showing ; or again there would be nothing but a dim adumbration of undefinable shapes, such as no other mind could have conceived ; yet all of marvellous beauty."

The British Museum painting is certainly not an original. The Ch'ien Lung Collection possessed his " Nine Dragons " dated 1244. Of the very numerous paintings in Japan which are attributed to Ch'ēn Jung, the best authenticated is probably Count Tokugawa's Dragon, reproduced in *Kokka,* 266.

---

[1] 1253–1259.

CHAPTER XVIII
YÜAN AND AFTER

CHAPTER XVIII
YÜAN AND AFTER

The Mongols were merely policemen. They did not influence the development of Chinese civilization any more than the officials at the gate of the British Museum influence the studies of the gentlemen who work inside. The " Mongol drama," the great innovation of the period, had nothing whatever to do with the Mongols. It was written (with the exception of one piece by a naturalized Tartar) entirely by and for Chinese. It had grown up naturally and inevitably out of various forms of recital, mimic dance, ballad, variety-turn, etc. It would have come into being if the Mongols had never conquered China, nor did they, so far as I know, give it any particular encouragement.

There was a tendency towards archaistic revival. The Court painters and poets felt that nothing less than the large *allure* of the T'ang dynasty was suitable to the triumphant times in which they lived. Moreover, their Mongol masters were as anxious as any American at Rome to get hold of the real, the hoarily traditional thing. In the suave and competent Chao Mēng-fu the conquerors found an ideal link between their own crude barbarism and the age-long civilization of their victims.

Chao Mēng-fu. He was a descendant of one of the sons of the first Sung Emperor. Born in 1254, he had already served for several years as secretary to the Treasurer of Chēn-chou (Marco Polo's Sinju), when the Sung dynasty fell. In 1286 Kublai Khan sent an envoy to the south of China to seek out prominent survivors of the late dynasty. Chao was persuaded to present himself at Court, and Kublai at once perceived his unusual force of character. " He seemed like a god come down to dwell among men. The Khan was delighted with him and pressed him into a seat above that of the Chancellor. Some murmured that Mēng-fu, being a descendant of the fallen Sungs, ought not to be admitted to the Court, but the Emperor did not heed them. It happened that at this time a proclamation had to be framed. Mēng-fu composed it, and when the Khan read it he exclaimed, " You have written exactly what I wished to be said." Many of the memorials written by Chao Mēng-fu still survive. He seems to have spent a great deal of his time in composing the elaborate proclamations by which the Emperor invested obscure Mongol princesses with high-flown Chinese titles.

He next distinguished himself as an economist. A rapid decline in the value of money had introduced various anomalies into the operation of the penal code. Mēng-fu proposed that the code should reckon in rolls of silk instead of strings of cash. He was violently opposed, his enemies alleging that the advice of one who was both a southerner and so young could not be of any value.

As a Cabinet Minister he found himself in very mixed company. The Cabinet was presided over by an Uighur named Sanga. When Sanga took his seat a bell was rung, and any Minister who arrived after the bell had ceased ringing was flogged. One day Mēng-fu arrived late, and was whipped. He was willing to put up with a good deal of barbarian eccentricity, but this was too much for his ex-Imperial feelings. He complained to the Chancellor, who was a Chinaman, and it was arranged with Sanga that henceforward only the minor officials should be flogged for unpunctuality.

In 1316 he became secretary of the Han-lin Academy. For some years, although not actually holding the position of Prime Minister, he had been the Emperor Ayuli Palpata's confidential adviser. His anomalous position caused great discontent in Court circles, but the Emperor used to say, " A Minister who was chosen by the great Kublai Khan is good enough for me."

In 1321 Ayuli Palpata died. The new Emperor, Sotpala, sent a messenger to Mēng-fu's house requesting him to make a calligraphic copy of the *Book of Filial Piety*. He did so, and was richly rewarded by Sotpala. A few months later he died at the age of sixty-nine.

Many of the Chinese who took office under the Mongols did so reluctantly, offering a somewhat sulky assistance to the new government only because they considered it to be in the interest of their country that they should do so. The Chancellor Yeh Li belonged to this category. Chao Mēng-fu's attitude was quite different. He expressed it in a well-known couplet: " The past is over and done with; let us speak of it no more. All that remains is to serve the Imperial Yüan with loyalty and devotion." The Mongol rulers, engaged in the difficult task of transforming themselves into Chinese Emperors, found in Chao Mēng-fu an invaluable assistant. He was the link between Sung elegance and Mongol barbarism. He was not a great writer or scholar, but he was good enough for Ayuli Palpata, who enthusiastically dubbed him " the Li Po of the Yüan dynasty."

Fundamentally Conservative and Confucian in his ideas, he yet possessed a good general knowledge of Taoism and Buddhism. He practised every branch of painting and possessed so high a reputation as a calligrapher that " an Indian priest travelled thousands of miles in order to procure a specimen of his handwriting." Mrs. Chao Mēng-fu[1] and Chao Yung, the son, were also great favourites at Court.

The following passage illustrates his view of art:

" It is essential that a picture should be based on the antique. Otherwise the painter's skill will not avail him at all. The men of to-day are quite pleased with themselves if their line-work is minute and their colouring rich. They forget that if a picture is not based on the antique, it is bound to be faulty in a hundred ways and scarcely possible to look at. The pictures which I produce may be simple and clumsy, but persons of taste esteem them, because they know that my work is closely modelled on the antique."

Out of this attitude grew up the code of rules which afterwards governed the Learned Men's School, to which I shall return later.

Chao Mēng-fu as a Painter. Europeans are apt to regard Chao Mēng-fu exclusively as a horse-painter. Considering the immense part that horses played in Mongol life and in Chinese life as organized by the Mongols, it would have been strange if Mēng-fu had never painted horses. But it is worth noting that among twenty-one paintings by or after Mēng-fu that Ch'ien Lung possessed, only five were horse-subjects. The other titles suggest something quite different from the current conception of his style : " Summer Trees Drooping their Shade " in ink, " Elegant Rocks among Sparse Trees " in ink ; " Water-village," " Epidendrum and Orchid," " Trees and Rocks," all in ink ; " Landscape Album " in light colours.

It has for some reason become the habit of Chinese picture-dealers to put the name of Mēng-fu on all the horse-paintings that come into their possession. Some of the painters thus labelled are obviously modern forgeries ; others are ancient anonymous paintings which have been furnished with seals, " ancient inscriptions," etc., to enhance their interest. Among all these horses there may be some that are actually by Chao Mēng-fu. But to say, " This horse-painting is obviously more ancient than most, and is obviously the work of a competent master, therefore it is a genuine Chao Mēng-fu," seems to me to be a quite unconvincing argument. Many other artists during the Mongol dynasty were famous for their horse-paintings ; for example, Jēn Jēn-fa, of whom I shall speak later.

Wang Yüan (Wang Jo-shui). Before the fall of the Sung dynasty Wang Yüan, who was a Hangchow man, took lessons in painting from Chao Mēng-fu. " Accordingly all his paintings are in the style of the Old

[1] Known as Kuan Tao-shēng. She excelled in painting bamboos.

Masters; there is not a trace in them of Sung Academy style. In landscape he imitated Kuo Hsi; in birds and flowers, Huang Ch'üan; in figures, the T'ang painters." His name is very well known in Japan, where collectors attribute to him realistic brightly-coloured flower-pieces. Chinese sources, however, tell us that it was in ink-sketches that he excelled.

Wang Chēn-p'ēng. This versatile Court painter was probably somewhat younger than Chao Mēng-fu, though he too worked for Ayuli Palpata. He excelled in " ruled and measured " paintings of palaces in full colour; but he also worked in the outline style of Li Lung-mien, copying many of that master's more phantasmagoric subjects, such as " Demons Fighting for the Bowl."

Ch'ien Hsüan. Ch'ien Hsüan, better known as Ch'ien Shun-chü, was born in 1235 and died about 1290. Thus most of his life was lived under the Sung dynasty. Like Chao Mēng-fu, he was a native of Wu-hsing (Huchau) in Chekiang. They quarrelled when Chao took service under the Mongol conquerors. Ch'ien Hsüan was best known for his bird-and-flower paintings; Chao Mēng-fu tells us[1] that these coloured " solid " paintings belong to Ch'ien Hsüan's first period. Later he took to painting landscape in light colours, somewhat in the manner of the 10th-century artist Tung Yüan. He is perhaps best known in Europe for his picture of the flute-player Huan I, reproduced in *Kokka*, 66, and there wrongly called " Portrait of the Emperor Huan Yeh."[2] In this exquisitely graceful figure the painter has summarized the delicate æstheticism of Ku K'ai-chih's age. I do not know if this work may be taken as the standard for Ch'ien Hsüan's figure-painting. Its credentials have not yet been critically examined.

A somewhat similar touch is seen in a painting belonging to Monsieur Vignier of Paris, which represents a son taking leave of his parents. This too is attributed to Ch'ien Hsüan.[3]

Just as the picture-dealers have put the name of Chao Mēng-fu on all the horse-pictures they could lay hands upon, so the name of Ch'ien Hsüan has been indiscriminately scrawled on paintings of birds and flowers and on many miscellaneous figure-paintings. Soochow was during the 19th century the headquarters of the picture-faking industry. Hence the signatures of Chao Mēng-fu and Ch'ien Hsüan, who were both natives of

---

[1] *Shu Hua P'u*, 85, 19.

[2] This description has been repeated by subsequent writers. Huan I lived in the second half of the 4th century A.D. See *Biog. Dict.*, 839.   [3] See Plate XLVII.

the district, came to be regarded as indispensable adjuncts to " Old Masters."

Ch'ien Hsüan's pictures had become rare in the 18th century. Ch'ien Lung possessed only five originals as against about a dozen copies.[1]

Jēn Jēn-fa. Jēn Jēn-fa, better known as Jēn Yüeh-shan, is another horse-painter who deserves mention. A native of Sung-kiang, he rose to be Assistant Governor of Eastern Chekiang. He was the author of a work upon irrigation, the *Shui Li Shu.* His pictures, like those of most of the Chekiang artists of his time, found their way to Japan. The Ch'ien Lung Collection, however, contained a long roll by him, representing " Dragon Steeds," and a similar picture (classified as a copy) which was dated 1314.

THE FOUR MASTERS

During the 14th century various categories of the " Four Great Landscape-Painters " were formulated. But posterity has fixed them as Huang Kung-wang,[2] Wang Mēng,[3] Ni Tsan,[4] and Wu Chēn.[5] They are regarded by Ming critics as the true transmitters of the Southern Style. They worked chiefly in the south, in Kiangsu and Chekiang, not taking office under the Mongols. Their work survived in countless copies, and doubtless also in many originals. It does not seem to have found its way to Japan except in isolated and doubtful examples. They worked in a free technique, chiefly in ink and light colours. The first two were almost exclusively landscapists. Ni Tsan was also famous for his ink-bamboos, and Wu Chēn is perhaps best known for his bamboos. The quality which all alike sought was *i* (Japanese *itsu*), " aloofness,"—the opposite of *schwärmerei*, turgidity, facile emotionalism, popular appeal.

Huang Kung-wang. He was born near Soochow. His youth was devoted to the study of the literary classics and to an impartial survey of the various philosophic schools. It was at this period that he built the Hall of the Three Doctrines at Soochow. One authority[6] states that for a while he served the Mongol Government. We soon find him living in retirement upon the Fu-ch'un Hills in Chekiang. He took to landscape-painting late in life, at first imitating the 10th-century master Tung Yüan. In his coloured paintings (as in those of Tung Yüan) the transparent brownish red wash called *ch'ien-chiang* played an important part. He seldom used the full green-and-blue colour-scheme of Li Ssŭ-hsün, nor the pure ink-style.

---

[1] For a reproduction of his portarit of T'ao Ch'ien the poet, see *Chung Kuo Ming Hua Chi*, IX.   [2] 1269–1354.   [3] Died 1385.   [4] 1301–1374.   [5] 1280–1354.
[6] *Shu Hua P'u*, 54, 1.

" But in his few ink-pieces folds and contours were marked by very delicate, minute brush-lines." Though a member of the Southern School which scorned the Hangchow Academy and sought its models in the 10th century, Huang Kung-wang had " picked up something from Ma and Hsia."[1]

Wang Mēng. He was a son of Chao Mēng-fu's daughter and, like his grandfather, was a native of Wu-hsing, the modern Hu-chou in Chekiang. Soon after the fall of the Mongols he was made prefect of T'ai-an, in Shan-tung. His window looked on to the great Mount T'ai. Tu Mu[2] tells a story of how Wang Mēng covered one of his walls with silk and began painting a huge picture of Mount T'ai, adding a touch whenever he felt in the right humour. Three years passed ; the panorama was complete and the colouring finished, when one day a heavy snowstorm fell. So beautiful was the effect that Wang Mēng determined to change his coloured view into a snow-scene. He tried dabbing on white paint with a brush, but this had not a happy effect, so he fastened his brush to a small bow and twanged a shower of white dots on to the silk—in fact, created a miniature snowstorm. . . .

This story tells us something about the mentality of the writer who admiringly repeats it, but nothing about the art of Wang Mēng, for there is not the slightest reason to suppose that it is true. It belongs to the folk-lore, not to the history, of art. A very large number of such stories have been translated. They reflect a view of art which has always been that of the great majority at every period and in every country.

In 1380 Wang Mēng became involved in Hu Wei-yung's attempt to over-throw the Ming dynasty, and died in prison in 1385.

It is said that he always painted on paper, but not much importance can be attached to this standard, for very early sources mention paintings by him on silk. The Chinese art journal *Shēn Chou Kuo Kuang Chi*[3] repro-duced a tall kakemono attributed to him, representing a party picnicking under pine-trees at the foot of a wooded hill down the sides of which a torrent pours.

The Northern School landscape-painters sought—at any rate, in their more intense works—to inspire us with the feeling that Nature is a god, stupend-ous and inscrutable. The Southern School, as represented by this picture, shows us Nature rather as a charming companion, affable and alluring.

Ni Tsan. The first two of the Four Masters were both to some extent men of affairs. The other two were pure Bohemians. Of Ni Tsan's roaming life an account will be found in Giles's *Pictorial Art.*

---

[1] *Shu Hua P'u,* 86, 2.　　　[2] 1458–1525.　　　[3] V, 13.

He is the only one of the four who occupies a distinguished place in letters as well as in art :

I sit and watch the green moss
Till it almost grows upon my dress,
All day, till the spring pond
Is dim in the evening light.
To this wild village from dawn to dusk
No traffic comes ;
Only the passage of a broken cloud
Guides the cranes to their home.

That is his most famous poem, barely recognizable as poetry in this rough translation.

As a painter he seldom worked in full colours. Out of thirty paintings in the Ch'ien Lung Collection all were in ink, save one in light colours. In the landscapes of his contemporaries human figures played an important part. They served as a link between the spectator and the scene depicted. But Ni Tsan in many of his paintings dispensed with them altogether, being, I imagine, the earliest artist in the world to do so. Like Mi Fei, whom he somewhat resembles, he was fanatically frequent in his ablutions, and like Mi Fei he had a small collection of choice paintings, the list of which has been transmitted to us. Among them were " The Constellations," by Chang Sēng-yu ; " The Birth of Shākyamuni," by Wu Tao-tzŭ ; " An Autumn Mountain," by Ching Hao ; " The Wedding of the River-god," by Tung Yüan ; and paintings by Mi Fei, Li Lung-mien, and other great artists. The following is an extract from his writings :

" What I call painting is no more than a careless extravaganza of the brush, not aiming at resemblance, but only at the diversion of the painter. Recently, on the occasion of one of my rambles to the capital, people came to me begging for paintings. I found that they all wanted them to be like something in particular, seen at a particular season. Then they went away angry. But this is like scolding a eunuch for not growing a beard ! "

Wu Chēn. Wu Chēn[1] was a complete recluse, a Taoist in the 4th-century style. He painted some landscapes, but chiefly rocks, bamboos, and pine-trees in ink. A picture[2] by him, reproduced in the Chinese art-journal which I have mentioned above, shows a pine-tree stem enlaced by a clinging creeper.

[1] " The Plum-blossom Priest."   [2] *Shēn Chou*, II, 15.

CHINESE PAINTING

KINDRED PAINTERS

I have already mentioned Kao K'o-kung as a 14th-century imitator of Mi Fei. A rather interesting artist of whom no account has been given by European writers, is Fang T'sung-i, better known as Fang Fang-hu, a native of Kuei-ch'i in Kiangsi. Like Wu Chēn he was a mystic and recluse. He believed that he was able to visit at will and without stirring from his seat all the world's most marvellous scenes, the great mountains of T'ai-hang, the precipice of Chü-yung, every wild sublimity of Nature. And not that only; he could also converse with heroes, handle every strange ingenuity of human art, even see the lost masterpieces of the great painters of antiquity.

It is said that there was in his pictures (and one may well believe it) an immaterial unearthly quality, the reflection of his mystical experiences.

The *Kokka*[1] has published a very beautiful landscape by him, dated 1368. It was acquired by Professor Ogawa during a visit to China a few years ago.

BUDDHIST PAINTING

The official religion of the Mongols was Tibetan Lamaism. We know that during the 14th century a great deal of Tibetan Buddhist art was imported into China, and we know that it was imitated by Chinese artists. It is doubtful whether any of it survived the fierce anti-Mongol reaction that followed the establishment of the Ming dynasty.

Among artists who continued the native tradition of Buddhist and Taoist painting was Yen Hui, a native of Chiang-shan in the south-west of Chekiang. Like so many Chekiang painters he is better known in Japan (particularly by his " Gama " and " Tekkai " in the Chionji, Kyōto) than in China. But his Chinese obscurity has been exaggerated. At least one of his works, the " Procession of Demons on New Year's Eve," was well known to Chinese critics in later times. It is at present quite uncertain which of the very numerous works attributed to him in Japan are genuine.

Another Buddhist painter who represents a problem which has not yet been solved, is Chang Ssŭ-kung. He is quite unknown to Chinese art records; according to one Japanese tradition he lived under the Northern Sung dynasty, according to another, under the Mongols. Finally, a Chang Ssŭ-kung is known to have been an official in the Yung Lo (1403–1425) period of the Ming dynasty. He painted highly coloured old-fashioned Buddhist cult-pictures; such subjects as the Amida Trinity, the Shākya-

---

[1] No. 348. The artist is there mistakenly called Fang Fang-k'un.

muni Trinity, the Peacock King. His style is gentle, restrained, even somewhat timid. Mr. Taki[1] sees in the colouring of the Shākyamuni Trinity traces of Tibetan influence.

Wang Li, who died about 1370, was a doctor of medicine. He made important discoveries about cold-catching and fevers, publishing several well-known medical works. But he was also a poet and painter. On one occasion he climbed the Hua Mountain (in Shensi) and painted forty pictures of it. He also composed 150 poems to commemorate his excursion. In his " Introduction to my Pictures of Hua Mountain " he writes :

" Though painting represents forms, it is dominated by the ' idea ' (of the object represented). If the idea is neglected, mere representation cannot avail. Nevertheless, this idea is embodied in forms and cannot be expressed without them. He who can successfully represent forms will find that the idea will fill out those forms. But he who cannot represent them, will find that not form but all is lost. He who sets out to paint something wants his picture to resemble that thing, and how can it, if he does not even ' know his subject by sight ' ? Did the old masters achieve their success by groping about in the dark ? These fellows who spend all their time copying and tracing, most of them know the subjects they choose only by other people's drawings of them, and go no further. Each copy marks a wider removal from the truth. The forms are gradually lost, and the ' idea ' is not likely to survive them.

" In short, till I knew the shape of the Hua Mountain, how could I paint a picture of it ? But after I had visited it and drawn it from nature, the ' idea ' was still immature. Subsequently I brooded upon it in the quiet of my house, on my walks abroad, in bed and at meals, at concerts, in intervals of conversation and literary composition. One day when I was resting I heard drums and flutes passing the door. I leapt up like a madman and cried, ' I have got it ! ' Then I tore up my old sketches and painted it again. This time my only guide was Hua Mountain itself. I thought nothing at all about the schools and styles which ordinarily obsess the painter.

" Now schools and styles must be founded by some one. A man gave them their fame ; and am I alone not a man ? "

MING

Tung Ch'i-ch'ang and the Literary School. Yüan reaction against the brooding mysticism of Southern Sung continued under the Mings, who, amused by the glittering surfaces of life, did not desire to probe them. The Ming dynasty, with its passion for the tangible, is a revival of T'ang, but it is a T'ang without verve, without grandeur. Under the Mongols

[1] *Kokka,* 149.

China had been cosmopolitan. Now just as fast friends, after a stranger has at last left their company, draw up again round the fire to enjoy the pleasures of exclusion, so China withdrew into the comfortable glow of her own self-sufficiency.

There are in Europe at present two kinds of art. The chief characteristic of the first kind is that it must always be mixed with something else ; normal people cannot take their art " neat." Not only must art always be diluted by such extraneous elements as religion, patriotism, or pornography, but the different arts must also as far as possible be blended together. Hence the popularity of opera in which each art magnanimously supports the other.

In Ming-dynasty China there was a similar division, but the line of demarcation was not quite the same. The average Chinaman could not take his art undiluted, but he could stand more than the homœopathic dose which satisfies the European. In literature the discovery was now made that by the omission of anything demanding thought or sustained attention " the many " could be reconciled to classical poetry. Hence the elementary anthologies consisting of short, pretty pieces which are now all that the average educated Chinaman knows of Chinese poetry, and which Europeans who study Chinese literature insist on regarding as canonical.

Painting of the popular kind had its own technique. Highly finished detail was demanded (the purchaser likes to feel that he has bought up the largest possible quantity of human labour), and the artist was usually called upon to illustrate well-known legends or novels. That is to say, painting was diluted with literature.

But there was another kind of painting designed also for a large public—the Learned Man's Painting (best known to Europeans by its Japanese name, *Bunjingwa*). This was the hobby of State officials who, like the members of our own executive departments, were chosen for their proficiency in Classical learning. Owing their position to assiduous study, they believed that knowledge was also the key to art. Painting was to them a complicated ritual, like the Court functions in which so much of their lives were spent. Only " recognized " pictures could be painted, and they must be painted in the " recognized " way. The *Book of Odes* mentions a certain river in connection with autumn. Accordingly this river must always be represented by the painter under its autumnal aspect. The same code of usages demanded that each part of a picture should be in the style of the particular master whose work was regarded as canonical in this branch of painting. The nature of the code cannot be better

246

explained than by introducing to the reader the arch-master of these curious ceremonies.

Tung Ch'i-ch'ang was born in 1554 and died in 1636. He rose to be President of the Board of Rites, and may in this capacity have had to deal with Matteo Ricci, who died in 1610.

He held, at various times in his life, provincial posts in Shantung, Honan, and Kuangsi; but for the most part worked, in the service of four successive Emperors at the capital, Nanking. He was one of those immensely gifted and vigorous characters whose happy careers spread like a vast tree over a whole century. (One thinks of Bernini, who also died at the age of eighty-two.) To these facile giants failure is, it would seem, impossible; but so also is the highest achievement.

As a statesman, as a painter, as a calligrapher, as an archæologist, and as a writer on art, Tung Ch'i-ch'ang enjoyed for fifty years the highest reputation. No ancient picture was genuine till Tung's seal had made it so. Travelling *en grand seigneur* through the provinces which he governed, he was met at every posting-station by the possessors of would-be masterpieces. Gifts, naturally, were showered upon him, and his own collection assumed vast proportions.

But in all his journeys he was dominated by one desire—to discover a painting by the great 8th-century master Wang Wei. For many years he could get no nearer his idol than we can to-day: it was in a copy by Chao Mēng-fu that he studied Wang Wei.[1] And it was only an intuition which informed that Wang was in this case the painter of the original.

" Yang Kao-yu at Pekin has a small Snow picture by Chao Mēng-fu. He makes a free use of gold-powder. There is in his treatment of distances a tranquillity and elegance quite out of the common. As soon as I saw the picture I knew that it was after Wang Wei. Asked why I thought so, I replied, ' From T'ang till Sung the different methods of ' wrinkle ' are clearly distinguished in the different schools. It is like the five divisions of the Dhyāna (Zen) sect in Buddhism. A single phrase, often a single word, is enough to tell the listener to which sect the speaker belongs.'

" Now in this picture the ' wrinkles ' are not like those of Chang Sēng-yu nor of Li Ssŭ-hsün, nor yet like that of Wang Hsia, nor of Kuan T'ung Nor does it resemble the eclectic styles of Tung Yüan, Chü-jan, Li Ch'ēng, and Fan K'uan. Whose, then, can be its manner, if it be not that of Wang Wei?"[2]

[1] Cf. the copy by Chao Mēng-fu of Wang Wei's *Wang Ch'uan Roll*, now in the British Museum. See L. Binyon, *Burlington Mag.*, Vol. XVII, p. 256.

[2] Part of this passage has been quoted above, p. 148.

At last his search was definitely rewarded.

" In the autumn of this year I heard that an original by Wang Wei, *Hills by the River, after Snow,* was in the possession of Fēng Kung-shu. I at once sent a messenger to Wu-lin to ask if I might see it. Kung-shu valued it more highly than the eyes in his head or the marrow of his brain, but, knowing of my passionate interest in Wang Wei, he complied with my request. I fasted for three days before examining the picture. As soon as I saw it I realized that the style resembled that of the small picture by Chao Mēng-fu. . . .

" I had never seen Wang's pictures, but I had dreamed of them. And now when at last I saw one I found that it corresponded exactly to my dreams. Surely in some previous existence I must have entered Wang's house, seen his brush at work, and carried away a recollection of that encounter which even to-day has not wholly dimmed ! "

Tung Ch'i-ch'ang was not, as might have been expected that he should be, an orthodox Confucian. From his earliest years he was devoted to Zen Buddhism, not merely in a dilettante way, but studying the curious scholastic of the subject and indulging in the half-colloquial jargon of the professional adepts. He also shows definite knowledge of Christianity, and compares a remark made by Matteo Ricci to the tenets of Zen Buddhism. He could look upon new religions with a friendly and interested eye, but as regards painting his formalism and conservatism knew no bounds :

" In calligraphy it is possible to create new styles ; but in painting the familiar is essential. In calligraphy a man may start with the familiar and go on to the experimental ; but in painting he must begin and end with the familiar. . . . In painting distances one should imitate Chao Ta-nien ; in mountains and crags piled one above the other, Chiang Kuan-tao[1] should be the model. For outline use, Tung Yüan's Hemp-skin method or the dotted style of the Hsiao Hsiang views. For tree-outline, go to Tung Yüan or Mēng-fu. As Li Ch'ēng sometimes painted in opaque greens and blues as well as in ink, he may be copied in either style.

" Different styles must not be mixed. However, in tree-painting some mixture is possible. Here are the styles of Li Ch'ēng, Tung Yüan, Fan K'uan, Kuo Hsi, Chao Ta-nien, Chao Ch'ien-li, Ma Yüan, Hsia Kuei, Li T'ang—in fact, right down from Ching Hao to Huang Kung-wang and Wu Chēn—may be freely used in combination.

"*It has been said that in tree-painting one is free to make one's own style. Nothing could be more untrue !* For willow-trees Chao Po-chü is the standard ; for pines Ma Ho-chih ; for withered trees Li Ch'ēng. These

---

[1] I.e. Chiang Ts'an, c. 1200. The other artists mentioned in this passage have all been referred to in previous chapters of my book.

laws are of great antiquity and cannot be changed. Slight modifications may of course be introduced, provided they do not impinge on the essentials. How absurd to speak of abandoning the old method and creating a new ! . . .

" It is most important that a landscape should include some withered trees. They should appear occasionally in among healthy trees, as a foil. . . .

" The prime essential is that the painter should imitate the Old Masters. After that he may go on to the imitation of natural objects."

We have seen that Tung Ch'i-ch'ang was a devoted adherent of the Learned Man's School. He thus describes its origin :

" The Scholars' style began with Wang Wei. It was continued by Tung Yüan, Chü-jan, Li Ch'êng, and Fan K'uan, who were the true descendants of Wang Wei. Li Lung-mien, Wang Shên, Mi Fei, and Mi Yu-jên all derive from Tung Yüan and Chü-jan. This style goes straight down to the Four Painters of Yüan—Huang Kung-wang, Wang Mêng, Ni Tsan, and Wu Chên. In the present dynasty (Ming) Wên Chêng-ming[1] and Shên Chou[2] have from ' times long past received in trust the sacred relics of the School.'

" But Ma Yüan, Hsia Kuei, Li T'ang, Liu Sung-nien, and the like are followers of Li Ssŭ-hsün, and ' our people ' ought not to imitate them.

" When educated men paint they ought to use a style based on ornamental characters in cursive or ceremonial calligraphy. Their trees should be like twisted iron, their mountains like painted sand. They should exclude anything pretty or commonplace. For such is the scholarly spirit. Otherwise, however great their talent, they will fall into the purgatory of Professional Painting."

In another place he says :

" The Southern School began with Wang Wei, who was the first to use light washes. He completely revolutionized the minute and laborious technique which had hitherto prevailed."

He even recommends the non-professional style on hygienic grounds :

" The art of painting, which has been called ' holding the Universe in the hand,' keeps constantly before the eyes the Works of Nature. Consequently many practicants of this art have lived to great old-age. But where a laborious and minute technique is practised the painter becomes a slave of Nature, and she soon wears him out. Huang Kung-wang, Shên Chou, and Wên Chêng-ming all lived to a great age, while Ch'iu Ying[3] died quite young, and Chao Mêng-fu was not much over sixty.

[1] I.e. Wên Pi, 1470–1567.   [2] 1427–1509.   [3] *Circa* 1522–1560.

" Though Ch'iu and Chao were quite different in character, yet both belonged to a school which makes a business of painting. The use of painting as an amusing relaxation began with Huang Kung-wang. . . .

" Chao Po-chü was extremely minute in his technique, but nevertheless had a scholarly spirit. His subsequent imitators attained to the same skill, but not to the same degree of refinement. Examples of this defect will be found in the work of Ting Yeh-fu[1] and Ch'ien Hsüan of the Yüan dynasty. Five hundred years later came Ch'iu Ying. Originally he was very much advertized by Wēn Chia.[2] But in this class of painting Wēn could not compete with Ch'iu, and his praise does not enhance the value of Ch'iu's pictures.

" Now when Ch'iu Ying was painting he would not have heard the beating of kettle-drums nor the din of horses' hoofs. He was like the legendary character who, when a lady was dressing behind a screen, refrained from peeping—that is to say, self-absorbed to an exaggerated extent. Such an art becomes absolute hard-labour ! "

I will conclude by quoting two miscellaneous paragraphs :

" Scholars in discussing a painting seem to take for granted that they are discussing an homogeneous whole. But no painter who is not competent in all the various branches can produce all the elements of a picture. Fan K'uan's landscapes are ranked in the Divine Category ; yet he found it necessary to get his figures put in by special figure-painters."

" When I was young I imitated Huang Kung-wang's landscapes ; but in middle life I left off and copied Sung masters. Now I occasionally copy Huang again and manage a tolerable imitation. I am over fifty ; any trees, rocks, peaks or hillocks that I come across I can sketch quite successfully ; but I still cannot do human figures, boats, carriages, or architecture ; and this vexes me. I am glad, however, to recall that Ni Tsan suffered from the same defect."

Tung Ch'i-ch'ang completely identifies the Learned Man's Painting with the Southern School. But in the 17th and 18th centuries it became a separate branch of Southern School painting, wild, rapid, and purely calligraphic. It is to these cursive eccentricities that the Japanese apply the name *Bunjingwa*.

In the second half of the 17th century the pure Southern School style of the Yüan landscapists was revived by the " four Wangs," whose solidly constructed compositions are far superior to the academic elegances of Tung Ch'i-ch'ang and his school. Mr. George Eumorphopoulos owns a

---

[1] See above, p. 185.   [2] 1500–1582. Son of Wēn Chēng-ming.

most interesting landscape by Wang Yüan-ch'i.[1] The work of this 17th-century school is almost unknown in Europe, collectors showing a preference for the antique.

Perhaps the most original of these early Ch'ing painters was the Nanking master Kung Hsien,[2] better known as Kung Pan-ch'ien. He must, I suppose, have been born about 1635, for he is sometimes classified under the Ming dynasty; he probably died about 1700. Like Albert Samain, " il aimait passionément les feuilles mortes." He saw Nature as a vast battlefield strewn with sinister wreckage. His rivers have a glazed and vacant stare; his trees are gaunt and stricken; his skies lower with a sodden pall of grey. Many of his pictures contain no sign of man or human habitation; he once said that mankind had no existence for him. Such houses as he does put into his pictures have a blank, tomb-like appearance; his villages look like grave-yards. With this tragic master I conclude : *Hactenus dictum sit de dignitate artis morientis.*

[1] Born 1642; died 1715. President of the commission which compiled the *Shu Hua P'u,* the great encyclopedia of painting so often quoted in these pages.
[2] *Shēn Chou,* II, 24, xi. 25. *Shimbi Taikwan,* XVIII. *Tōyō,* XII. *Bijutsu Shūyei,* XVIII. *Kokka,* 379 (landscape dated 1686, not 1746 as the *Kokka* states). For the artist see *Journal Asiatique,* 1918, p. 330.

BOOKS

The following have been referred to in the above pages :

(1) Professor H. A. Giles : *Chinese Biographical Dictionary*, 1898.
Professor H. A. Giles : *Introduction to the History of Chinese Pictorial Art*, 2nd ed., 1918. Cited as " Giles."

(2) Friedrich Hirth : *Scraps from a Collector's Notebook ;* being notes on some Chinese painters of the present dynasty, with appendices on some Old Masters and Art Historians. Leiden, 1905. Cited as "Scraps."

(3) Chavannes and Petrucci : *Ars Asiatica*, No. 1 (La Peinture chinoise au Musée Cernuschi). Paris, 1912.

(4) *The Kokka*, an illustrated monthly journal. Tōkyō, 1889, etc. (Nos. 181–313 in English and Japanese ; the rest in Japanese only).

(5) *Shimbi Taikwan* (" Selected Relics of Japanese and Chinese Art "). Kyōto, 1899.

(6) *Tōyō Bijutsu Taikwan* (" Masterpieces selected from the Fine Arts of the Far East "). Tōkyō, 1902. Referred to as Tōyō.

(7) *Bijutsu Shūyei* (" Selected Masterpieces of Old Paintings and Sculpture of the Far East "). Tōkyō, 1911, etc.

(8) *Shēn Chou Kuo Kuang Chi.* An art journal published 1908 *seqq.*, at Shanghai.

(9) *Chung Kuo Ming Hua Chi.* " Famous Chinese Paintings." A number of fascicules published at Shanghai. Unfortunately I have been unable to procure the series and only know part of it.

(10) Ōtani : *Sai-iku Kōko Zufu.* (Central Asian antiquities.) 2 vols. Kokka Co., 1915.

The only short general introduction to Chinese painting is Petrucci's *Les Peintres Chinois,* Laurens, Paris, 1912 (pp. 116). By the same author :

La Philosophie de la Nature dans l'Art d'Extrême Orient. Laurens, Paris, 1911.

Encyclopédie de la Peinture Chinoise. Laurens, Paris, 1918. (An annotated translation of the Chieh-tzŭ-Yüan Hua Chuan, " Mustard Seed Garden Painters' Manual," a 17th-century popular treatise on the technique of painting. For the bibliography of the treatise see Chavannes in *Journal Asiatique*, 1918, I, p. 300.,

For easily accessible reproductions consult Dr. William Cohn's admirable series *Die Kunst des Ostens*, No. 1 *Die Kunst Ostasiens*, by O. Kümmel ; No. 6 *Das Ostasiatische Tuschbild*, by Ernst Grosse. (The latter contains many " Zen " paintings.)
The following contain sections on Chinese painting :

E. Fenollosa : *Epochs of Chinese and Japanese Art*, 1912.

L. Binyon : *Painting in the Far East*, 3rd ed., 1923.

J. C. Ferguson : *Outlines of Chinese Art* (The Scannon Lectures for 1918.) Chicago 1919.

I have not used the above books as " sources,"[1] nor does the fact that I mention them here imply that I consider them all reliable or useful. Most of my information has been drawn either direct from Chinese texts or from the citation of such texts in Japanese works. The following is a list of the principal native sources which I have consulted :—

(1) The Dynastic Histories : lithographic reprint, 1878.

(2) *Li Tai Ming Hua Chi*, by Chang Yen-yüan, completed in 847 A.D. Edition issued without date by the Chi-ku-ko, kindly lent to me by Professor Osvald Sirèn. Cited as *Ming Hua Chi.*

(3) *Hua Shih*, by Mi Fei, *circa* 1105. Chi Ku Ko edition.

(4) *T'u Hua Chien Wēn Chih*, by Kuo Jo-hsü, *circa* 1080. Shanghai edition.

---

[1] I have however taken from Giles's *Biographical Dictionary and Chinese-English Dictionary* a few unessential dates.

BOOKS

(5) *Lin Ch'üan Kao Chih*, by Kuo Ssŭ, *circa* 1100 or later. Reprinted in the *Mei Shu Ts'ung Shu* (" collection of works on fine arts "), Shanghai. In the colophon Kuo Ssŭ calls himself Kuo Ssŭ Jo-hsü, and for this reason I identified Kuo Ssŭ with Kuo Jo-hsü in my *Index of Chinese Artists*. It seemed to me unlikely that two Kuo Jo-hsüs, both writers on art, lived at K'ai Fēng Fu in the same period. Yet such was the case; for the author of the *T'u Hua Chien Wēn Chih* speaks of Kuo Hsi in a way which makes it clear that he was not his son; and of his own father in a way which makes it clear that his father was not Kuo Hsi.

(6) *Ch'ing-ho Shu Hua Fang*, by Chang Ch'ou, 1616 (a description of paintings, etc., seen by the author). Cited as *Shu Hua Fang*.

(7) *Kēng-tzŭ Hsiao Hsia Lu*, composed in 1660 by Sun Ch'ēng-tsē (born *c.* 1590). Chapters 1–3 discuss pictures and calligraphy in his collection; Chapters 4–7, stone inscriptions of which he possessed rubbings; Chapter 8, paintings and calligraphy which he had seen.

(8) *Chiang-ts'un Hsiao-hsia Lu*, 1693. A catalogue of paintings seen by Kao Shih-ch'i, a favourite of the Emperor K'ang Hsi.

(9) *Ch'in-ting P'ei-wēn-chai Shu Hua P'u*. Imperial encyclopedia of calligraphy and painting, issued by order of the Emperor K'ang Hsi in 1798. Cited as *Shu Hua P'u*.

(10) *Nan Sung Yüan Hua Lu*. Academy paintings of Southern Sung. By Li Ē, 1721.

(11) *Ch'in-ting T'u Shu Chi Ch'ēng*, 1726. The great general encyclopedia published by order of K'ang Hsi. Cited as *T'u Shu*.

(12) *Shih Ch'ü Pao Chi*. Catalogue of the secular pictures in the Emperor Ch'ien Lung's collection, first published at Shanghai, 1918.

(13) *Pi Tien Chu Lin*. Taoist and Buddhist pictures in Ch'ien Lung's collection. Shanghai. N.d. (*c.* 1916 ?).

(14) *Kuo-ch'ao-hua-chih*. Painters of the Manchu dynasty by Fēng Chin-po, originally published in 1794. The revised and enlarged edition in the British Museum is dated 1831.

(15) *Mo-hsiang-chü Hua-chih*, originally published by the same author as the above in 1794. The British Museum possesses an undated reprint.[1]

(16) *Ming Hua Lu* (Biographies of Ming Painters). By Hsu Ch'in, 1817.

(17) *Hua Shih Hui Chuan*. Biographies of painters down to the beginning of the 18th century. By P'ēng Yün-ts'an, 1825. Cited as *Hua Shih*.

(18) *Sung Yuan i-lai Hua-jēn Hsing Shih Lu*. Biographies of painters from the 10th to the beginning of the 19th century, in 36 books. By Lu Tung-shan, 1830.

(19) *Hua Hsüeh Hsin Yin*, collected essays on painting. Edited by Yang Han, *c.* 1870.

(20) *Ssŭ T'ung Ku Chai Lun Hua Chi K'an* (" Collection of Reprints of Essays on Painting from the Studio of the Four Bronze Drums "), 1908. Contains Tao-chi's *K'u Kua Ho-shang Hua Yü Lu*.

(21) *Shina Gaku*, a Japanese journal of Chinese studies, 1921, etc.

Neither of the above lists is intended to be a bibliography; for fuller information see H. Cordier's *Bibliotheca Sinica*, with the Supplement which is in course of publication.

---

[1] In my *Index of Chinese Artists* I have reproduced the bibliographical information concerning these two books which is given by Hirth in his *Scraps*. Professor Pelliot (*T'oung Pao*, 1922, p. 332) has shown that this information was inaccurate, and I here embody his corrections. They have of course been very little used in this book, which does not treat of the periods with which they deal.

INDEX

(The index contains some additional book references.)

INDEX

INDEX

258

INDEX

259

INDEX

INDEX

INDEX

PLATES

PLATE II

PAINTED VASE. 3rd century A.D. (?). Height of
vase, 13¾ in. Diameter of lip, 5¼ in. Width
of decorated band, 4 in. (See p. 39.)
British Museum.

PLATE III

LADY FÊNG AND THE BEAR. By Ku K'ai-chih.
Height, 9¾ in. (See pp. 50.)
British Museum.

PLATE IV

LADY PAN REFUSES TO RIDE. By Ku K'ai-
chih. Height, 9¾ in. (See p. 50.)

British Museum.

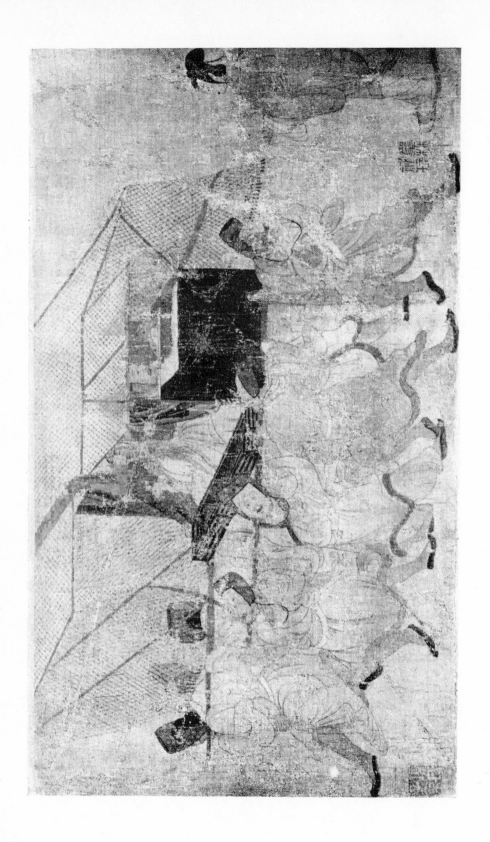

PLATE V

BED SCENE. By Ku K'ai-chih. Height, 9¾ in. (See
p. 51.)

British Museum.

PLATE VI

INSCRIPTION ON THE TOMB OF WU YEN-
LING. Said to have been designed by Con-
fucius. (See p. 70.)
From the " Chin Shih So," Vol. VII.

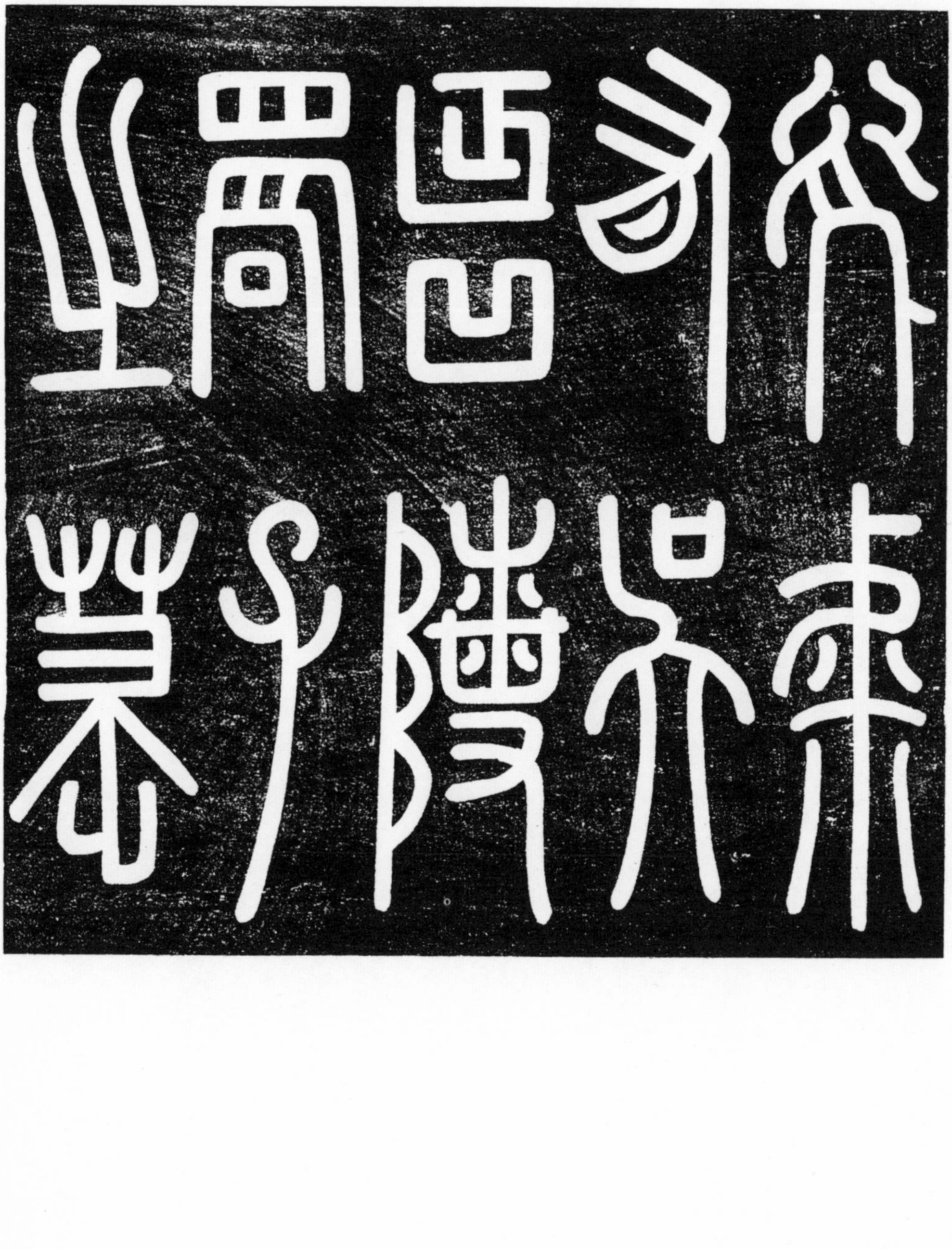

PLATE VII

THE PIAO-LAN SCRIPT. 8th-century copy of a
letter by Wang Hsi-chih. "Hsi-chih bows
his head and announces that the civil disorders
have reached their climax. . . ." (See p. 71.)
Japanese Imperial Household.

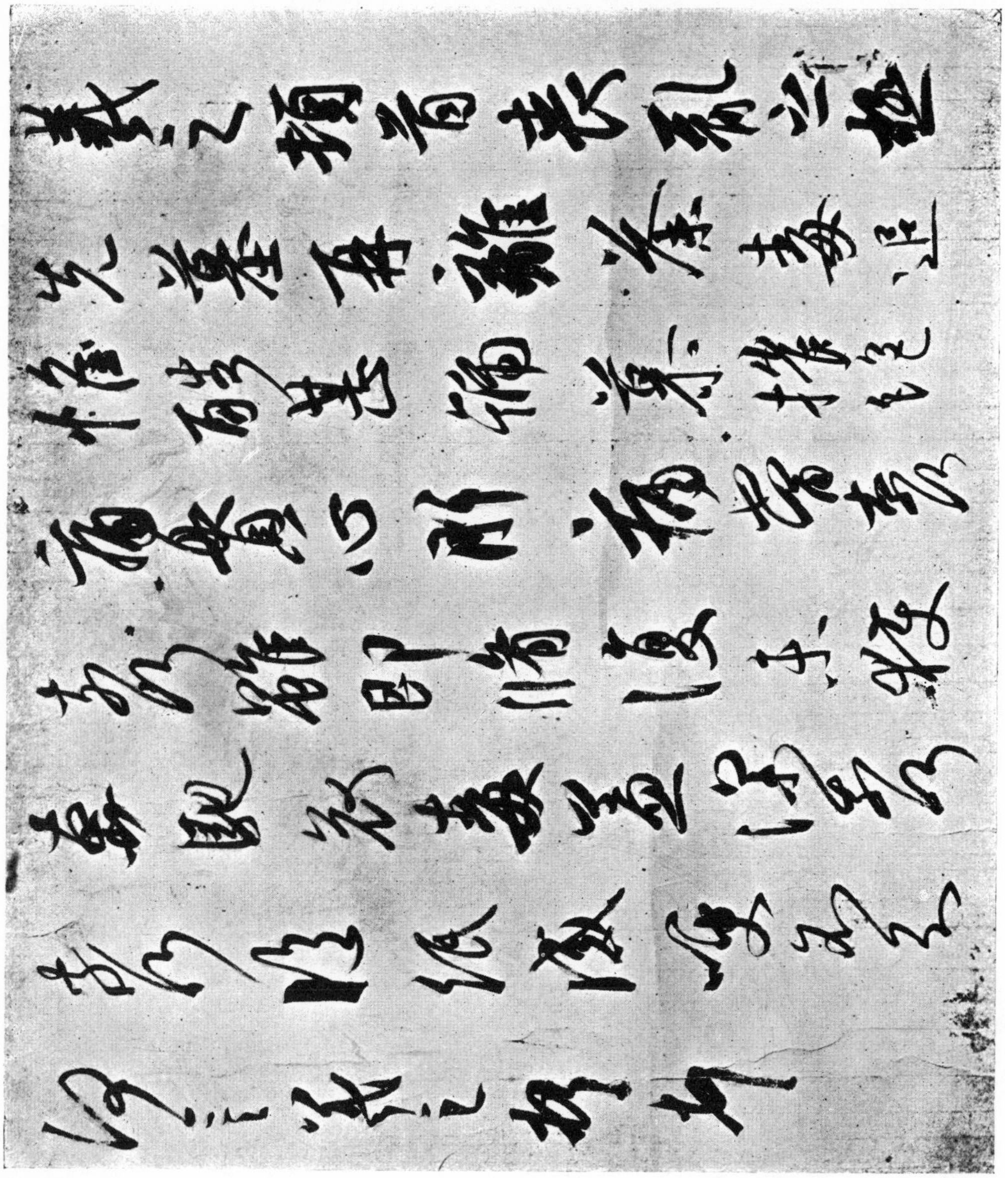

PLATE VIII

WALL-PAINTING. Cave 135 (*circa* 530 A.D. ?). (See
p. 81.) The Tun-huang photographs were
taken under extremely difficult circumstances
and cannot be expected to yield first-rate
reproductions.

Grottes de Touen-houang, Vol. V, Plate 280.

PLATE IX

WALL-PAINTING (Chariot of the Sun).   Cave 120 N
(*circa* 550 A.D.).   An example of the Turfanese
style.   (See p. 81.)
Grottes de Touen-houang, Vol. V, Plate 266.

PLATE X

WALL-PAINTING (Battle).   Cave 120 N (*circa* 550
A.D.).   (See p. 81.)
Grottes de Touen-houang, Vol. IV, Plate 253.

PLATE **XI**

DRAGON. Painting on wall of the Great Tomb at
Gükenri (Ŭ-hyŏn-ri), Pyong-nam province,
Korea. (See p. 84.)
Chōsen Koseki Zu-fu, Vol. II, Plate 612.

PLATE XII

THE EMPEROR HSÜAN OF THE CH'ÊN
DYNASTY (reigned 569–582 A.D.). By Yen
Li-pĕn (much repainted). (See p. 111.)
Collection of Lin Wei-yü.

PLATE XIII

SNOWY MOUNTAINS. Attributed to Yang Fei
(end of the 8th century). 4 ft. 8 in. × 1 ft.
6 in. (The picture is certainly not a T'ang
painting ; but it may contain some remote
echo of Wu Tao-tzŭ's landscape style.) (See
p. 113.)

Messrs. Yamanaka.

PLATE XIV

SNAKE AND TORTOISE. Rubbing from an incised stone, after a painting by Wu Tao-tzŭ. 3 ft. 1 in. × 1 ft. 7 in. (See p. 115.)

PLATE XV

WALL-PAINTING (The Eight Perils). Cave 70.
Background *circa* 700 ; monk, middle of the
9th century. (Avalohiteśvara fulfilling his
promise to save all those who call upon his
name from the perils of fire, water, wind,
chastisement, demons, prison, brigands, and
the curse of being born a woman. See *Lotus
of the Good Law*, Book 25.) (See p. 123 *seq.*)
——— *Grottes des Touen-houang*, Vol. II, Plate 122.

PLATE XVI

WALL-PAINTING (The Procession of the Donor).
Cave 17 *bis* (*circa* 800 A.D.).   (See p. 124.)
Grottes de Touen-houang, Vol. I, Plate 44.

PLATE XVII

WALL-PAINTING (The Fight for Buddha's Relics).
Cave 70 (*circa* 700 A.D.). (See p. 124.)
Grottes de Touen-houang, Vol. II, Plate 124.

PLATE XVIII

WALL-PAINTING (Visit of Manjuśrī to Vimalakīrti).
Cave 1 (end of 9th century). (See p. 124.)
Grottes de Touen-houang, Vol. I, Plate 11.

PLATE XIX

WALL-PAINTING (Donors). Cave 120 X (8th century ʃ). (See p. 123 *seq.*)
Grottes de Touen houang, Vol. V, Plate 270.

PLATE XX

DETAIL FROM PARADISE OF BHAISHAJYA-
GURU. 9th century (?). Height of detail,
15 in. (See p. 128.)
British Museum, Stein Collection, No. 36.

PLATE XXI

BUDDHA AND MONKS. 9th century. 4 ft. 6 in.
× 3 ft. 4 in. (See p. 129.)
British Museum, Stein Collection, No. 6.

PLATE XXII

AVALOKITESVARA. 9th century. 4 ft. 8 in. ×
1 ft. 10 in. In Chinese, Kuan-yin ; in
Japanese, Kwannon. (See p. 129.)
British Museum, Stein Collection, No. 13.

PLATE XXIII

THE SEARCH.   9th century (?).   7¼ in. × 5½ in. (See
p. 130.)
British Museum, Stein Collection, No. 95.

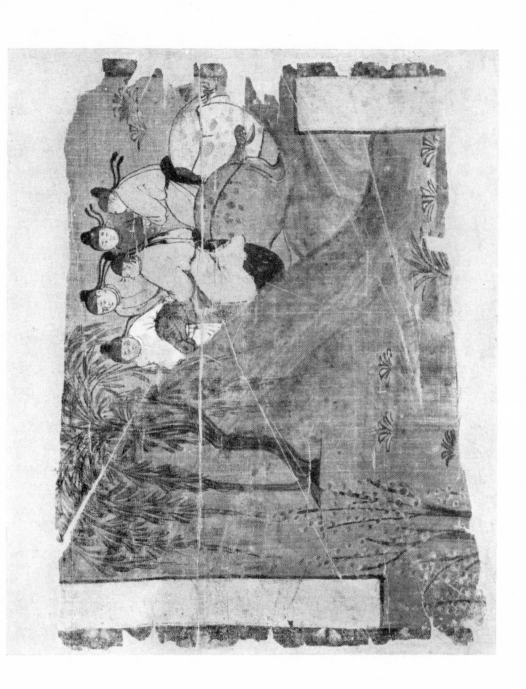

PLATE XXIV

THE CELESTIAL HAIRDRESSER. 9th century(˙)
11 in. × 7¼ in. (See p. 130.)
British Museum, Stein Collection, No. 97.

PLATE XXV

DEMON-QUELLER. 9th century. 2 ft. 7 in. × 1 ft.
The identity of this demonic Bodhisattva is
discussed in the text. (See p. 131.)
British Museum, Stein Collection, No. 40.

PLATE XXVI

THE SEARCH FOR BUDDHA. Japanese copy, made in 735, of a 6th-century Chinese scroll. Height, 10 in. (on paper). From near the beginning of Scroll III. Compare with Plate XXIII. The text refers to the colloquy between Buddha and the messenger whom his father had sent to recall him from the life of austerities: Then the messenger said : " The great King your Father has long known of Your Highness's deep desire to leave the World and has realized that from this purpose you cannot be deflected. Yet so great is the King's love towards you that the lambent flames of sorrow kindle perpetually within him, and only your Highness's return can extinguish them. He bids you come back at once to the Palace, and promises that even if upon occasion duties should arise which you ought to perform, he will not ask you to give up the religious life altogether. Peace of heart can surely be found elsewhere than in the mountain forest ? Your aunt Mahā Prajāpatī, your wife Yaśodharā, and all your kind friends and relations are plunged in the great ocean of despair. . . ." (See pp. 133–134.)

Imperial Museum, Kyōto.

憂惚大海思太子還
內外眷屬皆悲沒於
波閻波提耶輸陀羅
之慶不必山林摩訶
太子全棄道業靜心
宮城雖有物務不令
之耳顧便迴駕還及
熾燃須太子歸以滅
情深憂愁盛火常自
迴然王於太子恩愛
子深樂出家此意難

PLATE XXVII

LISTENING TO MUSIC. By Chou Fang. Height
of original, about 16 in. (See p. 158.)
Shĕn Chou Kuo Kuang Chi, Vol. VI, Plate 15.

PLATE XXVIII

PORTRAIT OF LADY LIEN. Sung (anon.). 21½ in. ×
16¾ in. I have a recollection of coming
across this lady as a poetess ; but I cannot
verify it. (See p. 160 *seq.*)
Collection of Mr. Oscar Raphael.

宋珠夫人像

PLATE XXIX

PORTRAIT OF THE PRIEST WU-CHUN. Anon.
(dated 1238). 4 ft. 1 ft. 7½ in. This portrait, which bears an inscription in Wu-chun's
own writing, was brought back to Japan in
1238 by Shō-ichi Kokushi, founder of the
Tōfukuji. It has been attributed to Mu-ch'i
(see p. 238). Wu-chun (best known to the
Japanese as Bukkan Zenji) was one of the
greatest Chinese ecclesiastics of the Southern
Sung period. (See p. 160 *seq.*)

Tōfukuji, Kyōto.

大宋國日本國天無

根地無極一句定千□老

府□□□□□□□□□南

□□頌出浩□清風

守□□

日□文□□長老

□子□賀讚

嘉□戌中夏□

大宋徑山□□老僧書

PLATE XXX

PORTRAIT OF KUBLAI KHAN (born 1214 ; died 1294 A.D.). (*On paper*.) Anon. After a 13th-century original. Kublai was a great bene-factor of the Confucian Temple, which he restored in 1278. (See p. 160 *seq*.)
In the possession of the Confucian Temple at Confucius's birth-place, Ch'ü-fou in Shantung.

PLATE XXXI

LOHAN. Attributed to Kuan-hsiu (much repainted).
4 ft. 2½ in. × 2 ft. 2 in. This painter is known
in Japan as Zengetsu Daishi. (See p. 167.)
Collection of Baron Takahashi, Tōkyō.

PLATE XXXII

LOHAN. Attributed to Kuan-hsiu (much repainted).
4 ft. 2½ in. × 2 ft. 2 in. (See p. 167.)
Collection of Baron Takahashi, Tōkyō.

PLATE XXXIII

KHOTANESE HORSE AND GROOM. By Li
Lung-mien. (*Ink.*) 1 ft. × 5 ft. 11⅜ in.
(See p. 198.)

Collection of the Manchu Imperial Family.

PLATE XXXIV

THE CLERICAL ORGY. Possibly by Li Lung-mien. 1 ft. 1 in. × 2 ft. 7½ in. (See p. 198.)
Collection of M. Adolphe Stoclet, Brussels.

PLATE XXXV

DETAIL of Plate XXXIV.

PLATE XXXVI

DETAIL of Plate XXXIV.

PLATE XXXVII

THE THREE INCARNATIONS OF YÜAN-TSÊ
(left-hand portion. Attributed to Liu Sung-
nien. 9¾ in. × 3 ft. 3 in. (whole picture).
(See p. 206.)
Collection of Mr. George Eumorphopoulos.

PLATE XXXVIII

THE THREE INCARNATIONS OF YÜAN-TSÊ
(right-hand portion).

PLATE XXXIX

LADY FÊNG AND THE BEAR. After a Sung design. 1 ft. 8½ in. × 2 ft. 11¼ in. (Compare with Plate III.)

British Museum, No. 9.

PLATE XL

PUPPY.   Attributed to Mao I.   9¾ in. (widest diameter).
(See p. 208.)
Collection of M. Charles Vignier, Paris.

PLATE XLI

BIRD ON BOUGH. Sung dynasty (anon.). $10\frac{1}{2}$ in. × $8\frac{3}{4}$ in. (from album).
Collection of Mr. George Eumorphopoulos.

PLATE XLII

BOATING BY MOONLIGHT. Attributed to Ma
Yüan. (*Ink.*) 5 ft. 9½ in. × 2 ft. 9 in.
Collection of Mr. George Eumorphopoulos.

PLATE XLIII

RAIN. After Hsia Kuei. 6 ft. × 3 ft. 7 in.

Messrs. Yamanaka.

PLATE XLIV

PERSIMMONS. By Mu-ch'i.   1 ft. 2½ in. × 11¼ in.
(See p. 231.)

Ryūkō-in, Kyōto.

PLATE XLV

WINTER BIRDS.   By Liang K'ai.   9¾ in. (greatest
diameter).   (See p. 231.)
Collection of M. Charles Vignier, Paris.

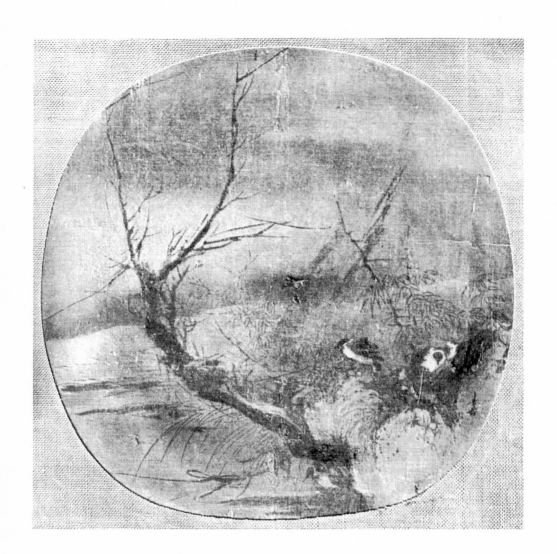

PLATE XLVI

TWO HORSES. Signed " Tzŭ-ang," i.e. Chao Mĕng-
fu. 1 ft. 3¼ in. × 2 ft. 1¼ in. (For Chao
Mĕng-fu, see p. 237 *seq.*)
Collection of Monsieur A. Stoclet, Brussels.

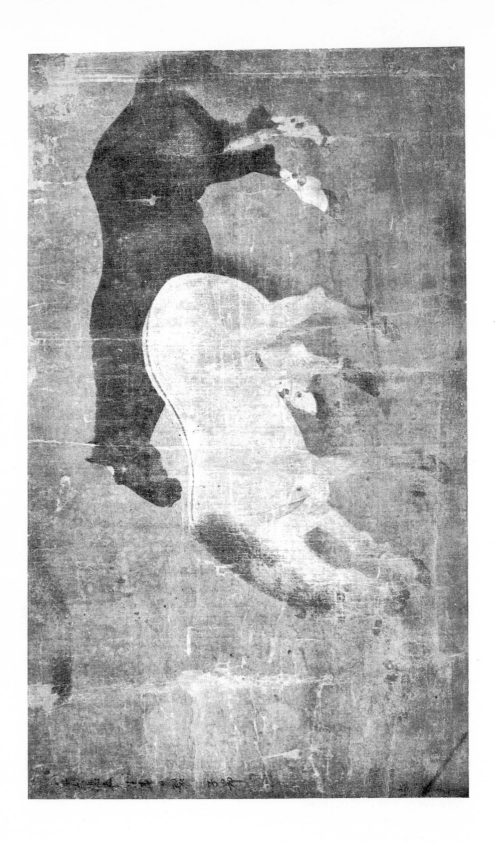

PLATE XLVII

SON PARTING FROM HIS MOTHER. Attributed to Ch'ien Hsüan. 10¼ in. × 1 ft. 3¾ in. (See p. 240.)

Collection of M. Charles Vignier, Paris.

PLATE XLVIII

BIRD ON BOUGH. Attributed to Wang Jo-shui.
1 ft. 7½ in. × 1 ft. 1½ in. (See p. 239.)
British Museum, No. 68.

PLATE XLIX

GEESE AND RUSHES. By Lin Liang (*circa* 1500).
(*Ink.*) 6 ft. 2 in. × 3 ft. 3 in.
British Museum, No. 77.